Changing Giants
The U.S. and China

Changing Giants
The U.S. and China

MAINSTREAM AND ORGANIC VIEWS

Dr. Ifay F. Chang

ISBN: 0977159450
ISBN-13: 9780977159451
Library of Congress Control Number: 2017903367
TLC Information Services, Katonah, NY

Air Defense Identification Zone (ADIZ)
Air Sea Battle (ASB)
American Exceptionalism
Arms Race
Asia Infrastructure Investment Bank (AIIB)
Asia Pacific Economic Conference (APEC)
Australia
Balance of Power
Brazil
Cambodia
Chinese Exceptionalism
Comfort Woman
Corruption
Crimea
Currency
Cyber Security
Defense Budget
Democracy
Diaoyu Islands
East China Sea
Economy
Energy
Environment
Financial Crisis
Gas and Oil
Global Warming
Hackers
India
Inflation
Indonesia
Islamic State of Iraq and Syria (ISIS)
Japan
Laos
Malaysia

Naval Blockade
Network Security
North Korea
Nuclear Threat
Okinawa
One Belt One Road (OBOR)
Pakistan
Paracel Islands
Philippines
Pivot To Asia
Pratas Islands (Dongsha Islands)
Rebalance
Regional Development
Russia
Trade Deficit
Scarborough Shoal
Singapore
South China Sea
South Korea
Space Technology
Spratly Islands
Taiping Island (the largest of Spratly)
Thailand
Trans-Pacific Partners (TPP)
Trump Phenomenon
Ukraine
Vietnam
World Elections
WW II
Xi Jinping

Table of Contents

Acknowledgment ·xi
Preface · xv

Introduction ·1

Chapter 1   Seeking Honest Discussion on U.S. Welfare and
            Healthcare Issues · 13

Chapter 2   Obama's China Policy and Looking Beyond 2016 · · · · · · · · 18

Chapter 3   American Dream and Chinese Dream – Immigrants'
            Perspectives · 23

Chapter 4   China's Ten Point Water Plan · 27

Chapter 5   Will the Next Automobile Revolution Happen in the U.S.
            Europe or China? · 31

Chapter 6   What Does the U.S. Want from the South China Sea? · · · · · · 36

Chapter 7   US-China Relation Does Not Need Another Lawyer · · · · · · · 40

Chapter 8   Chinese Foreign Minister Wang Yi's Speech at CSIS · · · · · · 44

Chapter 9   Why Does China Keep Increasing Her Defense Budget? · · · · 49

Chapter 10 Interpretation on the South China Sea Dispute by History
            and Law · 54

Chapter 11 China's Military Strategy - Interpretation of Her
            White Paper · 59

Chapter 12 Historical Evidence Prove South China Sea Islands Belonging
            To Chinese · 63

Chapter 13 Sino-Vietnam War (1979) Deserves Serious Reflection - A
            Tipping Point for the Collapse of the Soviet· · · · · · · · · · · · · 67

Chapter 14 Liberalism and Conservatism and Proper Balance · · · · · · · · · 71

Chapter 15 The Philippine Foreign Relation under 'Pivot' and
          'Freedom of Navigation'· 76
Chapter 16 HONY Facebook's Open Letter to Donald Trump · · · · · · · · 81
Chapter 17 The Invisible Money Hands behind World Economy and
          International Stock Markets · 86
Chapter 18 GOP Changes Three No Trump to Four Diamonds But
          Needs One More Diamond to Win (The Bridge Game) · · · · · 90
Chapter 19 Will The Warm UK-China Relation Be A Long-term One? · 95
Chapter 20 Taiwan's Fate Not Dictated by Hegemony Theory · · · · · · · · 99
Chapter 21 Connections of Government and Mafia in Japan · · · · · · · · · 104
Chapter 22 Will China Overtake the U.S. as the Superpower? · · · · · · · · 108
Chapter 23 Leadership Transition Must Occur on the World Stage · · · · 112
Chapter 24 The Importance of Transparency in National Security,
          Core Interests and Foreign Policy · · · · · · · · · · · · · · · · · 116
Chapter 25 The U.S. Legislative Process and the Asia-Pacific
          Maritime Security Bill · 121
Chapter 26 Tibet and Tibetans We Come to Understand· · · · · · · · · · · · 126
Chapter 27 The Right to Speak and the Art/Effect of Diplomatic
          Speech - 2016 IISS Shangri-La Dialogue · · · · · · · · · · · · 131
Chapter 28 Are We Addressing the U.S.-China Confrontation
          Correctly?· 137
Chapter 29 Accepting Multi-Polar World Order Is Inevitable And
          Beneficial · 141
Chapter 30 Comment on The End of Eras: Donald Trump and the
          TPP - The E.R. Podcast · 145
Chapter 31 'Soft Landing' Makes Great Sense in the Sino-Philippine
          SCS Dispute · 149
Chapter 32 Is Taiwan a ticking time bomb for the United States? · · · · · · 154
Chapter 33 Recipe for World Politics – Old Cold War to
          New Cold War· 159
Chapter 34 Hiroshima and South China Sea - Truth Be Told and
          Justice Be Served to Correct the Military Culture · · · · · · · · 163
Chapter 35 What is the Impact of Brexit to Everyone? · · · · · · · · · · · · · 168

Chapter 36 From the Republican Convention Projecting to the
            November Presidential Election · 172
Chapter 37 From the Democrat's Convention Projecting to the
            November Presidential Election · 176
Chapter 38 Can Taiwan Practice An Honest Democracy Leading to a
            Successful Reunification? - Taiping Island a Test Case · · · · · 181
Chapter 39 Understanding of China's World Development Program,
            OBOR· 186
Chapter 40 Condition for US China Cooperation Leading to Better
            World (I and II) · 191
Chapter 41 Americans Should Understand What Spoils A Friendly
            US-China Relation · 199
Chapter 42 Diagnosis and Solution of Cross-Straight
            Reunification Issue· 204
Chapter 43 Space Law Should Be Established Before Space
            Colonization Takes Place· 208
Chapter 44 Historical Development and Future Significance of G20
            Following The Meeting in Hangzhou, China · · · · · · · · · · · 212
Chapter 45 Why People Say Donald Trump Is the Peace Candidate · · · · 216
Chapter 46 China's New Work Permit System for Foreign
            Employees· 220
Chapter 47 From President Obama to Dr. Sun Yat Sen on Political
            Philosophy · 224
Chapter 48 The Real Effect of the 2016 Presidential Debate · · · · · · · · · 229
Chapter 49 Why Do the U.S. and China Do War Studies Against
            Each Other? · 233
Chapter 50 Americans Have the Right to Know Why the U.S. Treats
            Japan So Differently· 237
Chapter 51 Macao and the Philippines – Implications on Political
            Governance · 241
Chapter 52 The Final Presidential Debate and Election Outcome
            Analysis· 246
Chapter 53 Where and What Can the U.S. And China Collaborate? · · · 250

Chapter 54 The Immigrants and Minorities in the United States and
            China - A National Issue Needs A Correct Policy · · · · · · · · 254
Chapter 55 A Citizen's Open Letter to the Next President of the U.S. · · 258
Chapter 56 Singapore - Colony to Independence to the Future between
            the U.S. and China· 262
Chapter 57 Trump Movement, Phenomenon and Victory - Post
            Election Analysis on Why, How and What I. Why
            Trump Represented a Movement and a Phenomenon?· · · · · · 267
Chapter 58 Trump Movement, Phenomenon and Victory - Post
            Election Analysis on Why, How and What II. Why and
            How Trump won the Election? · 272
Chapter 59 Trump Movement, Phenomenon and Victory - Post
            Election Analysis on Why, How and What III. How and
            What Does the Trump Victory Mean to the U.S. and the
            World? · 277
Chapter 60 From Kissinger-Trump Meeting to APEC to US-China
            Cooperation · 284
Chapter 61 Can We Compare Trump's Future Foreign Policy and
            Obama's Past Performance? · 288
Chapter 62 Fidel Castro, His Legacy and Future US-Cuba Relationship 292
Chapter 63 Meaning of Burning Flag and Mocking Swear-in · · · · · · · · 296
Chapter 64 Must A 'Change' PRESIDENT Take 'Strange' Actions to
            Accomplish 'Changes'?· 300
Chapter 65 Not All Trump's Cabinet Members Are Gold Fixtures · · · · · 304
Chapter 66 Will Tweeter Trigger Or Prevent Nuclear War? · · · · · · · · · 308

Conclusions· 311
Appendices (I)   Essays Written in Chinese Language · · · · · · · · · · · · 315
Appendices (II)   Why Did I Publish the Book Series on US-China
                    Relations? · 322
Appendices (III)   Table of Contents of US-China Relations · · · · · · · · 328
                    Table of Contents of Understanding the
                    U.S. and China· 333
Notes and References · 339

Acknowledgment

—w—

As I BEGAN WRITING COLUMN articles for newspapers I only dealt with a small number of people. When the US-China Forum established its websites (www. us-chinaforum.org and www.us-chinaforum.com) two years ago, my articles under the column of Mainstream and Organic Views were published on the websites in addition to the weekly newspaper pages. (Taiwan Daily, Washington China Daily News, Dallas Daily News, Southern Chinese Daily News, and Chicago Chinese News) The fact that these Chinese newspapers are willing to give their limited print space to publish my English articles on current events and US-China relations shows that the interest and attention of the Chinese American community has changed. Although the China towns are still existing and vibrant throughout the U.S., but the Chinese American population are more becoming bilingual, educated, affluent, and professional as well as more politically savvy than their elder generations. This expanded exposure of my articles increased my interaction with many more people, editors, webmasters, and a lot more readers now communicating with me through emails, mailing lists and blog forums.

I am in debt to all of them. First I would like to thank the Forum's English editors, Richard Chen, Paul Tung and Nelson Ma who worked as a team supporting me. I most appreciate their prompt response which has kept my work schedule steady. I also would like to than k the Forum's Chinese editors, Prof. Wenji Chang, Thomas Fann, Paul Shui and Sam Chen. I thank the two teams for their meticulous editing, careful proof reading and timely publishing my weekly column. I also would like to express my appreciation to a few who worked diligently on US-China Forum websites. First is Betty Tsang, who is the official webmaster since the beginning of the forum. Kevin Shin initiated the English website along with Christine Mei and Paul Tung. Maintaining websites and posting articles on time with no errors are tedious work with time pressure. As an author I thank them for myself and my readers. I also would like to thank Jennifer Wang for her patience in making proof corrections on my articles. It is because of their support that I was able to maintain my weekly column writing continuously for the past three years. These writings are the basis for my book publishing which I hope will provide more value than my weekly writings.

My deepest appreciation goes to my readers, especially many of them I know through correspondences. They gave me encouragement, suggestions on topics to write and many helpful criticisms and discussions on numerous subjects such that I could include different views on controversial topics. Thanks to Internet, my readers, though scattered all over the world, can communicate with me day and night on any current event happened just minutes ago. My reader correspondence list is my treasure and pleasure. In my previous book, I listed some of my readers' user names on the acknowledgment page but I will not do it here again since it has grown to be a huge list. I just want to say to my readers, thank you all and I promise, if you correspond with me, I will always reply promptly.

I had set my goal to publish one book a year. I have kept my promise so far. I am very happy to say, I have managed to complete this third book within 12 months of the publishing date of my previous book. I owe this deed to my family, especially my wife, Teresa, who has taken good care of my daily needs and let me work long hours to beat my self-imposed deadline. Of course, in order to meet a shortened publishing schedule, I have to work with an efficient publisher. Indeed, my publishing agent, CreativeSpace, is very efficient. A third time around, the publishing process seems to be a breeze. Since my three books are topically related like a series, we opted out to use the same cover page graphics – the map and flag of the United States and China. Of course, the title font, the paper type and color background will easily tell the three books apart. The cover page of the first book, US-China Relations, is glossy dark navy blue. The second book, Understanding the US and China, has a matt grey background. I hope you would like this third book, Changing Giants – The U.S. and China, with a red cover background. My sons have voted for the choice of red color.

One very observing reader did ask me about why there was a dash line going through the middle of the Taiwan island in the map of China on the cover page which I never explained anywhere in my books. I will explain it here. The Taiwan issue, also known as Cross-Strait Unification issue, could have been graphically represented by a dash line drawn along and in the middle of the Taiwan Strait, but if one digs deeper into the Cross-Strait Unification Issue, one can see that it is never the Strait (ocean) that divides Taiwan from Mainland. Taiwan was in the sovereignty of China for many centuries. By and large the people on two sides are Chinese sharing the same culture, language, skin color, ancestries with same surnames, and lots of inter-marriages across the Strait; they are separated because of external influence (foreign powers and wars) resulting in a complicated modern history of Taiwan and an 'artificial politically divided' Taiwan. The dash line drawn across Taiwan in the middle dividing it into North and South two halves is an artist's abstract rendition of such a complicated reunification issue. When such a dash line is removed, it will mean that Taiwan is united politically together to face its future. When Taiwan is united, it will naturally reunify with Mainland as their Chinese heritage will so dictate.

I hope all my readers will enjoy this book.

Preface

—w—

"Other than serving as an ambassador, writing and publishing is the best way to learn the subject matter of International Relations."

~ Dr. Wordman

CURRENT EVENTS, DOMESTIC AND FOREIGN affairs, both are important in our lives. We all live in domestic current events, be it politics, economic issues, social problems or law and order, as they occur near and around us impacting our way of life. Seemingly we don't live in foreign affairs as they occur far away, but they do affect our country thus eventually affect our lives. Most significant international affairs have an impact on us, some immediately such as an attack of our embassy killing our ambassador and some delayed such as the melt down of Fukushima nuclear power plant in Japan caused by an earthquake and subsequent tidal wave. The debris with radiation drifting over from the Pacific Ocean to the California shore is a delayed impact. Radiation contaminated produce and food products from Japan, eventually being banned from import, exhibit a long term impact. Some impacts are direct such as an automobile trade agreement between two foreign countries may have a direct impact to the U.S. auto industry whereas other international relation issues may have an indirect impact on the US economy such as UK's recent vote for exiting the EU (BREXIT).

We live in a complex and globally intertwined world, thus we must keep in tune with current events including both domestic and foreign affairs. In today's world, we are fortunate that we have access to vast amount of information and thanks to Internet technology we can receive reports on current events, foreign policies and international relations worldwide. But unfortunately, we only have 24 hours a day and can only spare, at most, a few hours a day to monitor the current events and international affairs happening continuously. We are forced to rely on media to condense and interpret the news and events for us otherwise we will be overwhelmed by the vast amount of daily information and enormous amount of archived materials.

Having information is certainly better than not having any. However, when we are overwhelmed with information, deciphering its accuracy and truthfulness becomes very critical. We rely on our media industry to be diligent and honest to provide us true facts, impartial analyses and unbiased comments so that we can form our learned opinions on particular events or issues, especially concerning foreign nations. If our media industry is not trust worthy, then we do have a serious problem. Don't we? The trust index of the US media has decreased over the years according to an academic research study. This problem is accentuated recently through the election cycle of the 2016 US Presidential election. Americans' trust in Mass Media sank to a new low according to a Gallup poll especially among younger and older Americans.

One of the strong reasons for me to devote time to write a weekly column, called Mainstream and Organic Views, is because of the above observation. The mass media has become more integrated like an enterprise and yet separated like competing rival camps (of course with money behind driving and controlling) with different charted mission (other than a common mission - journalism) and opposing political view (preconceived and biased position) and preset objective (to impose opinions onto the public). Political correctness is supposedly to be a good thing, but when it is promoted by a media enterprise, it eventually backfires as we have seen during the last presidential election (media ganged up together against a candidate). Abraham Lincoln has said: "You can fool all the people some of the time and some of the people all the time, but you cannot fool all the people all the time." So long as the first amendment (freedom of speech and freedom of press) of our constitution stands, Lincoln's words are valid and the public, with some effort, can find truth and honesty in the media. This book is my effort to contribute to media truthfulness and honesty. I dedicate this book to Lincoln for honesty and I also dedicate this book to scholars, students and citizens who are interested in foreign affairs and international relations beyond mass media headlines.

Introduction

—꿈—

CHANGING GIANTS - US-CHINA RELATIONS

WHILE THIS BOOK IS WRITTEN, the US-China relation is changing from better to worse like a roller-coast ride, up and down, with uncertainties and fears. The author would like the readers to read this book bearing this in mind. The two great nations, the U.S. and China are changing and may be fast changing. Hence, in this introduction, the author would like to, in a short description, lay the background on 'changes' the two great nations have experienced alone as a nation and together as an international relationship in the past so that the readers will appreciate the chapters in this book, - current events related to the U.S. and China, more fully and understand how the two giants and their relation are fast changing. So please read this introduction on 'Changing Giants' before reading the rest of the book.

BACKGROUND ON CHANGING GIANTS
THE UNITED STATES

Since her independence in 1776, the U.S. has been evolving around a constitution-based democratic political system (federation of states) driven by capitalism for economic development. The nation enhanced her democratic system gradually: first, only land owner could vote (1776), States decided voting rights (1787), vote expanded to all white men (1856), first abolishing slavery (1862), repealing Fugitive Slave Law (1864), banning slavery (January 1865, 13th amendment rectified December 1865, April 1865 Lincoln assassinated and civil war ended), granting male blacks right to vote (15th amendment 1869), native Indians could not vote (1876), Chinese Exclusion Act barring Chinese ancestry to become US citizens (1882, repealed 1943), granting citizenship to native Indians requiring application (1890, no voting rights), then granting female right to vote (1920), repealing discriminating laws against Chinese immigrants (1943) and McCarren-Walter Act granted all Asian ancestry right to become citizens (1952). Finally the U.S. adopted socialistic laws such as social security, affirmative action and Medicaid to take care of the underprivileged, the poor, the minorities and the retired with the purpose of providing all citizens a minimum standard of living and closer social and economic equality as the capitalistic democratic system can offer. However, the wealth gap has persistently existed. This timeline review indicated one thing, civil rights and democracy came gradually and may not be rushed, therefore it is unreasonable to expect a change to whatever level of democracy overnight through regime change as the U.S. foreign policy seems to hope to achieve.

The U.S. has developed the Monroe doctrine (James Monroe 1823) to discourage intervention and invasion of foreign powers into weak nations in America, thus it is also known as the US policy towards West Hemisphere. The U.S. held the Monroe doctrine in general but less rigorous in her foreign action particularly in other continents. Although the U.S. was credited for advocating the 'Open China' policy in 19th century to ask the other powers (England, Russia, France, Germany, Italy and Japan) to show constraint in their aggression towards China and towards each other and to respect China as a nation allowing her to administer her own trade rules in her ports and on her land, but in practice, the U.S. had always placed her own interest above all. At that time, it was the trade interest. The British was guilty of forcing opium trade onto China, but the American traders participated in opium trade in China for profit as well (for example, see Forbes House Museum in Boston on Forbes trade in China).

The 'American first' political philosophy is understandable and even acceptable from nationalistic viewpoint. However, when American interest is interpreted as Justice for all, imposed on other nations, then the American foreign policy showed elements of hypocrisy. In many cases, the U.S. foreign policy backed by her military strength is "do as what I preach but don't do as what I do." This power backed foreign policy works, though not convincingly; so long no other nation can challenge the might of the U.S. The U.S. grew stronger through WW I and II and maintained her strong position since the end of WW II (1945). By leading the world against communism, the U.S. eventually gained her superpower status by making the Soviet Union to collapse completely in 1989-1991.

After the collapse of the Soviet Union, 'against communism' became less a binding force among the allies of the U.S. especially in Asia and Africa and to a lesser extent in America. The 'American interest' dominated international order has met resistance from various reasons all linked to contentions in resources, trade and economic benefits. The Middle East, Africa, even South America began to question the 'American interest'. Trouble, even war, started despite of the superior US military forces and her numerous military bases around the world. Since the collapse of the Soviet Union, instead of having world peace, the U.S. had engaged in numerous wars; in particular, the Middle East Wars had dragged more than two decades draining the U.S. Treasury.

In the meantime, China has risen to be the world's number two economy, holding a foreign reserve of $4 Trillion (2015) growing out of surplus of trade with the U.S. and the rest of the world. In addition to the pressure from foreign affairs, the U.S. faces domestic issues, economy, immigrants, unemployment, decaying infrastructure and burden of welfare system which all require large funds that the U.S. economy could not seem to produce. The world is experiencing that the American democracy and American interest may not be the ultimate answer or the only answer to the problems of the world. 'What is good for America is good for the world' can no longer be convincingly preached to other nations. Many nations, especially Asian countries were able to grow their economy with a rate of a factor of two or three higher than that of the U.S. and that of most EU countries. The American people somehow sensed (but yet silent) that there were something wrong about the political and social system of the U.S. That sentiment was amply demonstrated in the 2016 US Presidential election and proven by the election result - a non-politician businessman, Donald Trump, won the election with his "politically incorrect" approach and remarks which somehow resonated with the angry silent majority.

Yes, the U.S. has changed and is still changing, More likely to change more after the 45th US President has fully assumed the responsibilities of his office starting January 20ᵗʰ, 2017. However, one thing seems to be clear though, relationship between the two Giants would be better off for each other and the world if each side would make a sincere effort to understand the other. All citizens of the U.S. should make such an effort to make sure the US China policy is a sound one and the US-China relation will change for the better not for the worse. There are hawks targeting China and there are Panda huggers being friendly with China but no one has been able to articulate that a confrontational US-China relation will benefit either the U.S. or China or the world at large.

CHINA

One may not have to go back to 1776 to understand how China was changing, but one could get a better feel of why China was changing as she did and continued to change rapidly by reviewing her history back to 19th century. The changes in the U.S. as a nation were evolutionary after her revolution. The changes basically followed the time and were very much being reactionary to events. China on the other hand has made gradual changes in steps seemingly evolutionary but more so **driven and mandated by her revolution** – a unique history. China's changes are very different from the changes of the U.S. exhibited by her modern history since her independence. By historic mandate, it really means that the 1.4 billion Chinese people were bestowed by the 200 years or so 'national disaster' and the Chinese people endured with personal misery far more than any revolutionary war had ever given to a nation. Not lucky like the U.S., China's revolution to build a republic suffered from so much intervention from foreign powers and later foreign invasion and threats so that her revolution still has not been completed to this day, after more than one century. Thus, 'To complete China's revolution to build a United Republic

Nation' has become the historic mandate for all Chinese people throughout the last and current century. Of course, the image or destiny of a Republic China has been described by Dr. Sun Yat Sen, father of China (11-12-1866 – 3-12-1925) more than 100 years ago, in his famous book, Three Principles of People. This mandate - building China to be an independent and prosperous Republic - was sustained by Chinese political leaders (Chiang, Mao, Deng, Hu, Jiang) and clearly and artfully illustrated especially today by Xi Jingpin as the **Chinese Dream**. The world and US citizens should understand the Chinese Dream in the above context.

Fulfilling the Chinese Dream is a historical mandate for Chinese, even though many of the Chinese people are not sophisticated enough in under-standing any detailed doctrine behind the mission of fulfilling the Chinese Dream (Socialism, capitalism or something in between were too technical for the common mass). Ever since the founding of the Chinese Republic (1911), the Chinese wanted a strong China, getting rid of foreign aggression and providing peace and prosperity which the Chinese citizens ever cared and wanted throughout their thousands years of history* (*Some would say that the Chinese were the least nationalistic race who viewed government just as a tax collection institution, they don't care who comes to power they just hope the tax collection is fair and bearable. Of course this notion was wiped out by the Japanese atrocious invasion and ruling in the Japan-occupied Chinese territories. Subsequently, Mao in his teachings called for the awakening of nationalism to remove the infamous descriptor of Chinese people by foreign-ers, "a plate of loose sand".)

The U.S. has always been regarded as a friendly nation to China during her early revolution phase. Unfortunately, after WW II, China being ruined to ashes and rubbles by the war, was "helped" by Russia and the U.S. sepa-rately each with a selfish motive. The two sources of foreign 'assistance' were confrontational making the process of rebuilding China ominous. This sit-uation created division and civil war in China till Mao occupied the entire Mainland and Chiang retreated to Taiwan. Mao and Chiang both understood the motives of the two rivals, Russia and the U.S., but the division of China was done which had become a nightmare in the Chinese Dream and a thorn in the historic mandate of the Chinese people.

Even though China was divided but the Chinese Dream remains to be shared despite of a minority of pro-Japan people plotting Taiwan's independence today. Taiwan accepted the artificial temporary division and struggled to build her economy with the U.S. backing her (ROC) under the American Interest - prevention of the spread of communism. Mainland China also accepted the artificial temporary division and focused on feeding the huge population and repairing a devastated war-torn country. Mao was facing a tremendous challenge domestically as well as the pressure from the Soviet and the U.S. which forced China into the Korean War, a war with no benefits to China, other than keeping out Russian forces from the North East of China and stopping the U.S. occupying the entire Korean Peninsula posting a military threat at China's border.

Mao was a great but tyrannous leader forcing Chinese people to work hard to be self supporting. He made a number of mistakes in his policies but his goal was clear, well aligned with the historical mandate - the Chinese Dream. Fortunately, the Cold War between the U.S. and the Soviet Union gave China an opportunity – a window for self-development. The Chinese leaders, Deng, Zhao and Hu, followed Mao and took the opportunity emphasizing on 'careful national planning' and 'picking strategic regions for development' to demonstrate successful examples for other areas to follow and replicate, eventually making China an export based strong economy today. As China is growing in economy, profits were reinvested in China's basic infrastructure such as energy, transportation, roads, bridges, ports and basic human development in education, science and technology and industrial skill. These investments transformed China into an industrial nation gradually evolved into a manufacturing power house for the world. When China was on the sanction (especially technology) list, of course, China tried every means to acquire technology know how, but that policy was no different when the U.S. was eyeing technologies from Britain and Germany and Japan was stealing technologies from the U.S and Germany through espionage or reverse engineering. IP theft should not be condoned but it is a way of business unfortunately. In fact, signs are showing now that China are concerned with her advanced technologies (materials, laser, manufacturing, space and high speed rail etc) being spied on by other nations.

Part of the Chinese historic mandate was deeply rooted in the view that China was a victim of foreign aggression. China (both Mainland and Taiwan) felt that the post WW II international order was illegitimate, gerrymandered by the Western powers resulted in unfair arrangement regarding China's sovereignty and her deserved war reparation (Japanese atrocious war crimes such as Nanking Massacre, sex slaves/comfort women, bioweapon experiments on live human and POWs were not brought to justice). The gradual assertive attitude China exhibits today as she rises with economic power and military strength is easily understandable. However this attitude is neither derived from aggression like the past invaders done to China nor came from revenge which was quite absent in Chinese diplomatic history, but simply rooted in the Chinese historic mandate discussed above. That is why China always urges everyone to respect history - historical facts about war crimes and sovereignty and Chinese political philosophy on governance. Based on the Chinese historic mandate, one can understand why her claims, regarding sovereignty, is always backed by historic evidence.

Xi inherited China's historic mandate and took it on as a personal and national challenge. Xi articulated the mandate as the Chinese Dream emphasizing that China will rise peacefully and China will persistently develop and change to fulfill the Chinese Dream. China's challenge is to convince her neighbors that her rise is benign and harmless to anyone. Ironically, it seems more difficult for China to convince her strongest neighbor, Japan (a past aggressor to China) that China is trying hardest to develop win-win relation with her Asian neighbors. The historical baggage - Japan's invasion to China - of course is not a forgettable (but forgivable) history, but Japan's stubborn denial of her past war crimes in China was far more the reason for triggering Chinese people's anger and fueling Japanese people's insecurity than the assumption that China will take a revenge on Japan for her past sins. (*Number of Chinese tourists being the biggest in Japan should dispel the 'revenge' assumption) Japan really ought to understand this, so does the U.S. Understanding this national psychology will help US-China-Japan to develop a mutually beneficial rather than a hostile relation. In both countries, there are people understanding this historical baggage and advocating peaceful relations, but unfortunately there are still many believing in hegemony theory and striving for a belligerent national security strategy. The current right-wing Administration in Japan and the new US Administration should understand this.

How Can the Changing Giants achieve a friendly and productive US-China Relation?

Today China has risen as a great nation, economically, militarily and diplomatically. However, from the above description of the Chinese historic mandate, the notion of 'China Threat' proposed by some strategists seems to be baseless. There is no concrete evidence that China is threatening the security of the U.S. and world peace. Other than being more assertive in dealing with her sovereignty issue, China has not put effort into preparing military bases for offensive purposes. Her military development by and large is for defense and focusing on second strike capability. Thus, it is not wise for the U.S. or anyone else to target China militarily and pressure her into a mutually destructive arms race.

China has already become a strong nuclear power among the U.S., Russia, India and Japan. Therefore, applying nuclear threat to China (as Russia (President Putin) and the U.S. (President Trump) recently called for more nuclear capability development) has very little real deterrent effect, more likely to produce the opposite reaction and waste funds. Recalling a US-NATO military exercise in 1983 (under Reagan Administration) involving nuclear missiles nearly triggered a massive nuclear war with the Soviet Union (a possible total destructive world war), one must remember and conclude that reoccurrence of any such event has to be avoided. So far China has not joined in such rhetoric making nuclear threats, but this should be viewed as that China is being rational and sensitive not willing to engage in inflammatory rhetoric regarding nuclear threats, not as that China is being weak or timid when comes to a nuclear war. China has always maintained that she will never be the first to use nuclear weapon, but recently in response to foreign threats such as Japan's desire to rearm with encouragement from the U.S., China seems to be worried and warned that she might have to remove that pledge, a rather unfortunate path to take or even think about it. Any thought of rearming Japan to counter China and North Korea seems to be an obvious foolish destructive idea. Therefore while we are witnessing China's rise, we must not misinterpret China's resolve in her rights to fulfill the Chinese Dream and her rights to defend herself as aggression; any hostile and belligerent reaction would be a mistake and very dangerous.

At this point, China is governed under a decisive, experienced and visionary leader, Xi Jinping, who had made serious effort in reaching out to President Obama in the past four years to open dialogs on issues and to reach agreements regarding conflicts while dealing with the 'Pivot to Asia' policy initiated by Obama-Clinton, which is perceived by China as targeting her. World leaders have shown concern about such an ambiguous US-China relation; they rather see a stable friendly US-China relation for the sake of world peace and prosperity. It is expected that Xi will try to maintain a collaborative approach with President Trump based on Xi's speeches, even though Trump has kept being elusive in declaring foreign policies particularly his China policy. In the 2017 Davos Conference in Swaziland, Xi has made a clear speech on China's position regarding globalization and world development. President Trump is yet to make a major policy speech to a world audience to clarify the fuzzy impressions he created in his campaign speeches and tweets. Trump has issuesd a number executive orders regarding immigrants and refugees which had caused many angry protests in domestic and foreign lands. The change of US Administration has cast more uncertainty to a changing U.S. As said above, we must reemphasize again, relationship between two 'changing' Giants would be better off for each other and the world if each side would make a sincere effort to understand the other.

Trump's surprise victory does reflect the desire of a silent (questioning political correctness) majority to forego legacy and make some changes.

Instead of adhering to a U.S. dominated international order and trying to maintain it with reactionary foreign policies, the U.S. may want to start from fresh to take a proactive approach to define what is really good for the U.S. and understand that what is good for the U.S. may or may not be good for other nations or the world. Trump and his team should take their time to articulate and develop a clear answer to what is the best China policy, a workable trilateral US-China-Russia relationship and a win-win foreign policy, since they seem to have a resonance with the hidden silent majority in the U.S. (consider it an election mandate) on the one hand and a serious clash with an open mass of protesters domestically and worldwide (consider an accountability check). We certainly hope that the Trump team can figure out a proactive policy to lead the U.S. first to make the America great again, but not at the expense of the world peace and harmony.

The US-China Relation is at a crossroad. Both countries are facing their domestic and international challenges. Thus, each must continue to change. While change will produce uncertainty, each nation must take careful steps in plotting the change. The real conflict between the U.S. and China is the imbalance in trade. Trump is right about using smart negotiation to reach favorable trade agreements for the U.S. However, negotiation requires understanding. Citing a famous phrase from Chapter Three in Sun Tzu strategy book, "Know yourself and know your opponent well, you will always win.", this phrase simply says that one must try to understand your competitor or opponent to develop a winning strategy. Of course, one must realize that both sides can adhere to this famous phrase, so it may be wise to develop a win-win strategy rather than just focusing on a one-sided winning strategy. China seems to understand this philosophy; she has been preaching it in her foreign relations. China's "One Belt and One Road" program seems to be based on the win-win principle. The change of heart in the attitude of the Philippine's President towards China's South China Sea policy seems to reflect on that principle as well.

Therefore, as you read this book, Changing Giants, I urge you to keep an open mind to seek win-win opportunities; we do believe by understanding each other and exploring win-win opportunities, the two giants can make changes for mutual benefits as well as for the prosperity of the world.

Author, Ifay Chang. Ph.D.
Producer/Host, Community Education - Scrammble Game Show, WeeklyTV
Columnist, www.us-chinaforum.org -Dr.Wordman
Trustee, Somers Central School District
President, IPO2U.COM, Inc. and TLC Information Services
Retired Professor, Polytechnic University (Now Part of NYU)
Retired Scientist, TJ Watson Research Center, IBM
Published books: US-China Relations(4/2015 ISBN 9780977159420),
Understanding the U.S and China (4/2016 ISBN 9780977159426)
Available from Amazon.com and other retailers
http://www.amazon.com/U-S-China-Relations-Mainstream-Organic/dp/0977159426
Facebook.com/ifaychang Websites: www.tlcis.uswww.ipo2u.com
Twitter: ifaychang@drwordman.com, DrWordman@scrammble.com
Email: DrWordman@gmail.com
Publisher
TLC Information Services
3 Louis Drive, Katonah, N. Y. 10532-3122, Tel. 914-248-6770

CHAPTER 1

Seeking Honest Discussion on U.S. Welfare and Healthcare Issues

—⁂—

PEOPLE HAVE CONSERVATIVE OR LIBERAL views based on one's upbringing and past learning. The media of course is very influential in shaping people's views. This is why Hollywood movies, Major TV broadcasts and Mass News publications are so critical in transforming citizens' ideological beliefs, social views and life philosophies. The media soft power is not only mighty in the U.S. but also worldwide. If the mainstream media were biased or neglect to report facts or truth, then the public would be misled. Hopefully, some organic media will offer missing information or revealing the truth for the public to digest. Sometimes, one must make effort to seek honest discussions in the media. In this paper, we will take the two important issues, social welfare and human healthcare, as examples to illustrate this point.

The standard of living is the absolute measure of a country's standing in the world. The social welfare and healthcare are the most important elements in characterizing the standard of living. The world has made tremendous stride in raising its standard of living through the globalization process. Nations open to other nations receive the benefits of globalization in communication, cultural exchange, and commerce and the benefits are reflected in the standard of living. We Americans have contributed significantly to the globalization process through our soft power in media, finance and trade. But come with globalization is global competition, even as a superpower, the U.S., for the first time in a long time, is being challenged in industrial skills and adaptability by world competition since the beginning of the new century. The U.S. social welfare and healthcare systems long admired by other nations have now exhibited unsustainable financial problems. Although there are plenty of reports about these problems, but an honest discussion seems to be lacking in the mainstream media to provoke deep thinking and decisive actions to come up with solutions.

SOCIAL WELFARE SYSTEM

The U.S. attracts millions of immigrants for many good reasons including her welfare system, but in the same breadth, we should state the stark-naked truth about the possibility of collapsing of the great American social welfare system. The American welfare system evolved from the social safety net in the depression era to the present state that eleven of fifty states, Maine, New York, Ohio, Illinois, Kentucky, South Carolina, Alabama, Mississippi, New Mexico, California and Hawaii, now have more people on welfare than people working, an obvious unsustainable trend. In a Senate Budget Committee report, we find that summing up the U.S. welfare benefit programs of food stamps, housing subsidies, child care support, Medicaid, and other benefits, the average U.S. Household below the poverty line received $168 a day in government support in the fiscal year of 2012 (the annual figure, $61320, is rising with inflation adjustment).

An honest discussion seems to be missing in the mainstream media on this issue. For example, another statistic data highlighting the significance of our welfare magnitude is the median household income, which is just over $50,000. This translates to an average of $137.13 a day, $30 less than the government welfare benefit of $168 stated above. So being on the government welfare is getting more money than a worker paid $20 an hour for a 40 hour workweek (The seven day welfare payment $168x7 is equivalent to a 40 hour weekly pay at $30 per hour). These numbers explain why Americans are discouraged to work, especially to work on jobs paying minimum wage, which is capped at hourly rate $15 or less in all 50 states. Obviously, mandating a minimum wage increase to $30 per hour is not the solution.

Is it fair to say that one of the key reasons for keeping our unemployment rate high is the American social welfare system? The better the welfare system the more people give up seeking jobs thus distorting the unemployment rate to be lower than the actual. The American social welfare system is also likely the reason for attracting illegal immigrants coming across our borders to fill low wage jobs which Americans has no incentive to perform. The immigrant issue and the welfare system are related and must be honestly analyzed in order to come up with a viable solution.

HUMAN HEALTHCARE SYSTEM

From technology, patient care and clinical achievement standpoints, the American healthcare system has a lot to be proud of. Lots of medical advances are attributed to the U.S. medical and pharmaceutical research. Availability of healthcare service and equipment are the highest in the U.S. compared to other countries, for example in MRI scanning, Breast cancer screening or hip replacement. There is no question that the U.S. leads in medical research in many specialty fields such as cancer, diabetes and heart disease.

However, the above accomplishments do not speak about healthcare cost issue which has been escalating with above inflation rate for years, now stressing the U.S. citizens. According to OECD (Organization for Economic Co-operation and Development) report, the rate of increase in health care expenditure in the U.S. is growing as the fastest in the world, way above Canada and England. Canada and England both have national healthcare insurance but from service availability point of view they have an inferior healthcare system and most likely also inferior in outcome as well. The current administration of U.S. is pushing healthcare reform towards a national health insurance system without a clear understanding of how to deal with the real issue of stopping escalating healthcare cost. Some pointed out that the Obama leadership (the cabinet) was too zealous about advancing ideological concept of national healthcare and social welfare but had very little industry experience, corporate management skills and in-depth understanding to deal with the technological and financial problems involved.

In healthcare, a philosophical characterization of life, healthy life, expectancy of life and value of life must be clarified and incorporated in any meaningful healthcare reform. For example, the U.S. has highest increase of obesity rate among OECD countries. Obesity leads to over-weight, but is it really a health care problem or life style issue? Can healthcare be really effective with uncooperative patients? Likewise, in social welfare, a philosophical definition of minimum standard of living, future prospect or goal in life, governmental help to sustain self-help and transition to productive life must be deliberated and implemented into a regenerative not a degenerative welfare system. An analogy may be appropriate here: offering a man a fish is not as meaningful as teaching a man how to fish. These topics have to be honestly discussed in the open media to derive effective solutions.

Other countries such as China and India with large population are certainly facing more challenges in social welfare and healthcare problems. They look to the U.S. for hindsight wisdoms but yet what they see is only the mess and half-baked solution or indecision or bi-partisan bickering without any real answer. In fact, welfare and healthcare, different from other issues such as defense or commerce where competition may hinder cooperation, can be dealt with honest discussions to seek solutions with global cooperation. Just to lead the discussion in such a direction, let's make a hypothetic proposal for governments to consider: What if a sensible immigration and foreign worker policy involving collaboration between countries could be established. The U.S. can devise training and work program within her welfare system to train welfare recipients (say unemployed) to be trainers to train foreign workers from foreign country to become social and healthcare workers to work in the U.S. for a fixed period of time in the social healthcare domain where the U.S. has shortage of workers. Isn't this example a possible win-win solution (cost saving and productivity gain)? Shouldn't there be more specific examples to be discussed in the open media?!

Obamacare has not fared well and most likely the new Trump administration will appeal or modified it significantly. Trump was a surprise winner in the presidential election but his victory does represent a movement challenging the 'political correctness' and desiring an honest and effective solution for our social welfare, healthcare and employment issues. The new administration is facing a big challenge as well as a big opportunity to do the right thing for the American people.

CHAPTER 2

Obama's China Policy and Looking Beyond 2016

—⁓—

POST NOTE

THIS ARTICLE WAS WRITTEN AT the end of 2015 but the messages are still valid now after Trump has won the Presidential election. Trump has shown a tendency that he will not simply adhere to legacy foreign policies and he seems to prefer more bilateral interactions and dealing when comes to foreign relations. However, throughout the presidential campaign cycle, both candidates were adopting the 'traditional' bashing China and Russia rhetoric rather than turning a new page projecting into new US-China and US-Russia relations as this article suggests to do. We do sincerely hope that the new Trump Administration will keep an open and clear mind and sharp ears and keen eyes to search for sensible new leafs in US-China-Russia diplomatic policies for mutual benefits and world stability, prosperity and peace.

—⁓—

The U.S. has been the world's promoter of democracy, freedom and capitalism since the end of WW II. For the past 70 years, the U.S. has conducted her foreign policies under such a banner (DFC) with varying degree of rigor ranging from modest soft power influence to militant 'regime change' strategy. The end of Cold War, the collapse of Soviet Union, could be considered a major victory, but the DFC banner seems to be tarnished by various events such as 'color movements' taking place along the way. First of all, democracy has not been an assurance to a stable prosperous nation. Many examples of South American countries, EU and the Asian nations including even the U.S., have shown that limitations of making progress for a 'democratic society' and its inability in reducing wealth gap in the society persist. As for capitalism, many nations in the world, communist countries included, have adopted capitalism but with serious reservations and necessary dosages of socialistic modifications, practiced by the U.S. herself. As for freedom, the principal element is really the freedom of speech and mobility; all human rights, religious rights etc are visible and measurable via freedom of mobility and communication. The migration to cities from rural areas and immigration issues involving people moving to countries with better economic conditions indicate that mobility is more a social problem rather than a political freedom issue. With the advent of Internet, the freedom of communication has soared tremendously in the world, in China, particularly, with voices of hundreds of millions expressed daily, barring those concerning sensitive national security or anti-government opinions. On the other hand, the U.S. has found necessary to monitor citizens' communication (in violation of privacy rights) for security concerns caused by international terrorism.

The U.S. is still the most liberal country in media freedom; she has more publications than any other country in the world especially in the domain of national security and foreign policies, although many are not as independent as they claim to be. Information overload has become a serious burden to citizens; however having more is still better than having less provided people are willing to digest the different views to avoid being brain washed. Foreign Affairs, a prestigious magazine, recently published a special issue, entitled Obama's World - Judging His Foreign Policy Record. In this September/October 2015 issue, it contains an essay, Obama and Asia - Confronting the China Challenge, authored by Thomas J. Christensen, a Princeton professor and the author of The China Challenge: Shaping the Choices of a Rising Power (Norton, 2015). Prof. Christensen had served as the U.S. Deputy Assistant Secretary of State for East Asian and Pacific Affairs, a valuable experience for him to write a review on Obama's China Policy record. As American citizens are going to elect a new President in 2016, it is timely for us to discuss the important U.S. China policy topic with reference to Christensen's review article.

Let's first summarizes Prof. Christensen's main points with check marks in mind, right, wrong or debatable, then we will offer additional analyses and comments if appropriate.

Christensen rightly pointed out that China poses challenges to the U.S.; and China is powerful enough to be influential in the stability of East Asia and important enough to be relevant in solving global problems. Christensen acknowledged that President Bush ended his term heading the China policy to a right direction and President Obama made some progress with a mixed record. Obama was effective in placing US presence in Asia and managed tension but made mistake in rhetoric and in diplomacy with flip-flop languages from 'pivot' to 'rebalance', from agreeing to respect each other's 'core interest' (China's stability and territorial integrity and U.S. Anti-terror and world security concern) to selling arms to Taiwan and meeting Dalai Lama and from reassuring security to criticizing China's Internet and blaming each other on hacking. In Christensen's view, the tensions are up in the East and South China Sea but not manufactured by the U.S. even though she held military exercises in those regions. On global governance, Obama's record is also mixed: On the nuclear issue with North Korea and Iran, China is getting warmer to South Korea which may indicate China's inability to control North Korea. China's increasing investment in North Korea certainly weakens the US sanction (Note: perhaps the U.S. needs to understand China's strategy better for the Korean Peninsula). In conclusion, Christensen remarked that anytime the U.S. engaged in a regime change, China stopped supporting the U.S. in international affairs (e.g. nuclear, Qaddafi, Kim, ...) which should be noted. A bright spot in U.S.-China relation is on climate change with quantitative expectation as a result of mutual internal pressure (Note: Common interests between the U.S. and China, particularly on issues the people of two nations care about do exist. Leaders and politicians should stay away from rhetoric but listen to what people say!)

After reading the Foreign Affair's issue and Christensen's review on China Policy, I could not help raising some fundamental questions. First, is it correct for the U.S. to assume that the China challenge is a national security issue as we did on Russia? Is China really the destabilizing element in Asia or as the U.S. making her to be? For decades, there were no serious confrontations in the East and South China seas. It was in 2010 Japan first arrested a Chinese fishing boat that evolved into a series of drama including Japan's comic move of purchasing those non-inhabitable rocks historically belonged to China. The

U.S. is fully aware of this yet cowardly or shrewdly declares taking no position on this sovereignty issue, essentially encouraging Japan to take more provocative actions, and further condoning Japan by applying the article 5 of the US-Japan Defense treaty to those rocks. On this issue, leaders should listen to the people than follow the legacy think tank touting a fictitious enemy to drum up arms race and military alliances leading to tension rather than solving world problems. If one asks why is China making a big effort to conduct a parade to commemorate the 70th anniversary of the ending of WW II? The answer is simple, China is feeling insecure - the only nation was invaded and victimized by so many countries, from the West and the East, for so many years causing the world's biggest economy to become the poorest population on earth for decades. Now China is rising, what do the Chinese people see, they now have a dream but they see their country being targeted as the enemy by the U.S., worse by Japan even threatened by North Korea. Chinese people are no more belligerent and warmongering than the American people, why should they be targeted as the enemy? More than sarcastic is China being targeted as enemy by Abe Shinzo, a bloodline descendent of a Japanese war criminal.

Another fundamental question is that why is China accused of being reluctant to pay economic and political cost to deal with world problems and to contribute to the global prosperity? This is puzzling to the Chinese and American people alike. The Chinese believe more in the United Nations than the U.S. does. China's grand strategy of constructing a 'One Belt and One Route' connecting Asia to Europe has every element for stimulating economic development of half the world. China's foreign policy has been leaning far more towards economic development than military alliances. Why should the U.S. urge Japan to assume a larger role in global affairs in the direction of escalating her military strength? To add more pressure on an insecure China or to depend on Japanese troops to defend the U.S., a ludicrous logic in view of the historic facts how US-Japan fought during WW II and how Japanese textbooks describes Pearl Harbor, Nanking Massacre and the atomic bomb.

Finally, one questions why is the U.S. as the greatest power in the world not willing or unable to manage the U.S.-China security issue bilaterally without involving other nations? The U.S. has always been assertive in conducting her foreign affairs. China has become more assertive in a reactionary manner to provocation. In fact, China openly regards the U.S. as the greatest nation and wishes to have a friendly relation to avoid to be targeted as the enemy. Is it that difficult for the U.S. leader to deal with the Chinese leader in a frank and direct manner? It can't be the language, since the Japanese language and culture are probably more mystic than Chinese to Americans. This Fall, when Chinese leader, Xi Jingping, who had studied in the U.S. with fond memory and gratitude towards his American host family, visits President Obama, we hope they will open a new page of China policy to guide the U.S.-China relation onto a positive course.

As 2016 is approaching, the U.S. presidential campaign is warming up. The China Policy should rank high on the candidates' minds. It is so important for the candidates to leaf through the legacy pages of China policy and cultivate a new constructive dialogue rather than blindly iterating China bashing. The future of the U.S., China and the world depends critically on the outcome of the 2016 election as I have discussed in other chapters.

CHAPTER 3

American Dream and Chinese Dream
– Immigrants' Perspectives

—〰—

WE HAVE DISCUSSED AMERICAN DREAM and Chinese Dream before, generally from a historical perspective. After witnessing a couple of unusual elections last year that brought in a new administration in the United States and that of Taiwan government, we witnessed some policy changes impacting Americans and Chinese people. Amazingly, in a short period of time, these changes have shaken the core beliefs of the people, especially the value system of immigrants. This prompts me to talk about the 'Dream' topic again. People's dream is an important concept defining a nation's destiny and people's life goals; it is a topic deserving our attention.

People take for granted that the United States is a country of immigrants. Surely, since the arrival of May Flower from England, North America has become the land of immigrants, though mostly from Europe. The blacks from Africa were imported in as slaves and the Asians, mostly the Chinese, were admitted as coolies. To Americans' credit, the US revolution gained total independence and established a constitution-based government system. This political system gradually, over two centuries, abolished the discriminative laws against the blacks, the Asians, the Mexicans and the South Americans. In 20th century, the U.S. benefitted from a systematic immigration policy achieving the world's no. 1 economy and a superpower status leading the world. Up to the end of 20th century, the U.S. is considered a dream country of immigrants. All Americans, including old and new generations of immigrants, cherish the American Dream - in the land of opportunities,

Americans can do anything and fulfill everyone's dream, from having a happy life to becoming the US President.

Entering 21st century, the world has changed, many nations rise economically. The globe has become more integrated in commerce, communication and culture (3C) and yet more competitive (4th C), pursuing multiple dreams - Chinese Dreams, Indian Dream, Brazilian Dream, European Dream, African Dream, etc..... In contrast, the American Dream has visibly lost some luster as her internal problems of decaying infrastructure, shrinking industrial base, mounting national debts and budget deficit for decades. This stress and pain created a movement and phenomenon resulting in the victory of Trump's presidential campaign, characterized by the slogan, "make America great again". Trump's new Administration, considering their campaign slogan as their mandate, proceeded to define a new American Dream - a dream where new immigrants are discriminated and future immigrants are shut out.

Since Trump's inauguration, he has issued a number of executive orders. His order banning Muslims entering the U.S. from seven Muslim countries (affecting foreign workers and international students entering the U.S.) and his plan to overhaul the immigration law: i). restrictions on H1-B visa (which allow US corporations to hire foreign talents), ii). new rules on issuing green card (permanent resident status) and iii). limiting immigrants receiving welfare benefits, are destroying the traditional American Dream. Based on the above actions and Trump Administration's philosophy of making America great again at the expense of immigrants and other nations, there is no rosy picture for the new American Dream, at least from immigrants' perspective. We seriously doubt that this new American Dream can make America great again.

Another election in 2016 produced a overwhelming victory for Ms Tsai Yin Wen, leader of Democratic Progressive Party (DPP) in Taiwan. Her victory did not produce any mandate because she got elected by pledging to stay the course regarding cross strait relation but reneged her promise by leaning towards promoting separation from Mainland China and more dependence on Japan and the U.S. The people in Taiwan can also be considered as immigrants in the same sense as Americans in the U.S. The Taiwan aborigines were nearly wiped out by the Dutch and Japanese during their intermittent occupation in 17-18th and 19-20th centuries respectively. Chinese immigration to the island originated long before 15th century (Ming Dynasty). These Chinese immigrants are the old generation of immigrants in Taiwan (majority, like the white immigrants in the U.S.). The Japanese immigrants to Taiwan during the 50 years of Japanese occupation (1895-1945) and their descendants are a minority even less than the new Chinese immigrants from Mainland after WW II (post 1945) and their descendants.

The Chinese Dream was quite modest because the Chinese suffered nearly two centuries of atrocities from foreign aggression and invasions; they simply desire to have a stable government without foreign power interference permitting them to pursue a peaceful modest life. The Chinese Dream is shared by the Chinese people in Mainland and Taiwan; they separately pursued economic development despite of their different governments being ally of Russia and the U.S. respectively. Fortunately, the two sides never waged war or any serious battle hence allowing them to fulfill their Chinese Dream. Taiwan developed faster and brought prosperity to the islanders sooner than Mainland did owing to a big task of lifting a huge population from poverty. However, with diligence, the Chinese mainlanders persistently pursued their Chinese Dream. Today, the Mainland China has raised her economy on par with that of the U.S. and has made Taiwan's economy dependent on the Mainland.

The Chinese Dream like American Dream are more economically oriented, however, there is a political element. The political element in the American Dream is the American Exceptionalism applied to foreign affairs and international relations. This aspect of American Dream may also change because of Trump's redefinition of American Exceptionalism, a new NATO policy (EU and Russia) and Asia policy (China and Japan). The political element in the Chinese Dream is Unity applied to sovereignty and foreign diplomacy. China has relentlessly pledged that she will rise peacefully and rigorously defend the One China policy. Therefore, the Chinese Dream including both the economic and political element (Unity) will be pursued by the Chinese people.

Any challenge to the Chinese Dream from other big nations or China's competitive neighbors is carefully handled diplomatically by China by repudiating the 'China Threat' theory and by proposing Win-Win international development programs such as the One Belt and One Route (OBOR). However, Tsai's election victory in Taiwan and her policies since her inauguration on 5-20-2016, surprised many Chinese people on both sides of the Taiwan Strait and posted a challenge to Chinese Dream. Her continued effort in 'distancing China' through textbook revision, manipulating media, unfriendly to Mainland tourists, shifting away economic dependence on China and pro-Japan diplomatic actions (allowing nuclear radiation contaminated food import from Japan) have awakened some of the majority immigrants in Taiwan and the mainlanders. More Chinese in Taiwan are participating in anti-Tsai protests and many mainlanders are becoming vocal and urging the government to use military force to unite with Taiwan. It seems that the division between the long-generations immigrants and recent-generations immigrants from Mainland are uniting and the division between the pro-Japan immigrants (affiliated with Japanese occupation) and the rest of immigrants are widening. China seems to be quite secure and Tsai's plots seem to be backfiring. Therefore, we may predict that the Chinese Dream shared by Chinese not only in Mainland, Taiwan but also worldwide has a rosy picture ahead.

CHAPTER 4

China's Ten Point Water Plan

—⚊⚊—

WATER HAS BECOME A PRECIOUS commodity for developed and developing countries alike. The draughts occurring in California in 2014 and in China in 2010 affecting nearly all plants (especially wheat) growing regions are serious problems on the one hand and the water pollution to natural water resources is a deadly issue on the other hand. These issues certainly call for effective measures from governments to deal with the fresh water problem. Recently, I came across a Chinese federal government notice (dated 4-2-2015) to local governments and directs departments reporting to the Chinese central government, a one sentence directive: We deliver the "Water Pollution Prevention and Action Plan" to you, please seriously implement the measures. What a simple and weighty executive order that will not only have impact to the livelihood of 1.3 billion Chinese people, but will also raise the welfare of the world. We certainly wish this mandate, with milestones set on 2016-2018, 2020 and 2030, will be successfully carried out for mankind's sake. I feel that it is worthy of our time to review China's Ten Point Water Plan and cheer the Chinese on.

Chinese government documents tend to be concise, in contrast, for example, to the 20,000 pages (11,588,500 words) Obama care. The lack of details in China's water plan might signify an inadequately thought-out plan which could allow loopholes to fail the implementation. However, if a plan was developed on a sound and broad basis, it might allow innovation and ingenuity to take place at the implementation level. Judging on the past achievements in economic development by the Chinese central and local governments (despite of corruptions), China's water plan may get effectively implemented in the usual manner that local governments are expected to work in a competitive mood to show measurable performance. Since China's water plan is such an important program of great interest to the entire world, this paper shall present in the following a summary and a condensed description and commentary of the Ten Point Water Plan. For more details, special mandarin terms and legal interpretations, the readers are referred to the original Chinese language document available from the Chinese State Council or through online search.

Priority conservation, physical balance, systemic management and balanced control with safety, cleanness and health are the four principles and three directives behind China's Ten Point Water Plan. Goals on quantitative measurable improvements of water environment and pollution reduction are set to be achieved by 2020 and 2030 focusing on China's seven major river-lake regions with quality level III as the yardstick mandating 75% regional water and 95% urban city drinking water to have quality better than level III, which is presumably a global industrial standard. The policies and directives are categorized under ten points as follows:

1. Pollution Control: By the end of 2016, China will outlaw all pollutions in over ten major manufacturing industries; by 2020, will establish city-urban water pollution and recycle control with waste water treatment reaching 85 95% range, agricultural and rural water pollution prevention through fertilization control, and water pollution regulations on ports by 2018 and in-land ports by 2021.
2. Industry Conversion and Upgrade: removing outdated businesses and issuing permits for pollution control, by 2020, completed all city-urban-rural water environment assessment; implementing water based space planning and promoting recycle, reclaim and closed cycle water usage. Apparently, China is coupling the water plan with the industry transformation and upgrade program to sustain China's economic growth, a smart move. Here more details perhaps will be forthcoming.
3. Conservation: Control total water usage, by 2020, limit to 670 billion cubic meters, raise water usage efficiency as one performance measurement of local governments; by 2020, achieve 30-35% reduction in

industrial water usage below 2013 level, and apply scientific protection to water resources.

4. Technology Support: Promote and demo applicable technology, initiate R&D on advanced technology and encourage investment in environment protection industry. One would expect more concrete steps will be defined on points 3 and 4. These areas present opportunities for the U.S. to offer goods and services.

5. Market Driven: Develop reasonable water tax and prices, attract investment into water environment protection businesses and provide incentive plan for energy conservation and water pollution reduction. Presumably, China will welcome foreign investment; foreign investors must follow up China's incentive plans.

6. Legal Measures: Complete needed legislations, increase legal power for pollution control and improve control effectiveness across all departments and municipal governments. Hopefully, this part of plan will take advantage of the anti-corruption and justice system reform programs to safeguard the effectiveness of pollution control laws.

7. Water Environment Management: Strengthen water quality goal management, total water pollution control, and water environment risk management; and implement pollution permit system, completion by 2017. This is an aggressive milestone to be watched.

8. Water Environment Safety Protection: Protect source of drinking water, prevent water pollution at all industry regions, strengthen coastal water environment protection and fix city dirty water problem, by 2017, no sizable floating debris on rivers, by 2020 complete dirty water control and protection of water resources and wet lands. Certainly, more definite description of floating objects and method of monitoring must be defined.

9. Accountability: strengthen local governments' responsibilities and inter-departmental coordination, clarify responsibilities of pollution prevention department and apply rigorous measurements on performance of all governments and departments. This is a common problem in other nations; China has the advantage being able to take some lessons from the U.S. and elsewhere.

10. Encourage Public Participation and Oversight: open pollution and environment protection information to the public, strengthen and train public knowledge for oversight purposes and cultivate all people care attitude and behavior. This is hugely important and a key element for the Chinese society to exercise democracy to hold governments accountable.

I was quite impressed after I managed to summarize this high level China's Ten Point Water Plan. If the set goals and quantitative measures were achieved, China would have made another impressive national development milestone for the Chinese people. For the next fifteen years, there are tremendous opportunities for the U.S. and her global corporations focused on environment protection to participate in China's quest for a better living environment. These opportunities will be not only beneficial to many businesses, exports of goods and services and investment firms but also helpful in stimulating and accelerating the development of the environment industry in the U.S. which in turn will improve the environment of the U.S. The best part, of course, is that China's quest for a better environment would create a win-win collaboration between the U.S. and China, two great nations, cooperating to lead the world to be a better place for mankind. In late 2014, when President Obama visited China, an agreement on Climate change control between China and the U.S. was announced. In 2015, during the state visit of President Xi Jinping of China to President Barack Obama of the U.S., further discussion on climate change and environment protection was on the agenda of their presidential meeting. The high level attention and energy spent between the United States and China on clean environment and pollution control is certainly more preferable and worthwhile than time and energy spent on arms development. As global citizens we all should cheer on the Chinese on this significant ten-point water plan.

CHAPTER 5

Will the Next Automobile Revolution
Happen in the U.S. Europe or China?

—⁓—

THE RECENT CONSUMER ELECTRONICS SHOW (Las Vegas) and the auto show (LA) in the U.S. have generated speculation about a major growth in the auto industry. Separately, the well-known consulting company, McKinsey & Company has released a report, entitled Disruptive Trends That Will Transform the Auto Industry, written by Paul Gao, Hans-Werner Kaas, Detlev Mohr (Directors of Hong Kong, Detroit, and Stuttgart Office respectively) and Dominik Wee (Principal in the Munich office) and contributed by nine other McKinsey staff. This report is signaling an 'automotive revolution by 2030' stimulated by four disruptive technology-driven trends: diverse mobility, autonomous driving, electrification and connectivity, so claimed. As a typical good consulting report, this long article made perceptive observations on the rise of technology that has disrupted other industries and so will the auto industry. This report pointed out the shared mobility (for example, Uber model), connectivity services (telecommunication and computing supported services), and feature upgrades will bring as much as 30% more business revenue in addition to its traditional auto-units growth which was estimated to be at 2% considering the changing business model for new cars (increasing demand) and consumer behavior shifts (decreasing demand).

The above study report touched upon an important fact that automobile consumers in the cities will have changing individual mobility behavior because of multiple modes of transportation available, thus preferring to have car services rather than car ownership. E-hailing, having millions of cars today, will influence new car design for utilization, robustness, additional mileages driven and passenger comfort and will make ten percent of new cars as shared cars in 2030, thus making cities replacing countries as the most relevant segment to determine mobility behavior and scope of automobile revolution. This paradigm shift to "mobility as a service" will change and force the auto industry and new players to compete on multiple fronts as well as to cooperate in exploiting the technologies to realize advanced driver assistance system (ADAS) to auto-auto (self-driven AA cars) and to focus on software based differentiator in new features. The report mentioned Tesla, Apple, Google and Uber as new players and Chinese car manufacturers to play a significant role, but the report did not answer my title question where the automobile revolution will take place, in the U.S., Europe or China?

McKinsey may have saved information beyond this public report for paid private customers, but as a technologist myself, I must say, there is a lot more can be said about automobile industry revolution beyond the above report. There are numerous articles that have come my way which are relevant to 'automobile revolution'; these include research reports on energy, environment, public policy as well as technology and social behavior studies. Inevitably, some of these materials came from organic media not necessarily with authentic authorship. One must read these reports with a grain of salt, placing one's own judgment to piece together a story making common sense. After reading the McKinsey report, I am motivated to review my collection of materials and deduce a possible "Automobile Industry Revolution" by synthesizing information principally from the organic media. The readers can simply treat it as an entertaining story or compare it seriously with the McKinsey report to ponder what and where the automobile revolution may occur. The new automobile revolution is likely to take place in China, not the U.S. nor in Europe, by my hunch.

The automobile industry has sustained a steady growth since the invention of gas engine by Gottlieb Diamler (1885) and a gas fueled car by Karl Benz (1886), although combustion engines were invented many centuries ago. Gasoline has dominated the auto industry as the principal fuel. Fossil fuel was plentiful enough to support car growth. Over the 130 years of automobile history, from 30 car manufacturers producing 2500 cars in 1899, it went through mass production process introduced by Henry Ford (1913) eventually resulted in the domination of the US Big Three in car manufacturing post WW II. However, by 1980, Japan had become the no. 1 car manufacturer. In the past three decades, more competitors entered the industry; by 2011, the ranking has changed to be China (14.5M), Japan (7.2M), Germany (5.9M), S. Korea (4.2M), India (3M) and U.S. (2.5M) with China becoming the largest automobile market and producer today.

One cause for the rapid technology-driven trends for disrupting the auto industry is the fact that the fossil fuel can no longer be used as the principal energy source, one for its diminishing supply and two for its carbon emission effect causing global warming likely to flood half of the habitable land on Earth. The U.S. used to be the number one contributor to carbon emission, now China has become the number one. With China's 1.4 billion people moving upward economically, it puts a tremendous pressure on the demand for cars. If China ever let her population own 2-3 cars per family like the U.S. does, the consequences would be unthinkable. So China is very much motivated to do something about it. The recent agreement between the U.S. and China to reduce carbon emission and monitor climate change is a good thing but hardly adequate to eliminate the global warming problem. China must move to clean energy and provide a mobility solution for her population which is congregating to cities creating smog.

Fortunately, China has had foresight and made significant progress in her national high-speed rail infrastructure in many parts of China and developed advanced mass transit systems in her major cities. However, the mobility problem remains to be challenging. What will China do? China will seize the new automobile revolution and develop a holistic solution for solving the mobility problem of her vast city-urban population. In the following, I describe an unverified government-dependent plan to embrace head-on with a technology-driven Auto Industry Revolution. The plan is more visionary than the McKinsey report mentioned above and its implementation is extremely challenging. However, if any country could implement this plan, it would be China, judging on her success on mega-projects in the past, I will bet more than 50:50 chances for the plan's success. The essence of the plan is as follows:

1. Twelve major cities in China are selected to participate in this Horse-Dragon (HD) Plan, the total population of the twelve cities is close to one billion. Without this plan, the population may demand one hundred million cars.

2. The city shared-bicycle model is elevated to automobiles between mega-cities after mathematic analysis. Citizens with valid ID can take out a HD car from a depot station and return to another depot station in the same or other city. Depots are designed with fully automated parking, maintenance and service system functioning 24 hours a day easily accessible from mass transit. The plan expects AA car available in a decade to auto-deliver.

3. The process of reserving a car and return is done with an online system with smart phone. Commuting routes are automatically matched and offered first priority.

4. The HD cars are designed with most advanced technologies providing navigation and driver assistance (ADAS) moving from gas engine to hybrid to electric to AA within one decade.

5. Citizens can purchase car service contract based on miles to be driven and time to possess the car. A fee algorithm is worked out based on a sophisticated model of efficient utilization formula and all HD cars are self-insured with self-fault detection system (accidents will be judged by the "black box" monitor in the HD cars. Drivers will be charged accordingly).

6. Governments of the participating cities will design highways with HD lane(s) and separate commercial vehicle lane as well as developing traffic rules for AA to selfdeliver. The Central Government will implement appropriate highways between the participating cities.

7. Car models are provided by manufacturers meeting government specifications (commodity PC model), modular design with parts standardized and replaceable at all depot stations by trained technicians.

Different models will satisfy different private car needs for pleasure, business and vacation requirements and preferences. Car reservations can specify model and accessories needed (boats, bikes, camping equipment etc) with a 12 hours advance notice.

8. All car maintenance will be performed by technicians at car depots. Car owner must bring the car (except AA cars) for maintenance according to specified schedule.

9. Private companies, including car manufacturers, electronics and technology companies, appliances, auto parts companies and online service companies, can bid to participate in the HD enterprise. The total number of depots (about 0.5 million) will provide millions of jobs (technician and engineers offset replaced jobs such as taxi drivers) self-supported by the enterprise (modified McDonald model).

10. The first trial of the plan will start at Guangzhou and Shanghai before 2018. The net savings is an ultimate reduction of cars needed from 50 million to 8 million (based on HD cars driven 20 hours per day vs private cars driven 2 hours per day).

Although the above plan is speculative, initiating such a plan in China is likely to kick off an automobile revolution with great impact and benefit to the world.

CHAPTER 6

What Does the U.S. Want from the South China Sea?

——ɯ——

SOUTH CHINA SEA WAS so named because it has been recognized as far back as 7th century A.D. as a part of China. Yes, there is dispute today but it can be easily traced from historical events. In 1884-85, there was the Sino-France war, when France was extending her colonial power to Asia, namely into China and Indochina; at the end, France got what she wanted in Indochina but recognized that those islands in the South China Sea (including Paracel Islands, Woody Island, Duncan Island and Spratly Islands) belonged to China. In 1933, while China was suffering from foreign aggressions from Japan and Russia, France seized the islands in the South China Sea. Then Japan began a war plan to conquer mainland China and in 1938 seized the South China Sea Islands from France. As the WW II ended in 1945 with Japan declared unconditional surrender to China and her Allies, the islands in South China Sea as well as Taiwan and its surrounding islands were reverted back to China. The U.S. as the leader of the Allied forces was not only a witness but instrumental in constructing the Potsdam proclamation and San Francisco Peace Treaty which demanded Japan to return all seized territory from China back to China. In 1947, the Republic of China publicly announced the 11-dash line to define the Chinese territory of South China Sea. The 11-dash line was adopted and revised to 9-dash line by People's Republic of China in 1949. The U.S. an ally with Republic of China at that time was fully aware of this part of history about the South China Sea and its islands.

The division of China with two governments may have contributed to the low level attention paid to the islands by both governments. However, the ROC government has governed the Taiping Island (part of the Spratly Islands) where an airport has been built, a garrison is stationed and tourists are welcome whereas the PRC government has maintained control of the Paracel Islands, where the Woody Island, one of the largest island, has an airport, hospital, school and bank serving about 2000 residents. The neighboring countries in the South China Sea, principally Vietnam and Philippines have made claims to these islands and made attempts to make landfills to enlarge the squatted island or docking stationary vessel to facilitate occupation. In response to these foreign claims, the PRC government has increased its own well engineered landfill and infrastructure constructions in the Spratly Islands. Although the Chinese island construction efforts on her own islands are perfectly legal, but it raised concern and envy from the neighboring countries, namely Philippines and Vietnam.

Ever since the U.S. initiated her "Pivot to Asia Pacific" policy, one can see the increasing diplomatic maneuver the U.S. is engaging with Asia Pacific nations. The elevation of the US-Japan Mutual Defense Treaty permitting Japan to make first attack on behalf of its ally and encouraging Japan to revise its Pacifist constitution and to strengthen its military power is the first deed. The finalizing of the decade long negotiation of a Trans-Pacific Partnership Agreement (TPP) governing trade and investment between 11 signed members excluding China is the second deed. (Although it is now scrapped by the Trump Administration) The increased military exercises conducted in the Pacific involving the U.S., Japan and other Asian nations and the development of several bilateral defense treaties between either Japan or the U.S. with another AP nation is the third deed. Most recently, the U.S. has plunged into the South China Sea dispute arena even though the U.S. is not a claimer in the South China Sea. The U.S. by raising the flag of freedom of navigation, entered into the South China Sea by sending spy planes and naval ships into the region to challenge the 12 nautical mile security zone sanctioned by the United Nation Convention Law of the Seas (UNCLOS). This is the fourth deed of the U.S. that has raised the temperature of the AP hot spot.

As a US citizen observing the above deeds, one cannot help but wonder what does the U.S. want in the South China Sea or in the Asia Pacific? A recent article, entitled American Aggression Against China written by Christopher

Black, an international criminal lawyer in Toronto, and published in Neon Easten Outlook on February 7, 2016, had given a thorough analysis of the U.S. actions in the South China Sea. He concluded that the U.S., never ratified UNCLOS but recognized the international law on 12 nautical miles security zone, was acting purely as an aggressor to provoke China. Mr. Black pointed out the sovereignty timeline regarding the islands and interpreted the legal significance of UNCLOS laws applicable to the islands; China was within her rights to do what she was doing. On the other hand, Black raised the question why is the U.S. adopting a double standard and practicing hypocrisy regarding UNCLOS and freedom of navigation. There was no maritime issue (freedom of passage) in the South China Sea other than the force entry by US navy vessel breaking into the 12 mi security zone without permission. This deliberate aggression (and bragging) is making the U.S. looking like a gangster nation. Black's article has prompted me to ask why is the U.S. doing this? What does the U.S. want from the South China Sea?

More than half of China's import and export goods sail through the South China Sea; it is to China's interest that the sea lanes are open to everyone without obstacles. In fact, South China Sea is safe and has never had any incidence such as pirates. So there is no need for a maritime cop patrolling, never mind having more military vessels coming from afar to crisscross those sea lanes in the South China Sea. So what does the U.S. really want from the South China Sea then? As I understand, when the U.S. Congress blocked the ratification of UNCLOS (proposed by President Bush in 2007 and promoted by Secretary of State Hillary Clinton, Joint Chief of Staff, Martin Dempsey and Defense Secretary Leon Panetta in 2009), the objection was that UNCLOS would restrict the U.S. freedom in deep-sea mining. Could it be that the U.S. had discovered some valuable minerals in the bottom of those South China Sea islands? Even so, China had declared welcome to partnership with other nations to explore energy resources in the South China Sea, wouldn't a partnership negotiation a better approach than sending battle ships to the region?

Another unthinkable scenario is that the U.S. simply does not want to see China rise peacefully. What the U.S. is doing is using South China Sea as an excuse to provoke China into a confrontation. If that is what the U.S. want out of the South China Sea, then we should not be surprised that China will fortify her occupied islands with defense weaponry. If this were the U.S. strategy, I believe more Americans would oppose such a strategy simply because the U.S. citizens could not see the justification for such a war. Recalling the Vietnam war in the 70's, it was justified under an ideology confrontation, but eventually it was opposed by American citizens when they realized the war was not in the best interest of the U.S. In the South China Sea situation, a war over a few rocky small islands could not be in the best interest of the U.S. Based on the above discussions, I do not know an answer to the title question and I will challenge anyone to come up with a good answer backed by rational thinking and justice.

CHAPTER 7

US-China Relation Does Not Need Another Lawyer

—᙭—

It has become obvious even to school children that the US-China relations is not on good terms based on mainstream media reports, although no one has a clear idea why it is so, not even the children's teachers. The mass media seem to be spinning a picture that China is a threat to the U.S., but in what way and to what extent? It is all speculations with hardly any evidence. We can clearly see the threat from terrorists because there were terrorist's events happening not only around us in the world but also in the U.S. homeland. The San Bernardino shooting (12-2-2015), killed 14 and injured 22, has rekindled Americans the fear and resentment towards the terrorists since the 9-11 tragic terrorists attack. In contrast, China shows no aggression to the U.S. other than being competitive economically in trade and development. Russia or the former Soviet Union had planned to establish a missile base in Cuba which no doubt posed an obvious security threat to the U.S. but China never wanted to have any foreign military base nor intended to place any weapon near the U.S. It is the U.S. who would place a Terminal High Altitude Area Defense (THAAD) system in South Korea causing concern in China. China's rising economy and competitive pressure to the U.S. economy is no different from the time when Japan's economic growth threatened the US economy in the late 1980's to 1990's. Through industrial transformation and serious trade negotiations, the U.S. eventually fended off the Japanese economic threat.

The title of this paper is a statement borrowed from Ms Abigail Washburn, a claw hammer banjo player, folk song singer and Grammy winner for the Best Folk Album in 2016. The interesting life story of Ms Washburn would explain why she said that "the US-China relation does not need another lawyer". Ms Abigail Washburn as a college student majored in East Asian Studies at Colorado College in Vermont and took an intensive Mandarin language training at Middlebury College (Vermont). She visited China in 1996 and exposed to Buddhism studies. After college graduation she was ready to go to China to study law and become a lawyer (with an ambition to help China in judicial reform, a goal was changed by her music talent). She became a musician and singer instead.

As life is always full of unpredictable twists and turns, Abigail by chance was stimulated by American folk music and the banjo instrument. She then bought a banjo and intended to bring it to China. As fate dictated, she was discovered at a Kentucky folk music festival and invited to Nashville for making an album. That was certainly a life-changing event and she had to tell her friends in China that she had changed her mind to pursue a music career rather than to be a lawyer. Her friends told her, great, when you are ready, bring your banjo and come to perform in China. As a matter of fact, she did and she learned and performed Chinese folk songs as well, for example, Tai Yang Chu Lai Le (太陽出來了, The Sun Rises) is one that can be heard from YouTube. Her music career is not very different from many other musicians, touring the country and earning her recognition; except in her case, her Mandarin knowledge and ability to sing Mandarin folk songs have distinguished her from other American folk song singers.

Ms Abigail Washburn kept her promise and visited China and performed her bilingual folk music. She even taught in Sichuan University American folk music; she had learned that the Chinese folk singers would use a lot of hand gestures when singing. She understood that the gestures would simply add to the expression of emotions. As a successful musician, she understood that the music could connect hearts better than anything else. She had toured in Tibet in 2006 and she performed in the 2008 Summer Olympics in Beijing. Often in her music, the lyrics addressed social issues and current events. Her work had made her an ambassador for American culture to China and deservingly, she was named as the first US-China Center Fellow of Vanderbilt University in 2013.

The statement, "US-China Relation Does Not Need Another Lawyer", was made in a TED talk by Ms Washburn as a TED Fellow in 2012. She wanted to be a lawyer to improve US-China relations and yet she became a musician and discovered the power of music. She had formed remarkable connections touring across the U.S. and China while playing banjo and singing American and Chinese folk songs. She had met so many people who all had a story to tell related to US-China relations, adopting children, romance and love story, interesting encounters during travel, etc., etc., but none related to a 'China Threat' or 'the U.S. Threat'. This makes one wonder why there is so much hostility in the mass media, is it because they have no good stories to report or they are simply pursuing a hidden agenda to push the two great countries to be enemies?

Ever since the U.S. recognized the People's Republic of China, the cultural exchange activities and interaction between the American people and the Chinese people have improved the US-China relations steadily, yet the official dialog in diplomatic language between the two countries are full of intrigue, suspense and even hostility. Often, the so called conflicts had no direct impact to each other rather they were only indirect geopolitical implications. It is hard for citizens to understand the hidden agenda behind diplomatic language and actions, but it is not difficult for citizens to appreciate (through music, for instance) that the people of two great countries are peace loving and friendly towards each other. Neither Chinese nor the Americans are war mongers.

Of course, there were differences in culture, history, and language, but the friendship among citizens could be built regardless. There have been quite a number of adopted Chinese children in the U.S. There is a national organization called Families with Children from China with over 100 chapters in nearly all states. These families are the proof that there is no threat but love between American and Chinese people. From 1999-2013, there were 71,633 adopted Chinese children in the U.S., the highest percentage in adoption far exceeding that of any other sending nation. Based on this number and at least 6 friends per adopted child (2 parents, 4 grandparents, and possible siblings), we can estimate that there are over half million Americans being friends of these adopted Chinese children today. How would they feel about the deteriorating US-China relations?

The governments were supposed to serve the people, shouldn't the citizens of the U.S. and China question their governments why do they portrait a hostile country to country relationship and yet their citizens obviously do not share such hostility? Why do the mass media try to brain wash the citizens with confrontational news and for what purpose? This paper represents the organic media challenging the mainstream media: don't spin the news! Do focus on evidence and balance the media with positive stories!

CHAPTER 8

Chinese Foreign Minister Wang Yi's Speech at CSIS

—w—

FOREIGN LEADERS' SPEECH AT CENTER for Strategic and International Studies (CSIS) are significant because CSIS is a platform for foreign leaders to declare and explain important policy statements to the American people. For example, in 2013, the Japanese Prime Minister gave his speech, which was nicknamed "Japan Is Back!"(CSIS, 2-22-2013), declared Japan's intention to return Japan to a "normal country" meaning to revise Japan's Pacifist Constitution, to enhance Japan's military strength and to be ready to engage in warfare on behalf of Japan's ally as born out later. We have commented on that speech before and the reason why Abe Shinzo's militaristic policy worries leaders in Asian countries. In this paper, we review and comment on the Chinese Foreign Minister, Wang Yi's speech, The Developing China and China's Diplomacy, at CSIS on February 25, 2016. I nickname this speech as "Peaceful Transformation and Development in Non-Threatening Chinese (Philosophy and Style) Manner" to capture the essence of Mr. Wang's speech.

Minister Wang started his speech by acknowledging China's successful economic development but an unsustainable one calling for a transformation to take an energy efficient, environment protective, green, recyclable and sustainable path. This change has already showed some progress although unavoidably it lowers the economic growth to 6.9% in 2015 (each percentage point is equivalent to 2.6% of 2005's economy). To sustain such a growth is a challenge but China is confident that she can do it because of the following three conditions: 1. China has an enormous market potential (four times of the U.S. population), 2. China's urban development is only at 40% (developed country usually at 70%) and 3. China's service sectors are just about 50% of the total economy (developed country is above 70%). Hence China is confident in sustaining her economic growth and maintaining a great economic and trade partnership with the U.S. as well as providing opportunities to the international community.

On Foreign policy, Minister Wang was modest in characterizing China's steady development and success in foreign relations but emphasized that China's foreign policy is the extension of her domestic policy under a vision advanced by President Xi Jinping, "the Chinese Dream" - bringing Chinese citizens to a middle class standard of living. China's foreign policy is directed to help fulfilling the Chinese dream by developing steady and friendly external environment and attracting external resources. Since Xi Jinping assumed the leadership, China's foreign policy is guided by three principles, protecting justified national interest, fulfilling obligated international responsibilities and developing friendly and mutually beneficial (win-win) international relations. Wang said, looking forward, China has five missions in foreign affairs:

1. Make more nations and their people understand the Chinese style (manner) development, her chosen socialist system and development path. Regardless one's background, every Chinese citizen shall be offered opportunity to develop one's dream through one's own effort. China has no intention of exporting the Chinese system or style of development but China is confident that her 86,000,000 party members can accomplish any goal they set their mind to. (Referenced Xi 's book on governance in China, widely reprinted 5 million copies)
2. Maintain and support the international order established after the end of WW II, a peaceful condition earned with 35 million Chinese lives. China, as the first signed member of the United Nations, will not create an alternative order, rather she will fully support the UN mission and responsibility in maintaining world order. Wang urged the development of an open and free international trade system and extending to investment as advocated by APEC rather than having regional restrictive agreements. Wang further explained the purpose of the Asian

Infrastructure Investment Bank (AIIB) supported by 57 nations for supplementing the investment needs in infrastructure development in Asia.

3. Actively promote China's development and her joint development with partners, a focused mission to assist the fulfillment of the "one belt one road" project proposed by China. The project needs three pillars; the first is infrastructure connections between the participating nations. The second is collaboration in manufacturing and energy supply among nations with mutual dependency. The third is cultural exchange and mutual absorption leading to advances in human civilization.

4. Maintain and protect China's oversea investments and enterprises, ensuring their safety and security. China now has more than 30,000 companies and several million Chinese people living overseas, 120 million traveling abroad each year and non-financial direct investment reaching over $1.2 trillion in 2015. The Chinese government has obligation to protect these legal interests, however, with limited organizations and resources, the foreign ministry must work hard in cooperation with foreign countries to protect and promote these investments and enterprises.

5. Participate and resolve hotspot issues in the world, constructively solving international problems. China, as a permanent member of the UN Security Council, is obligated to maintain international peace and harmony. Solving hotspot issues provides healthy conditions for world development such as the one belt on road project. China has participated in resolving South Sudan's crisis, Afghanistan's issue, Myanmar's problem, and Syria's battles.

Minister Wang particularly pointed out the common concern about North Korea's nuclear weapon development and declared China's three principles regarding the nuclear threat, 1. N. Korea must not develop nuclear weapon, 2. Korea Peninsula must not have military conflict, and 3. Any action in the Korea peninsula must not harm Chinese security and interest. Following Wang's meeting with John Kerry, the U.S. Secretary of State and his CSIS speech, the UN Security council just unanimously passed on 3-3-2016 a resolution placing strict sanctions against N. Korea. This is a clear example that the U.S. and China can work together through the UN to find solution to a hotspot problem.

Minister Wang also made a clear statement regarding the South China Sea concern. First, there is no real problem with freedom of navigation. Although China has lost 42 small islands and rocks to squatters, China still insists settlement through negotiation according to the DOC agreement China and ten ASEAN members have signed which specifies that disputes are to be resolved through negotiation. Second, China urges non-claimant neighboring nations to help maintain peace and stability in the South China Sea. Third, external nations should support and make the disputing parties to resolve the issues by negotiation. Under these three conditions, China and the ASEAN nations will be completely capable of maintaining peace and stability in the South China Sea.

Finally, Wang addressed the US-China relation, emphasizing that a collaborative win-win relationship is beneficial to the world. President Xi has suggested the U.S. and China to establish a new great nation relationship. China is cooperating with the U.S. moving in that direction by having more dialogs and increasing mutual understanding. Wang rejected the notion that China will be the ultimate opponent of the U.S. as a non-existing issue. China is still a developing country. For a long time forward China must focus on her own development; China will not compete against anyone nor intend to replace anyone. China and the U.S. have become two closely mutually dependent nations with $558 billion trades and 4.75 million people visiting each other every year (more than 10,000 people flying each day). It is inconceivable that the U.S. and China will have irresolvable differences. China will not be another U.S. China has no aggression in her DNA or much desire to be the world's guardian savior. Even one day China has grown stronger with bigger GDP than the U.S., China will still have her oriental philosophy and tolerance to deal with other nations and at that time, the cooperation between the U.S. and China will be even deeper. What is needed today is to increase the two nations' mutual understanding.

Comparing Wang's speech with Abe Shinzo's speech, one cannot help but conclude that the U.S. has no justification to side with Japan to target China as the eventual enemy. It would be far easier to solve world issues by working with the rising China than treating China as an enemy. Wang in his final words on the CSIS speech was trying to get this message across to the American people.

CHAPTER 9

Why Does China Keep Increasing Her Defense Budget?

—⟁—

ABSTRACT

AS THE U.S. AND CHINA become the two largest economies in the world, the complexity of their relationship goes beyond trades, investments, cultural exchange, and education. The competition in the area of technology (including space) and military seem to be more of concern casting uneasiness into the future of the US-China relationship. The real important strategic question is: Why does China keep increasing her defense budget? Still dwarfed from the U.S. defense spending, China's increasing in defense budget is out of fear and insecurity. China's decision to reduce the size of her army, to modernize her navy and air force for quality and to focus on technology-driven defense system rather than offensive weapons including her construction in the South China Sea is consistent with the 'fear and vulnerability argument'. China will gauge her defense spending with her economic development. So long her economy is healthy she will keep up with defense spending unless she no longer feels fear and vulnerability.

—⟁—

As the U.S. and China become the two largest economies in the world, the complexity of their relationship goes beyond trades, investments, cultural exchange, and education. In fact, in the area of technology (including space) and military, there seem to be more competition and concern casting uneasiness into the future of the US-China relationship. If you sensed that the U.S. had begun to sound off a hostile voice towards China, it was because the U.S.

was surprised by China's rapid rise (in economy, technology and military) and was not ready to deal with China on the world stage. The U.S. maintains a policy restricting high tech export to China and yet China has made tremendous advances on her own including satellite technology, launching missiles and the Beidou system (a variant global positioning system with added communication function) as well as super computer technology needed in space and other advanced R&D areas, lasers, robotics etc.

The notion, 'China is a threat to the U.S.', was mainly touted by the military industry complex based on comparing the two nations' defense spending. China kept a double-digit increase in defense budget while the U.S. is suffering from defense budget cuts in recent years. However, we must examine the real numbers before drawing conclusions. Based on news reports, I have collected the following data:

U.S. versus China's Defense Spending: 1996 ($266B:$8.46B), 1997 ($270B:$10B, +18%), 1998 ($271B:$11B, +10%), 1999 ($292B:$12.5B, +14%), 2000 ($304B:$14.6B, +17%), 2001 ($335B:$17B, +16%), 2002 ($362B:$20B, +17.6%), 2003 ($456B:$22B, +10%), 2004 ($491B:$24.6B, +11.8%), 2005 ($506B:$29.9B, +21.5%), 2006 ($556B:$35B, +17%), 2007 ($625B:$45B, +28.6%), 2008 ($696B:$57.22B, +27%), 2009 ($698B:$70.27B, +23%), 2010 ($721B:$77.9, Y532.115B+11%), 2011 (*\$717B:$91.5B, Y602,4B+17%), 2012 (*\$681B:$106.4B, Y670B,+16%), 2013 (*\$610B: $114.38B, Y720.2B, +7.5%), 2014 ($614B:$131.57B, Y808.2B, +15%), 2015 ($637B:$145B, Y890B, +10%), 2016 ($651B:$156B. Y958B,+7. 6%).

The above data give us a lot of information. The defense spending is in billions. The *\ sign indicates a budget reduction which occurred between 2011-2013 for the U.S. The annual increase of the Chinese defense spending by percentage was indicated. Due to exchange rate and purchasing power variants the percent increases are not precise. China has truly maintained a double-digit increase of her defense spending for the past two decades until the current year. However, China started with a very small defense budget for the size of her country. In addition, China paced her defense spending with her economy. As her economy slows down, her defense budget is scaled down accordingly. One must notice that in terms of dollar spent, the US defense budget dwarfed China's 31.5:1 in 1996 to 15.9:1 in 2006 and 4.2:1 in 2016. The U.S. leads in spending and advanced weapon development for so many decades that the U.S. military is far superior to the Chinese military in equipment, personnel training and real battle experiences. Some analysts predict that even with double-digit increase in defense spending, China cannot come close to the U.S. military power for four decades or more.

The real important strategic question is: Why does China keep increasing her defense budget? By finding a logical answer to the above question, the U.S. can then devise a strategy to deal with the rising China. At present, it is unreasonable to assume China is a threat to the U.S. It is also foolish to think an arms race is a sound strategy. The collapse of the Soviet Union is a clear historical case demonstrating that arms race and military confrontation are too costly to be sustainable, eventually destroying the economy even with profitable weapon sales. Both China and the U.S. should have understood the Soviet case and the fact that there would be no winner if nuclear weapons were included in the arms race.

So, why does China keep increasing her defense spending then? Does China have an ambitious plan to replace the superpower U.S. or does China feel compelled to build up her defense just for real defense? In the following, I would like to establish a number of factors as the basic reasons for China to keep increasing her defense spending. These are: 1. China felt insecure, 2. China recognized her vulnerability, 3. China witnessed the settlement of world crises by brutal wars and 4. China realized her weak defense capability, a large army with little modern battle experience, outdated equipments and training and a huge burden to the economy contributing little productivity. I shall present some arguments below to support this line of thinking.

China is increasing her defense budget out of fear and insecurity. The fear factor always exists among nations especially between great countries. (John J.

Mearsheimer asserts that 'fear' drives nations to practice hegemony theory) I rather believe China's fear is born from historical nightmares rather than from hegemony theory. Since 19th century, China had been invaded and violated her sovereignty rights by numerous world powers, all developed western nations from Europe and America and Russia and Japan from Asia. China was not willing to expose her North East region to foreign military occupation again after WW II but she had no choice but to enter into the Korean War (The Soviet would be glad to march her army through northern China to the Korea Peninsula). Likewise, China would not like to see her South West border with Indochina constantly in turmoil but she had little means to stop the Vietnam war until the U.S. really wanted to stop. China is vulnerable to her 14 watchful neighboring countries with over 22000 kilometers of land border.

China's vulnerability is not limited to land only; she has over 15,000 kilometer coast line not counting the security zones defined by her islands in the East and South China Seas. For many centuries, Japanese pirates had always attacked China's mainland and fishermen with hit and loot tactics along the East China Sea extending into the South China Sea. The present disputed islands in the South China Sea historically belonged to China but were one time seized by the French and later by the Japanese until Japan surrendered at the end of WW II. As China raises economically, more than half of her $4 trillion trades, imports and exports, must pass through the South and East China Seas. It is comical for Japan and the U.S. to accuse China impairing freedom of navigation in the South China sea. Bringing more naval power into South and East China Seas simply reminds China her vulnerability and her inadequate navy.

Is China really a threat to Japan and the U.S.? Japan has a much stronger and more modern navy than anyone in Asia; whereas the U.S. fleets are matchless in the world. China not only understands her vulnerability but also has a genuine fear from witnessing world crises being settled by brutal wars and regime change being practiced as a legitimate foreign policy. China's repeated claims, 'China wishes to rise peacefully' seemed to fall on deaf ears. Following the US 'Pivot to Asia' policy, she saw Japan's eagerness in enhancing her military forces and anxiously revising her pacifist constitution to give her liberty to attack. She also saw many large scale military exercises conducted in the Asia Pacific which purposely or not could only remind China her need to modernize her military. Hence, came the reform to reduce 300,000 personnel in China's army, to upgrade to higher quality equipments and to develop more sophisticated communication systems. I would interpret China's continuous increase of her defense spending as a logical decision reacting to 'fear and vulnerability' caused by her neighbors and the U.S.

China's decision to reduce the size of her army, to modernize her navy and air force for quality and to focus on technology-driven defense system rather than offensive weapons is consistent with the 'fear and vulnerability argument'. The construction work done on her South China Sea islands is obviously for defense rather than for offense. China gauges her defense spending with her economic development. So long her economy is healthy she will keep up with defense spending unless she no longer feels fear and vulnerability.

CHAPTER 10

Interpretation on the South China Sea
Dispute by History and Law

—⟋⟍—

CURRENTLY, THERE ARE TWO HOT spots in the Asia Pacific region catching world attention, the Korea peninsula where North Korea is pursuing nuclear weapon development over the objections from her neighbors and the U.S. and the South China Sea (S.C.S.) where Vietnam and the Philippines are challenging China's sovereignty claim over the islands in the S.C.S. with the U.S. looking like a curator of the saga. The former issue is a real security threat to the region since North Korea not only places nuclear weapon development as higher priority than its economic development but also repeatedly makes reckless threats of using the nuclear weapon. The latter issue is almost a theatric play staged by naval forces brought into the S.C.S. There were no real maritime problems in S.C.S. other than a few disputes over small islands between Philippine and China and Vietnam and China.

Early this month, the United Nation Security Council has unanimously passed a resolution to place strict economic sanction against North Korea. The fact that the United States can work with China to orchestrate this sanction is indeed a good sign, not only from the viewpoint of achieving effective sanction but also from the perspective of demonstrating a good collaborative US-China relationship in dealing with world crisis. We can look forward to a better world, more harmonious and peaceful, simply because the two great nations can cooperate with each other.

However, the saga in the S.C.S. is gaining heat due to the following three continued developments:

1. Philippines' challenge on China's sovereignty claim, a U shaped ocean boundary in the S.C.S. including Spratly islands (On Oct. 29, 2015, the Permanent Court of Arbitration in Hague claimed jurisdiction over the case). Vietnam, Malaysia, Brunei and Indonesia all have disputes on islands near them.
2. China's construction efforts on her islands in the S.C.S. making some of them to be serviceable air and sea ports.
3. The U.S. gestures sending naval ships even a carrier to demand freedom of navigation as if the above two activities have restricted the maritime freedom in the S.C.S..

Tracing the origin of the S.C.S. issue really leads to a legal interpretation of the U shaped boundary line China has claimed and published in 1947 after WW II. The officially published U shaped boundary line is based on historical Chinese presence and territorial claims in the S.C.S. In Sino-French war (1884-85), France recognized China's claim of the S.C.S. in exchange for China's recognition of Vietnam as a French occupied colony. In 1933, France seized the Spratly and Paracel islands despite of China's protest and in 1938, Japan took the islands from France till the end of WW II. After Japan surrendered in 1945, according to the San Francisco Treaty and Potsdam Declaration, Japan had to renounce all the captured territory and returned them to their rightful owners. This includes Taiwan, Penghu, Spratly, Paracels etc. acknowledged by both the ROC and PRC governments. At present, ROC is in control of Taipin Island - one of the largest island in Spratly, where a garrison, school, hospital and bank all exist; whereas PRC has total control of the Paracels where China has built airport and seaport on some of the islands.

Although there were squatting activities in the S.C.S. but mainly by fishermen, there was no impact to freedom of maritime. China has taken a very low key in dealing with any disputes in the SCS islands. However, in the recent 2-3 years, more disputes in S.C.S. arose resulting in a confrontational situation as described by the three developments listed above. Many Chinese American organizations especially those familiar with the Chinese history felt necessary to diffuse the confrontation and mystery by revealing the facts. Hence, On March 4-7, 2016, a number of organizations sponsored a series of seminars on the hot topic, disputes in the S.C.S. by inviting two experts on international law, Professor Fu Kuen Chen of Xiamen University and Prof. Yang Cui Bo of Sichuan University to offer a number of presentations on their research at Los Angeles, CA and Flushing and Manhattan, NY and Wash. DC. On behalf of the organizers, I had the privilege to chair the seminar session on March 7th at NYU Kimmel Center. The room was fully packed and the presentations were very stimulating. The audience, including a number of well known professors such as Professor Jerome Cohen, Director of US-Asia Law Institute and his students, Professor James Chieh Hsiung, Professor Huang Chi Chao and Prof. Hua Jun Xiong and many legal professionals including Douglas Burnett of Square, Patton Boggs, Issac B. Kardon, U.S. - Asia Institute, and Shen Jianmin, a practicing attorney with international law background, engaged in a very lively discussion.

Professor Fu first presented numerous historical evidence to establish the de-facto presence of Chinese and their utilization of the S.C.S. over two thousand years through several dynasties. Then he gave a detailed description how the U shape line was drawn, published and recognized by the international community including Vietnam's official acknowledgment of China's definition of ocean boundary in the S.C.S., the U.S. navy requesting permission to survey Spratly island in 1960, and Philippine government returned stolen ROC flag on Taipin Island by Philippine citizens and apologized. He then traced the proceedings of the UN arbitration court, from Philippines' initiation of a false claim denying Spratly islands as real islands, to the problematic creation of the arbitration court when a judge is lacking real impartiality and to the interpretation of UN Convention on the Law of the Seas (UNCLOS) regarding island definition, jurisdiction, compulsory ruling and member's right to refuse acceptance of the ruling when sovereignty is in dispute. Professor Yang added more of his research in historical evidence of China's ocean boundary in the S.C.S. In summary, they concluded that from legal and historical inheritance point of view, China has ample proof for her claim in the S.C.S.

Professor Cohen made a comment during Q&A, "if the tribunal court ruled in favor of the Philippines, it would make China look very bad in the international community" and he asked "what will happen to China then?" Naturally, this is a hypothetical question; the Q&A did not arrive at an answer. As the chair monitoring the session, I could not engage freely in the discussion but Professor Cohen's question stayed with me. Here, I would like to offer my comment. Given the fact that the arbitration court's track record on impartiality and success rate in enforcing its decision are not good, I think in the case of S.C.S., the impact of the court ruling on China would be determined by the ability of the disputing parties to make a successful interpretation to the International community, a PR case I may say.

Since China is armed with more historical facts, research work and archived documents, she should be able to present arguments against the ruling, if necessary, discrediting the impartiality and due diligence of the court. The United States has the richest communication media/industry in the world; hence generally she has a hold on the communication media and platform. However, in recent years since the opening of the Internet, China has established a sizable media and communication network of her own. Therefore, China would not be shy in publicizing her research and due diligence in defending her position regarding S.C.S. In this process, not only the litigants but even the bystanders will be dragged in. If China is able to present a fool-proof counter argument to support her case, every party including sideline cheer leaders will have to face the consequences. To avoid embarrassment, not only China needs to do a thorough research job to defend her position, all litigants must do the same. If the United States is going to take side, then she must do due diligence as well..

Based on what has been known so far, it appears that China has done more research than anyone else in defining the S.C.S. case. The United States most likely has access to the same information. It is my opinion that the academicians and scholars in the U.S. should begin a due diligence to do research on the S.C.S. issue rather than accept blindly the media spin coming with any S.C.S. news. The American citizens and policy makers should be well informed and educated on the S.C.S. issue so that the U.S. will not take the wrong side of the justice. After all, there is no real advantage for the U.S. to take sides in the first place. The S.C.S. has no real security threat to the U.S. If the U.S. would casually or deliberately take the wrong side on the S.C.S. issue, it would no doubt hurt the US-China relations, with both ROC and PRC governments. Therefore, it is wise for the U.S.to stay neutral and impartial to digest all the PR work presented by the disputing parties rather than choreograph any act to compound the S.C.S. issue.

CHAPTER 11

China's Military Strategy - Interpretation
of Her White Paper

—ɯ—

GOVERNMENT WHITE PAPERS, ESPECIALLY ON defense, military and security, are significant because they not only contain policy statements but also include certain amount of details about a government's past deeds and future intentions. In the domain of military strategy, China's military white paper must be treated with care by thorough analyses and interpretation so that China's goals and purposes are understood and correctly interpreted. Only correct interpretation can help guide the U.S. to develop an appropriate China policy particularly related to military strategy. However, the U.S. being a superpower is used to publish her white papers for the world to know her positions but not to publicly discuss other nations' white papers to derive a comprehensive interpretation to help guide the government's diplomatic positions. A case at hand is that the U.S. seems to adopt a hostile anti-China policy, viewing China as a competitive economy as well as a military threat to the United States with little convincing evidence. The recently published Chinese military strategy white paper openly admitted her plans of military reform to upgrade her outdated military organizations and also to a large extent explained in detail her improvements in military strength necessary for peaceful purposes, based mainly on self-defense. There are clear hidden messages in that document: China is concerned with the U.S.'s China policy and her misinterpretation of China's defense strategy.

The document, 'China's Military Strategy', published by China's Information Office of the State Council last May, contains a preface and six chapters. Each will be summarized and commented on in the paragraphs to follow, with attempts to decipher the Chinese government's intention (and its assumption about the US Government's intention). The Chinese and American people's views regarding US-China military interaction will be kept as background in reviewing this document.

From the document's preface, it is clear the Chinese government presents an official position: Military preparedness is necessary for China's modernization and security as well as for active defense to meet new situations and to achieve China's "two Century" goal of realizing Chinese Dream and rejuvenating the Chinese nation. This 'statement' does not alleviate the Western powers' and some of her neighbors' concern that China was a dominating world power two centuries ago, now awakening. Is China rejuvenating to an awaken lion? What would the lion do? This fear seems to be ill-founded, since there is no evidence in the six chapters of this white paper to suggest such a fear. Let's examine the six chapters below.

I. China's national security situation. This chapter emphasizes that globalization has brought changes challenging world community, balance of power, global governing structure and geopolitical issues. New threats include hegemonism, power politics, neo-interventionism and terrorism, resulting in hotspot crises. China desires to have stability and peace to pursue her development but faces serious security threats including North Korea nuclear threat, Diaoyu Island and South China Sea territorial disputes, Sea Line of Communications (SLOCs), Taiwan and other independence attempts as well as competitions in outer space, cyberspace and world military transformation focusing on long range, precision, smart, stealthy, and unmanned warfare. China recognizes her deficiency and need in 'informationization' in her military.

II. The Missions of China's Armed Forces. To achieve and guarantee China's national goal and Chinese dream of having a moderately prosperous society by 2021 and a modern socialist state by 2049 seem to be reasonable and harmless missions. The strategic tasks of the Chinese military described are not much different from that of the U.S. military;

they include handling emergencies and military threats and safeguarding unification, national interests and national stability, deterring and countering nuclear threat, participating in regional and international cooperation for peace keeping, performing rescue, disaster relief, rights and interest protection and supporting national and social development.

III. Strategic Guidance of Active Defense. China's definition of active defense adheres to 'will not attack but will surely counter-attack if attacked'. China's strategic guidelines were revised on 1993, 2004 since 1949 with emphasis in winning informationized local wars, again a defense rather than an offense posture. One thing the Chinese military is different from that of the U.S. is its unique party (CPC) leadership making the military more connected with the Chinese people. The US military assembled under solicitation system is less connected with the people.

IV. Developing China's Armed Forces. China has her traditional army, people's liberation army (PLA), people's armed police force (PAPF), small modular PLA (PLAA), navy (PLAN), air force (PLAAF), second artillery force (PLASAF), outer space, cyberspace and nuclear force all under the CPC leadership with priority on ideological and political building, advanced weaponry upgrade and new personnel training to respond to informationized warfare. China seems to recognize her out-dated military; hence she is reducing up to 300,000 personnel and accelerating a modernization plan.

V. Preparation for Military Struggle (PMS). This is a transformation process to enhance combat effect and to use information system to integrate a wide range of operational forces for joint operation under central military command (CMC). Realistic training is emphasized to reach constant combat readiness for situation of military operation other than war (MOOPWs), emergency, disaster relief, etc.

VI. Military and Security Cooperation. The main concept is to achieve common, comprehensive, cooperative and sustainable security for China involving military partners but in a non-aligned, non-confrontational and not against third party manner. This seems to be pointing fingers at some of her neighbors developing military alliances. China particularly mentions relationship with Russia and ASEAN nations under the above principle and desires to form new model of major country relationship with the U.S.

After reviewing China's military strategy document, one can find the following conclusions: China certainly prioritizes her military strategy for defense and self-defense under the principle, 'We Will Not Attack, But Will Counterattack If Attacked'. China prefers to fulfill her international responsibility through UN, her cooperation with the U.S. in the UN sanction against the North Korea nuclear threat is clear evidence. China's effort in trying to maintain a healthy military budget increase each year is easy to understand from her security situation. China borders with 14 neighborong countries, some hostile, some brewing terrorism and some raising territory disputes. More than half of China's trade goods passing through East and South China Seas are vulnerable to even a small country's naval force intervention. China's military budget is only a fraction of that of the U.S. and her navy strength cannot come close to that of the US Navy probably for decades.

The US 'pivot to Asia' policy seems to ignore China's security concern and overplays the U.S. security concern. The U.S. seems to misinterpret China's geopolitical reality and her non-violence foreign policy; instead of promoting stability in Asia Pacific, the mighty U.S. navy and air force are actually agitating more conflicts and tension. Why and what for? If only the Americans could just swap places with the Chinese for a minute, they would see a very different light in Asia Pacific. Is the U.S. really threatened by China, her meager navy? Are we talking about a real military threat or a hurt of pride that we would rather fight battles than compete with China on economic terms?!

CHAPTER 12

Historical Evidence Prove South China Sea Islands Belonging To Chinese

—⚏—

COLOR REVOLUTION AND INDEPENDENCE MOVEMENT involving protesting citizens are very different issues from territory disputes where there is no unrest of residents. For example, Okinawa islands in the East China Sea were arbitrarily given to Japan for administration by the U.S. post WW II in 1972. According to history, Okinawa was an independent sovereignty with diplomatic tie with and protection from China for centuries until her kingdom was toppled by Japan (1872) and her anti-Japanese resistance was further weakened when Imperial Japan defeated China in the Sino-Japan war (1894). To this day, there are still residents on the island longing for independence and many residents oppose the U.S. having a large military base there. In this case, the ultimate status of Okinawa should be determined by the Okinawans.

The recent disputes about the South China Sea (SCS) islands are entirely different matters. Most SCS islands are uninhabitable and never have had natives. A few large islands now with people came from China or Taiwan. Why the Chinese claim of sovereignty rights over the SCS islands is an issue then? It shouldn't really be. The sovereignty issue on the SCS islands should be resolved by establishing the historical facts such as i. Which people from where came first (usually fisherman), ii. Historical claims made by government and iii. International recognition made by other governments. These historical facts supported with documents, maps and governmental announcements should constitute solid proofs of sovereignty. As for the definition of island versus reef and their rights associated with economic zone versus security zone, they are defined by UN Convention on the Law of Sea (UNCLOS) signed and agreed by international members. Not all nations ratified the UNCLOS, China did and the U.S. did not.

Not surprisingly, there will be disputes on SCS islands as contemporary fishermen desire to catch fish wherever and however far they can reach, but it is surprising that the disputes are elevated to high tension under the issue of maritime freedom. After all the SCS islands are small compared to the vast seas and there were never any incidence of obstruction of maritime freedom. Rather, when the mighty naval ships came from afar to patrol the SCS, the tension rose. Should these naval vessels make their frequent presence in SCS? Why and What for? If it was for island disputes, shouldn't we let the disputing parties to resolve the disputes according to the historical facts they can present and resolving any rights issue by bilateral negotiation? For helping world citizens (especially Americans) to understand the SCS island dispute issues, the following discussion referencing two articles in the Observer Magazine (Cheng Hai Ling, British Navy Records Prove That China Has Sovereignty over SCS, 3-19-2016 and Chang Chien Fong, Taiping Island Is Not An Abandoned Island Governed by Jungle Rule, 3-20-2016) would shed some light on the issue.

China, in her long history, has ample records documenting the historical facts related to every dynasty and every emperor. Many of these records include sovereignty matters including territories extending into the seas from shore. However, these Chinese documents tend to be ignored by the West partly due to language difficulties and partly due to prejudice. Regarding SCS, as early as Han Dynasty (206BCE-220CE), a geography book (Han Book Geography) recorded since Qin (221-206BCE) and Han, Chinese had sailed to SCS with Map (called Needle Map) and discovered the SCS islands. Tang Dynasty (618-906) included SCS in her sovereignty map. Ming Dynasty (1368-1644) famous for sending Cheng Ho out for seven sea fares to explore the world and one of his missions was to inspect the SCS islands. However, these historical records did not have as much impact on the West's understanding of SCS as the western records.

Through scholars' research, it was found that British ships had reached Canton, China in 1637 and since then the British had cumulated lots of maritime records including SCS confirming that only the Chinese fishermen were ever present in the SCS centuries ago. A more recent reference from the British Royal Navy, 'the Chinese Sea Directory' (1879), had plenty vivid descriptions about the Chinese fishermen working and living on the SCS islands taking advantage of seasonal wind to go there, sending supplies and returning with sea cucumbers and sea turtle shells items only Chinese people valued them. In volume II of this 1879 book, numerous pages were devoted to SCS, mentioning "Tizard Bank and Reefs" (Chinese fishermen settled there and trade sea products with Hainan boats carrying rice), "Huba Island" (Named Taiping Island today governed by Republic of China where the drinking water quality was noted to be better), "Thi-Tu Reefs and Island" (Zhong Ye Island, now squatted by the Philippines, where Chinese fishermen from Hainan were found getting drinking water from north east part of the island. There was no mention at all any presence of the Filipinos) and "Lan-Keeam Cay" is a name from Hainan Chinese not a Filipino name.

The British Royal Navy record described how the Hainan fishermen went to the South Sea of China Sea (i.e. SCS) to practice seasonal fishing, harvesting sea cucumbers, turtle shells and fish fins. One sea route was described that Hainan people in March would go to SCS dropping supplies and a few fishermen there to work and sailed on to Borneo then came back in June to collect the fishermen with their sea goods, apparently taking advantage of the weather and ocean wind. In this directory, it also made reference to Daniel Ross's comments (1817) on Hainan's fishing boats being solid and fast (made of special hard wood) and they could sail 700-800 miles. Another British publication, Nautica Magazine and Navel Chronicle (1842) even mentioned that the Chinese fishermen had reached the Indian Ocean.

In addition to British and French archives about SCS, Japanese had records as well. China lost in the Sino-France war (1884-85) and let France colonized Indochina, but France clearly recognized China's sovereignty over SCS. In 1933, France seized Spratly and Paracel islands but then in1938 lost them to

Japan. Japan renamed them New South Islands and later assigned to be part of KaoHsiung (Taiwan's largest southern city) expecting to permanently occupy them all. When WW II ended in 1945, Japan surrendered unconditionally and, per Potsdam Declaration and San Francisco Treaty, Japan had to renounce all her illegally captured territories including Taiwan and SCS islands which should be returned to China.

Japan not willing to share her relevant official government records on SCS is easily understandable (damaging to her ambition to occupy China's Diaoyu Island in the East China Sea), but there are some civilian records available. For example, a Japanese book, Hurrican Islands (published in 1940, JPNo. 46072746 and NDC 292.24, written by a retired Japanese Navy Lt. Colonel, 1890-, 小倉, 卯之助), describing his sea adventure from Okinawa to Taiwan and SCS. He traveled to Taiping Island on 1-13-1919, upon landing discovering that Chinese had been living there. He found a shrine with plaque written in Chinese with Chinese date, Year Seven of Republic of China (1918). In addition, there is government document from Vietnam officially recognizing China's U shaped SCS boundary.

The above and much more foreign documents and numerous Chinese ancient and modern history books and maps prove without doubt that SCS islands belong to China. Both PRC and ROC governments are united on this position, that is why President Ma Ying-Jeou had flown to Taiping island on 1-28-2016 and showed the world with his presence that Taiping is not only habitable (discredit Philippine's false claim) but is established with school, bank, hospital and sea and air ports. As an American, it is really puzzling to see the U.S. siding with the Philippines and hyping the SCS situation to a world crisis. Wouldn't the stability of SCS be far more important to China for her trades and security than to the U.S.? Are we playing an honest game?

CHAPTER 13

Sino-Vietnam War (1979) Deserves Serious Reflection - A Tipping Point for the Collapse of the Soviet

—ɯ—

AN ANONYMOUS 50-PAGE DOCUMENT DISCUSSING the brief Sino-Vietnam war (SVW) in 1979 came to my mailbox recently. The document implied that it was written by a Western analyst and translated to Mandarin by the analyst's colleague. The document was suppressed from publication because the superior of the analyst felt that too much credit and praise were given to the Chinese leader, Deng Xiao Ping. After examining this document, I found that the analyst had presented fairly accurate facts (events, dates, names, geographic locations and some statistics related to the war) which could be checked out by research. The analyses and comments in the document are quite logical, definitely making the paper deserving to see the daylight. Hence, I am summarizing this long article, Foreign Sources Revealing the Truth of Sino-Vietnam War, with my comments added in this paper.

This paper started with the notion that the changes with small nations could not make enough impact to the balance or struggle of world powers. China's strategic change from being a nominal member in the Soviet Union bloc to a de facto ally with the U.S. was the primary reason that had led the Soviet Union to collapse eventually. The Soviet and the U.S. leaders did not have any serious regard to China's presence in the world arena until Nixon-Kissinger (1972) realized and formulated a strategy of working with China against the Soviet Union. Deng Xiao Ping visited the U.S. on January 1, 1979, the date the U.S. recognized China, and seven days later China launched a massive but a short 28 days war against Vietnam.

The document went into depth describing Vietnam and her wars with France and the U.S. which had built her confidence in winning brutal wars; indeed, the Vietnam soldiers (even civilians) were credited as tough fighters, persistent, deadly and cruel. Though Vietnam essentially won the Vietnam war but she was resentful that China did not support her all the way and China was courted by the U.S. (1972-). Although receiving military aid from China, Vietnam acted alone and hostile to her neighbors, Khmer, Laos and Cambodia; She conquered the South Vietnam in 55 days (1975). Vietnam's over confidence in her ability to fight and her obvious ambition reminded China about Japan's behavior towards China and Indochina prior to WW II. The Chinese Premier Zhou En Lai was alarmed and passed on instructions to Deng to watch out for Vietnam and to prepare a strategy to check her ambitions.

The Vietnam leader, Li Yi, went to Beijing (11/1977) asking for more military aid, but Deng refused him, and then he turned to the Soviet Union. The Soviet wanted to suppress China and granted Li's full request; a year later they signed a peace and cooperation treaty. Then within one year, Vietnam armed all her military forces with Russian equipment. In 12/1978, Vietnam attacked Khmer, captured Jin Bian in 14 days and destroyed Khmer, but it was both a strategic and a tactic mistake. China was wary of Vietnam's ambition in Indochina and had been preparing for war with Vietnam. Destroying Khmer essentially enhanced China's resolve to teach Vietnam a lesson. Hence, during Deng's visit to the U.S., he told President Carter his plan of attacking Vietnam. Carter, with the Vietnam War experience, warned Deng and did not want to get involved in any battle against the war hardened Vietnam. Deng, of course, had all figured out how to fight Vietnam, including stationing troops on China's Northern border in case Russia invading in the name of helping Vietnam.

Deng originally planned to attack in January, 1980, but khmer's fall in the end of 1978, hastened Deng's plan. Tactically, military maneuver and fighting in the Monsoon season (March and April), are not desirable. Vietnam's attack on Khmer in December and won in 14 days gave China a whole two months to act. Since China had well prepared for a number of years, this two months window was perfect for China to move up her plan. Deng, an excellent and avid bridge player, after touched base with Carter and calculated Russia's inability to mobilize during the winter, then made a decisive decision to punish the Vietnam with a quick and devastating attack by moving 300,000 Chinese troops with overwhelming fire power across the border (7/8/1979). Though the Vietnam troops were tough and loyal, but they were caught by surprise, outnumbered, outgunned, ill trained for large scale war and poorly equipped with communication gear, thus, suffered great casualty.

In sixteen days, China took Liang Shan, threatening to sweep the open flat capital, Ho Nui, but next day Deng ordered troops to withdraw to return home, on the way back destroying any resistance and industrial bases. Deng regarded Vietnam as the Soviet's Cuba in the East but he only wanted to punish her not conquer her. Tactically, Deng did not want to prolong the war into the Monsoon season. Given Vietnam's fearless or martyr style resistance, the fighting would drag into the rain season. The SVW lasted only a total of 28 days; Deng essentially achieved his objectives, seriously if not permanently quenched Vietnam's ambition of conquering Indochina and her aggression in the Sino-Vietnam border. Vietnam would need a decade or two to recover from the SVW.

This brief war was regarded as a huge success and a brilliant strategic execution produced a lasting impact to Vietnam. After the war, China became firmer in defending any Sino-Vietnam border conflict including the dispute in the South China Sea; China threatened to teach Vietnam a second lesson. This pressure had kept Vietnam to keep one million troops along the border and cost the Soviet Union $2-2.5 million a day to support them. The Cuba show-down with the U.S. made Khrushchev lose face but the U.S. had to promise not attacking Cuba, hence Cuba was never harmed other than being sanctioned till President Obama Visited Cuba normalizing their relationship (2016). The SVW made the Soviet Union lose more than face. It caused the Soviet Union to decline because of her heavy burden in foreign aid. The Soviet Union's inaction during the SVW cost her so much prestige that many members in the Soviet bloc begin to defect.

Egypt was the first to defect. President Anwar Sadat was in talks with Menachem Begin, Prime Minister of Israel, but hesitated to sign a treaty, but three months after the SVW, Sadat became braver and signed a peace treaty with Israel on 3/26/1979. Next was Afghanistan where a coup removed the pro-Soviet leader; Russia had to send 100,000 troops to topple the coup. Then there was Iran where an Islam revolution started 6 days before the SVW to topple the pro-U.S. King. Due to the SVW and the Afghan war, the Soviet Union had no time to take advantage of the Iran revolution. Supporting Vietnam and Afghanistan was an unbearable burden and cost the East Europe a recession. Poland first rebelled (8/14/1980), although the union revolt was put down but a cleavage between Poland and the Soviet Union formed and others followed.

Post SVW, the Sino-Vietnam border conflicts continued until Liyi died (7/1986). Then Vietnam had a naval battle with China in the South China Sea in 1988 but was defeated; Vietnam officially recognized China's claim and occupation of the Paracel islands. Cambodia revived post SVW and kept fighting Vietnam, a bleeding wound for the Soviet Union. With Egypt's defection, the Soviet began to lose her advantages in the Middle-East; Afghanistan became another bleeding wound for her. Both SVW and Afghan war made the U.S. (Reagan) more confident to engage a struggle with the Soviet not only in the Middle-East but also in Africa (Angola, Mozambique and Ethiopia), then Africa became the third bleeding wound for the Soviet.

Tracing events back to 1979, we can conclude logically that the SVW was the tipping point for the decline of the Soviet Union. The SVW made the U.S. to see the weakness and vulnerability of the Vietnam and Soviet Union. The short SVW was the only war China initiated against a sovereign country in her modern history. In the other wars, China was either passive or being attacked. The 28 days SVW with low casualty on the Chinese side (<10,000) had two very significant consequences. One, It stopped Vietnam's ambition of conquering the entire Indochina and laid foundation for a peaceful Indochina. Two, due to Soviet Union's strategic mistake of supporting the Vietnam against China, the SVW was the tipping point for the Soviet Union to collapse. The U.S. working with China against the Soviet Union was a winning strategy.

CHAPTER 14

Liberalism and Conservatism and Proper Balance

—⁓—

RECENTLY, I CAME ACROSS A Chinese article by Xue Zong Zhang, Why is Hu Shi (a famous Chinese intellect and author in 20th century; he is regarded as a promoter of liberalism not only in his time but beyond through his writings) a Half Baked Liberal?, on the "Baodiao Forum" (an intellectual forum devoted to discussions on Chinese governance and Chinese Sovereignty issues such as the Chinese sovereignty over the Diaoyu Islands). Mr. Zhang criticized Hu Shi not really understanding liberalism, but the article written in a Q&A format did not leave a clear description of liberalism and how it should be promoted. Personally, I find myself constantly swinging between liberalism and conservatism when facing different issues. The above article with its fuzzy arguments on true liberalism has triggered my long time desire to define liberalism and its workability in real world. This desire is confined to define liberalism from basic philosophical principles and how it may be practiced under different real world conditions and political systems. The following is my attempt of doing an intellectual exercise to define liberalism and the constraints the real world will bring to limit liberalism. These constraints working against liberalism, for convenience, may be characterized by the term, conservatism, which often restricts and works against liberalism.

From dictionaries, liberalism has the following definitions:

1. quality or state of being liberal.
2. belief in the value of social and political change in order to achieve progress.

3. a movement in modern Protestantism emphasizing intellectual liberty and the spiritual and ethical content of Christianity.
4. a theory in economics emphasizing individual freedom from restraint and usually based on free competition, the self-regulating market, and the gold standard.
5. a political philosophy based on belief in progress, the essential goodness of the human race, and the autonomy of the individual and standing for the protection of political and civil liberties.
6. Liberalism is a political philosophy or worldview founded on ideas of liberty and equality. Whereas classical liberalism and European liberalism prioritize liberty, American liberalism and social liberalism stress equality.

The above definitions seem to be fine but they do not touch on the essential aspect of how liberalism can be easily understood and how it works when constraints are applied. Therefore,

I prefer to take the approach of starting with broad acceptable principles to define liberalism and then to add layers of descriptions from real world constraints to arrive at the workable (practical and conditional) liberalism. Let's begin with the following principles I assume that are generally acceptable:

1. Human is the most intelligent species on earth. Human desires physical and intellectual liberty.
2. Human beings are born as unique individuals with one's own intrinsic ability and one's acquired ability through one's own will.
3. Human beings with intelligence deserve to have intellectual liberty that is to freely exercise one's intellectual capability.
4. Following principles 1, 2 and 3, unconditional or unconstrained liberalism can be defined as individuals have rights to think, say and do anything according to one's desire and to one's ability. (Any individual has liberal rights to think, say and do anything or whatever one wants. For example, an individual living by oneself in one's own universe)

The above definition of unconstrained liberalism cannot work. Since no two individuals are completely (100%) alike, unconditional liberalism will have intrinsic limitations due to one's ability. Furthermore, human beings live in a society (not practical to live by oneself totally cut off from any society), then they face other limitations due to one's environment, such as natural and physical living condition and other man-made conditions imposed by marriage, family, society, nation and world organizations in terms of ethics, laws and regulations. If we add constraints to liberalism, we shall have the following definitions:

5. Come with the above discussed intrinsic limitations and other constraints are liberal rights infringement. Thus conditional liberalism can be defined as individual's unconditional liberal rights being reduced to avoid liberal rights infringement. For example, an individual lives with a family will have to reduce one's unconditional liberal rights (singing loudly at two o'clock in the morning) to avoid infringing liberal rights of other family member (sleep undisturbed under quietness).

6. Conditional liberalism can also be defined as individual's unconditional liberal rights being reduced to tolerate liberal rights infringement caused by one's environment one's in. For example, an individual lives with a family will have to reduce one's unconditional liberal rights (sleep undisturbed at any time) to tolerate liberal rights being infringed by other family member (practicing singing for audition) So conditional liberalism must have 'give and take' conditions.

7. Unconditional liberalism cannot be accepted in an environment where family, society or nation exists simply because an individual's unconditional liberalism will infringe on other individual's unconditional liberal rights. Therefore, unconditional liberalism is not a workable liberalism.

8. Avoidance and tolerance of liberal right infringement really define the degree of constraints placed on unconditional liberalism.

9. Conditional liberalism is thus defined as unconditional liberalism with proper constraints applied in an environment, family, society and nation. 'Proper Constraints' of course can be subjective.

10. Within a family, conditional liberalism is constrained by family struc-
    ture, hierarchy, generation, and sibling relationship. These relationships
    define responsibilities, range of liberal rights limited by constraints.
    Voluntary constraints are guided by human nature (good versus evil
    both exist), human knowledge (more or less by education) and infring-
    ing and tolerance trade-off (give and take). Involuntary constraints are
    defined by moral principles and laws.
11. Going beyond family to community, society and nation, more individu-
    als are involved and more constraints will apply. These constraints will
    be guided by community/society rules, laws and constitutions depend-
    ing on the social structure, political system and economic condition.
12. The constraints applicable to the liberal rights can be created, regulated
    and altered by political system, for example, a communist system tends
    to restrict individual's liberal rights more, thus limiting individuals to
    achieve their full capability and capacity; a socialistic system tends to
    make trade-offs in individual liberal rights with a bias to side with the
    poor and disadvantaged population. A liberal society tends to maximize
    tolerance (reduce avoidance) to enhance individual liberalism.
13. The methods employed in the political system to apply constraints to
    individual liberalism is democracy with a variety of practicing methods,
    from one person one vote to various hierarchical representation systems
    to only one person decides. (dictatorship, one supreme individual above
    everyone) The various representation systems define various degrees
    of democracy. How well does a political system work depend on how
    liberalism is practiced and what constraints are properly applied, which
    are dependent on economic condition.

Ideally, human liberalism should be promoted with minimal constraints
and maximal tolerance. Unfortunately, human beings have faulty traits such as
selfishness, greed, laziness and intolerance, therefore, ideal liberalism (minimum constraints and maximum tolerance) does not work. For example, under
a democratic system, voters tend to vote for getting the maximum benefits
(take more from the government than give to the government) until the system (government) breaks down (Greece is an example) Therefore, there must

be a proper balance to limit or constrain liberalism. To achieve this proper balance, conservatism comes to play. So liberalism must be counter-balanced by conservatism. I hope this column offered you some useful information to understand and interpret the dictionary definitions of liberalism and its necessary constraints. Hopefully this information can help voters calibrating, comparing and judging the workability of the liberal (versus conservative) ideas made by political candidates in their campaign statements.

CHAPTER 15

The Philippine Foreign Relation under 'Pivot' and 'Freedom of Navigation'

—⚏—

ABSTRACT

MAINSTREAM MEDIA MAY NOT BE blindly trusted is almost become an axiom. A couple of news excerpts related to the title subject are presented and discussed in this paper as evidence. Although the Philippines did not have the same treacherous fate like China had in the 19th to 20th century facing invasions by seven Western powers and the Imperial Japan, but she had her share of colonialism and occupation by the Spanish, American and the Japanese. In view of Philippine's past history and geopolitical position, it is illogical that the Philippines would engage military alliances with Japan and the U.S. to target her biggest neighbor China which never invaded the Philippines in her thousands years of history. It seems that having the right diplomatic relationship with China can only be beneficial to Filipino economy and the Philippines. A good Sino-Philippino relation may give the Philippines a leverage in dealing with her Asian neighbors.

—⚏—

Paul Mcleary with Adam Ramsley publish a newsletter Situation Report for Foreign Policy. The report focuses mainly on Middle East and battles and wars therein as they occur. Lately, it is noticed that the newsletter has increased 'situation contents about China and South China Sea'. The following two excerpts are examples appeared in their April 4, 2016 report:

"Japan just made a port call [Defense News, 4/3/2016], in the Philippines, in a sign of support to the country as it hedges its bets against China's territorial ambitions. Defense News [4/3/2016] reports that Japan sent two destroyers, the JS Ariake and JS Setogiri, and a submarine, the Oyashio, to Subic Bay on Sunday [4/3/2016]. The visit marks increasing cooperation between the two countries as both are locked in disputes with China over its claims to islands in the region. The visit also marks the growing importance of the Philippines as a base for operations in the South China Sea. The U.S. recently signed a deal with Manila that gives U.S. forces access to five bases in the country, marking a return to the country since it closed down the U.S. Navy base at Subic Bay in the early 1990s."

"The U.S. Navy might be gearing up for a third **freedom of navigation** exercise [Reuters, 4/2/2016 quote an unnamed source offered on 4/1/2016] soon near disputed Chinese territory in the South China Sea. An unnamed source tells *Reuters* [4/2/2016, US officials speaking after Reuters reported the plan...] that the operation will take place in early April but other sources say no such operation is scheduled to take place in the near future. The source says the exercise is likely to involve a smaller ship and not the aircraft carrier USS *Stennis* currently in the region. China has registered mounting displeasure with the U.S. flybys and sail-throughs in recent months. In a meeting on the sidelines of the nuclear summit in Washington last week, Chinese President Xi Jinping told [South China Morning Post – Diplomacy & Defence, 4/1/2016] President Obama that "China will not accept any act under the disguise of freedom of navigation that violates our sovereignty and damages our security interests."

From the second excerpt, it is interesting to point out that a reputable mainstream medium- Reuters, would report a claim made by an unnamed source on 4-1-2016 (April Fool's day) which was then denied by an unnamed US official right away. Reuters decided to publish these unnamable quotes anyway [4/2/2016]. McLeary cites Reuters but omits yet another unnamed quote in the Reuters report, ""Our long-standing position is unchanged - we do not take a position on competing sovereignty claims to naturally formed land features in the South China Sea," a senior Obama administration official said on Saturday [4/3/2016]. " I inserted the bracketed dates in the above paragraphs just to call readers' attention: An unnamable source's April Fool's Day story would get mainstream media such diligent reporting and following-up is amazing in Journalism. One must ask, what is going on here and what is the hidden agenda? Were the media being manipulated by the government or the media were anxious to fabricate catchy news to manipulate foreign relations?

From the first excerpt and its source of Defense News, it is clear that Japan is an eager player in the US-Japan-the Philippine joint 'freedom of navigation' exercise to show naval power. The port call came on the eve of war games between the United States and Filipino troops in the Philippines. The Philippine Navy spokesperson, Commander Lued Lincuna said: "The [Japanese Navy] visit is a manifestation of a sustained promotion of regional peace and stability and enhancement of maritime cooperation between neighboring navies." Earlier in the year, Japan agreed to supply the Philippines with military hardware in the categories of anti-submarine and reconnaissance aircrafts as well as radar technology. In 2014, the Philippines and South Korea announced the completion of negotiations for the acquisition of 12 lead-in fighter trainer jets from South Korea with the intention to convert them to fighter jets as the new fighter jets are too expensive. It is also interesting to point out that the Subic Bay, one of the military bases Manila agreed to let the U.S. use, was closed down in 1990 after unrest and two US airmen and one US marine were killed.

I am not an expert on Philippine history, but I assume that Filipino historians and government would not white wash history textbooks like Japan did to twist the facts and cover the Japanese Imperial Army's war crimes. Although the Philippines did not have the same treacherous fate like China had in the 19th to 20th century facing invasions by seven Western powers and the Imperial Japan, but she had her share of colonialism or occupation by the Spanish, American and the Japanese. There were wars with Spain, the U.S. and during the WW II with Japan. Just taking the Subic Bay and the nearby Olongapo for example, Philippines lost in the Spanish (Philippones)-American war (1898-1899). The

American Navy (destroyer Charleston, Concord, Montgomery, Supply ship Zafaro, etc.) overpowered the Filipino resistance at Subic and elsewhere. The Treaty of Paris signed (12-19-1898 effective 4/11/1899) between the United States and Spain basically forced Spain to cede Cuba, Puerto Rico, Guam and the Philippines to the United States. Thus Subic Bay became a US Naval base. During November, 1941, WW II, Japan attacked Olongapo and marched in on 1/10/1942 then captured Subic Bay. Under Japan's rule, forced labor and comfort women (including Filipino, Chinese and Formosan (Taiwan people) shipped in) were used to build wooden ships and to serve as sex slaves to the Japanese army. In the end the wooden ships were destroyed by US air force. The Japanese army used American prisoners to board their ship decks to avoid air raids.

In view of the past history and Philippine's geopolitical position, it is illogical that the Philippines would engage military alliances with Japan and the U.S. to target her biggest neighbor China which never invaded the Philippines in her thousands years of history. If the resources in South China Sea were the objective, it would make more sense for the Philippines to join hands with China to explore such resources than to prepare for war, especially a war in proximity to Philippine's territory. In modern warfare, for short decisive war, it is advantageous to engage the war in the enemy's territory rather than near one's own region. Japan's ambition is to regain her ability to attack far from Japan to exert her military power returning her to past glory. The U.S. has always smartly kept the wars far away from her territory. What would Philippine gain by drawing war close to herself? Weren't the Finopino-America and Finopino-Japanese wars good history lessons? Buying planes or military weapons from other country only benefit the other countries.

Considering Philippine's foreign relation, it seems that having the right diplomatic relationship with China can only be beneficial to Filipino economy and the Philippines. A good Sino-Philippino relation may give the Philippines a leverage in dealing with her Asian neighbors. History always provide good lessons, the Philippines should examine her own history and the modern history of Puerto Rico (under US administration and in debt), Hong Kong (liberated from British colonialism and a significant growing economy), Singapore (independent, neutral and a healthy economy) and China (a country that will lift the world economy, in peace, and drag the world down in war) to arrive at a win-win foreign relations with China instead of being a pawn in the 'pivot' and 'freedom of navigation' game.

CHAPTER 16

HONY Facebook's Open Letter to Donald Trump

—∿—

ABSTRACT

HUMANS OF NEW YORK (HONY) is a fairly popular Facebook page featuring individual New Yorker in the city with a nicely captured photograph of an individual and his or her story for the moment. An open letter to Donald Trump on HONY (letter made serious accusation on Trump and took a firm position opposing Trump to be a presidential candidate) had received more than 200,000 viewers in the first 90 minutes since first posted. This essay offers a fair discussion. Brandon Stanton took off the letter probably because it created an uproar not easy to manage. His letter sides with "political correctness" but millions of American voters are really tired of. The fact that the HONY open letter ignited a viral response is a good thing. We the American voters are ill prepared to place moral judgment on presidential candidates. If one must make moral judgment on political figures, then we must forget about political correctness. We should apply a single (never double) standard, moral correctness, to judge politicians on their past behaviors.

—∿—

Humans of New York (HONY) is a fairly popular Facebook page featuring individual New Yorker in the city with a nicely captured photograph of an individual and his or her story for the moment. I can understand why HONY gains popularity with some postings receiving hundreds of thousands readers. A daily story book or diary about individuals in the metropolitan New York bound to have enough readers, just counting folks in the city alone. The creator of HONY, Brandon Stanton, ought to be congratulated for his creative work. Though HONY is not a mainstream medium, it is not a typical organic medium either. When its 'Open Letter to Donald Trump' hit viral, it reached the impact level of the mainstream media.

According to Jacqueline Pine, a writer on politics, who quoted HONY's open letter at U.S. Uncut, the open letter to Donald Trump had received more than 200,000 viewers in the first 90 minutes since first posted. Ms Pine did not offer any comments other than stating that Brendon Stanton had taken elaborated effort to claim that he was not partisan, but his open letter opposes Trump strongly. Ms Pine simply attached the entire letter uncut in her publication. It is a good thing Ms Pine did reprint the entire letter, because I was not able to find the original piece on HONY at the time of writing this paper. After reading Stanton's letter I feel it calls for some comments in an objective manner since the letter made serious accusation on Trump and took a firm position opposing Trump to be a presidential candidate.

Stanton's letter pointed out the following 'faulty deeds' made by Trump based on his observations:

1. I've watched you retweet racist images.
2. I've watched you retweet racist lies.
3. I've watched you take 48 hours to disavow white supremacy.
4. I've watched you joyfully encourage violence, and promise to 'pay the legal fees' of those who commit violence on your behalf.
5. I've watched you advocate the use of torture and the murder of terrorists' families.
6. I've watched you gleefully tell stories of executing Muslims with bullets dipped in pig blood.
7. I've watched you compare refugees to 'snakes,' and claim that 'Islam hates us.'

Reading the above will get one's blood heating up, but if one keeps a cool head, one will find that "retweet" racist images and racist lies cannot be crime themselves since that has been done by the mainstream media all the time, sometimes with added inflammatory remarks. These statements listed in HONY's open latter and discussed here are in some ways like 'retweeting', by itself not an evidence against the tweeter. As for "taking 48 hours to disavow white supremacy", it is far stretching to condemn Trump to be a white supremacist since he did publicly rebuke numerous times on this accusation and said that he didn't want the votes of any white supremacist, a clear black and white statement as it can be. Trump has continuously gained so many popular votes since he began his Presidential campaign; it should have told Stanton not to make accusations based on partisan interpretations,

As for the rest of Stanton's accusations on Trump for encouraging violence, advocating torturing terrorists and telling hate story about Muslims, again, if one had kept a cool head one would not and could not conclude these accusations based strictly on his campaign speeches. There is no evidence to label Trump as a violent, torturous and hate-driven individual towards Muslims. His angry remarks are natural response to the public media showing that the terrorists have vividly tortured, and beheaded their captives even vowed to kill all Americans. One may fault Trump for using crude language and for knowing too well how the media work and using the same 'tricks in trade' to catch headlines of media coverage, retweets and commentators' follow-ups to get his main messages across to people, Trump's messages are (1) People are tired to be placed in the pressure cooker of "political correctness" and angry to be forced to accept and live in hypocrisy and (2) People are sick of a corrupt political system, from elections of legislators to executive officials, leading the country to an ever worsening economic state. And many people are responding to his slogan: "To make America win again". Basically people are resonating with these messages of Trump.

The positions above which Trump advocates are the backbone of his campaign success. The establishment of the two parties did exactly the 'wrong thing' to help Trump succeed. The Republican Party machinery continues to exercise 'corruption' in manipulation and prejudice ignoring the feelings of the American people. By favoring party elites' preferred candidate(s) before the American people had a chance to select, the GOP has created a resonance among American people responding to Trump's messages. On the other hand, the Democratic Party identified its favorite Hilary before giving the Americans an honest chance to select a Presidential candidate. Hence Hilary's 'political correctness' and 'America is great and we, the past administration, including Hilary, had done no wrong and would make America better' simply reinforced Trump's 'people resonance' and offered Bernie Sanders a chance to challenge Hilary.

Stanton's concluding remark in his open letter to Trump, "along with millions of Americans, I've come to realize that opposing you is no longer a political decision. It is a moral one", is too strong a statement ignoring the fact there are millions of Americans resonating with Trump. In this year's presidential election, Hitler and Mussolini have been used to depict the American presidential candidates, the front runners of both parties. Why is there such a depiction? The impression is created by the graphical appearance (tough language, fierce facial expression and body gesture) of the candidates appearing in too many heated debates. The American voters must look beyond that appearance and dig into the deeds each candidate did in the past, to find if there is any trace of Mussolini or Hitler in any candidate!

I suspect that Stanton took his letter off HONY because it created an uproar not easy to manage. His letter sides with "political correctness" but millions of American voters are really tired of. placing moral judgment based on appearance and language as too harsh. The media have reported that Trump has many lawsuits against him but so far he managed to succeed in pursuit without being put in jail, nor being ruined by any scandal. We don't know how high a moral standard Trump will hold in the White House until he gets into the White House. No one can be presidential until being a real president, Lewinsky affair and Watergate tape reveal more on a president's moral standard than any rough language and rude mannerism a candidate exhibits on his campaign trail can. Trump has a very respectable family and well mannered adult children who showed genuine affection and support for Trump, This suggests that Trump is a principled person and he has applied appropriate ethics standard to bring up his family. On the other hand, the American public rarely questioned the Clintons' moral standard(s), is that out of political correctness?

The fact that the HONY open letter ignited a viral response is a good thing. We the American voters are ill prepared to place moral judgment on presidential candidates. If one must make moral judgment on political figures, then we must forget about political correctness. We should apply a single (never double) standard, moral correctness, to judge politicians on their past behaviors. Then we hope for the best, a presidential candidate will not change once entered the White House and gained the political power. It is safer and easier for voters to stick to political issues to evaluate the presidential candidates. We should look forward to some real debates between the final candidates on every domestic issue and foreign policy after they surfaced from a fair competitive primary election process.

CHAPTER 17

The Invisible Money Hands behind World Economy and International Stock Markets

—◊◊◊—

IN THE ORGANIC MEDIA, THERE is a well-articulated theory that the complex world economy is essentially controlled by an invisible group of global financiers, principally consisting of powerful invisible money hands in the developed nations in the West. By labeling the money hands invisible does diminish the credibility of this theory. However, when the theory is applied to the real world situation, plausible conclusions or explanations supporting this theory can be made. In this paper, we will follow this line of reasoning to discuss who is behind the international stock markets and world economy and why the Trans Pacific Partnership (TPP) is promoted and for what purpose?

The world economy is complex but the world order is more or less under control. There were financial crises but so far the crises were managed without the total collapse of the world economy. Under the above theory of "invisible group of money hands", this group essentially controls the trade, finance and the economy through their control of the multinational corporations. This group has ability to influence national policies and even governance of nations. This kind of powerful influence is accomplished through promoting and application of 'democracy' to nations. Such a democratic machine can be greatly influenced (lubricated) by money as seen in many small and large countries.

So long the democracy can be influenced by money, the invisible money hands can work in the name of democracy to influence the elections (electing officials), legislations (enacting laws) and administration (executing policies) to benefit the multinational corporations and the financial institutions they own. Amazingly, even the United States, a super power, seems to be controlled by this invisible international money group via her democratic system. The powerful Federal Reserve System (FED, the central bank of the U.S.) guiding and monitoring the US economy is a system consisting of a board of governors. Although the governors are appointed by the U.S. President and confirmed by the U.S. Senate, the FED is a privately owned organization, not a part of the government. The governors are selected based on a "fair representation of the financial, agriculture, industrial and commercial interests" from the twelve geographically defined Federal Reserve Districts (each has a regional self-supported bank), they answer to a board not a government agency. The 'visible' FED is a politically appointed system appointed by a democratically elected president influenced by money hence in essence it is controlled by the invisible money hands.

The invisible money hands influence all key elections through controlling political action groups and mass media. Therefore, the invisible money hands will promote and defend democracy and advocate a value system in which the economical power is controlling the political power. In principle, this value system is not a bad concept. If people can exercise democracy wisely without being influenced by the invisible money hands, the voting people can be the master of their own destiny. Unfortunately, in the democratic world, the invisible money hands are always present but invisible. Through money spent on mass media and political action groups, voters are led by the invisible money hands to produce its favored results.

The above described process does not work in an authoritarian system unless the authority (dictator) is bought by the invisible money group. Often most small countries under a dictatorship can be easily bought by the invisible money group, then the country's economy would be essentially controlled by them. Large authoritarian countries such as Russia and China cannot be bought easily. Hence, the invisible money hands must topple the authoritarian governments if they couldn't be bought for the purpose of controlling the world economy or world order. Therefore it is no surprise that the invisible money hands only promote democracy selectively in different regions or nations in the world.

When China was a poor country with a small size of economy compared to the size of the world economy, she had no significant impact on the world economy. Hence she was left alone. Today, China's economy has grown to over ten trillion dollars, second largest in the world. It is obvious to the money group that in order to control the world economy they must control China's economy. However, China practices, under one controlling Chinese Communist Party (CCP), a tightly government planned and government controlled economic development plan, allowing little external influence, essentially shutting out the possibility of influence and control by the global invisible money hands.

China's central economic planning group practices a collective planning process gathering inputs from grassroots, local governments and government owned as well as privately owned enterprises. In China, political power controls economical power. People of China benefitted from China's rising economy through the political system – the government. If the government were corrupt, the economic benefits would not reach the people. People would eventually revolt. Apparently China recognizes this potential problem hence mounting a serious anti-corruption drive and system reform, but interestingly, the West does not seem to be jubilant or eager to assist China in her anti-corruption drive nor in her system reform.

Perhaps China also understands the value system of borderless free economy the invisible money hands are promoting, that is, an economy not under political control. In another words, the economical power controls political power. So China is gingerly conducting her financial and economic system reform, gradually privatizing government controlled enterprises and slowly opening for external investment. When trade and economy are mostly in the hands of the government established organizations and corporations, the Chinese economy is pretty much off the hands of external money, the invisible money hands. When China reforms and opens up, she is also vulnerable to the invisible money hands in more ways than one.

As said earlier, the borderless economic system is nothing wrong in principle, if the invisible money hands would play a fair game. Unfortunately, the powerful invisible hands are omnipresent, controlled by the West. They influence and control the economies and international stock markets and dominate the global financial institutions, such as international banks, International Money Fund (IMF) and the World Bank. Recognizing the unfair current environment, China fights for entering RMB into the currency basket of the IMF, proposes new banks such as BRICS Development Bank and AIIB to assist her economic development. Opening her stock markets to the world attracts investments to China but also invites the invisible money hands. Apparently, China is willing to take the risk and learning to regulate her stock markets to avoid manipulation by the invisible money hands.

The push for TPP is highly motivated by the invisible money hands following the philosophy of establishing a borderless economic system with economic power controlling the political power. By having twelve countries agreeing to a set of rules above national laws, the multi-national corporations (and the invisible money hands) gain the power and control the trade and economy. Even though TPP brings disadvantages to some nations from several aspects such as market access, tariff rules, IP protection and settling investment disputes, the Obama administration, despite of many protests, still promotes it. Why? The invisible money force is pushing it for the benefit of multi-national corporations they own and for curtailing China's economy. TPP presents other problems in the borderless economic system, for one, the employment/immigration issue and another, income and wealth inequality. A socialistic China is sure to be leery about these problems.

China needs time to develop her own sustainable economic system. It is understandable that China adopts a controlled and measurable reform agenda rather than throwing her system wide open. Correctly, China is establishing the RMB as one of the world trade currencies and opening her stock markets to the outside world carefully. China is wise to continue to develop her bilateral and local multilateral agreements to defy TPP and to develop an acceptable trade and investment system.

CHAPTER 18

GOP Changes Three No Trump to Four Diamonds But Needs One More Diamond to Win (The Bridge Game)

—⚏—

ABSTRACT

THE 2016 PRESIDENTIAL ELECTION IS full of surprises of which the Trump phenomenon is most exciting not only in its evolving process but also in its possible outcome in the end. This essay is written shortly before Trump had secured his Republican Nomination but its analysis regarding the GOP's gear switching from No Trump to Accepting Trump is valid. Using the terminology of Bridge Game to describe this change makes it easy to understand. Making a four-diamond bid is asking a five diamond response to make a game. Defining and constructing a collaborative and productive US-China relation is the Fifth Diamond that Trump would need to make a bridge game. I venture to say that the Republicans do have a chance to win the 2016 presidential election if Trump and GOP bid and play a 'Five Diamond' game.

—⚏—

The Trump phenomenon is gaining more momentum after the GOP candidate won a sweeping victory on 4/26/2016 in five primaries of Connecticut, Delaware, Maryland, Pennsylvania and Rhode Island. This impressive result on top of Trump's overwhelming win in the states of Arizona and New York, Trump had gained 956 delegates of the1237 required to snatch the GOP nomination. The 956 number represents 48.5% of the 1970 total delegates counted up to the last primary contest. Subtracting 124 un-committed delegates from the total count of 1970, the 956 number represents 52% of the committed delegates who will vote for Trump at the GOP convention in Cleveland.

In the 2016 presidential election, there had been over 17 significant Republican candidates starting the race. The GOP party establishment had its favorite and adopted a no Trump strategy - anybody but Trump strategy. Trump denounced this unfair play and his supporters grew as Trump began winning in the primary process. The GOP party seems to base the no Trump approach on the following three no trumps:

1. Trump is not an insider of the GOP organization
2. Trump has challenged the party establishment and its mechanism and
3. Trump comes from the New York State, a Democratic State having nearly zero chance to win for Republicans.

Therefore, the GOP elites stuck to the Three No Trump game plan. They pushed for Jeb Bush, Marco Rubio, Ted Cruz, John Kasich, and ignored Trump.

Reviewing the GOP primaries held up to now, Trump not only has remained in the race, he is winning. Despite of the media's (both left and right) bashing Trump's manners and rough languages, Trump gained momentum and the number of his followers at his campaign rallies exploded. Senator Ted Cruz and Former Governor John Kasich joining hands as a last ditch effort to stop Trump failed in the last Tuesday's primary contests. Trump declared himself a presumptive Presidential Nominee. The 4/26/16 GOP primary result may be a wake-up call to the GOP, even Senator Bob Corker (R-Tennessee), Chairman of the Foreign Relations Committee is publicly stating that he is very pleased with Trump's foreign policy speech, declaring it a broad vision with substance. This and other public comments in the GOP camp seem to suggest that the GOP is changing the three No Trump bid to a four diamond game.

What is the rational for changing to a four diamonds bid? The reasons may be summarized as follows:

Diamond 1. Trump is a billionaire but he is winning the support of the working class which can be very helpful in the general election. His supporters believe that he is telling the truth in contrast to his opponent Hillary.

Diamond 2. Trump is self-financing his presidential campaign which can save money for GOP to focus on contests for congressional seats. This is a great opportunity to rally both presidential and Congressional elections coherently.

Diamond 3. People's ultimate concern is still on domestic issues with first priority on jobs and money in their pockets. He who can create jobs will be the winner.

Diamond 4. Trump's business sense, negotiation skills and aggressive, conservative and bottom-line oriented problem solving approach are in line with GOP principles. Tough talk can be empty without real skills, Trump, making money through his business skills is favored over Hillary, made money through her delivering speeches.

These four diamond points seem to win plenty of supporters for Trump and the polls have been showing it.

On the Democrat side, despite of Bernie Sanders' courageous fight in the Democratic primaries, Hillary Clinton seems to have sewn up the winning pouch. Bernie had drawn more support from young people with liberal appeal; thus Hillary has to figure out a way to court Bernie's supporters and mindful not tilting too far left. It is for sure that Hillary's opponent Trump will be coming from the right, if Republicans would eventually rally behind him. At this point, Trump has created a momentum that is threatening Hillary's sure win status in the beginning of the race. Trump is fully aware of Hillary's playing the gender or woman card. Trump is riding on the momentum of defying the current and past administration's blunders of which Hillary is a contributor.

However, 'Four Diamonds' does not make a game in bridge game; the U.S. 2016 presidential election is like building a bridge to a better future, whether it is for the U.S. to win again or for the U.S. to be great again. For Trump to win the general election beating Hillary, he must bid and play a 'Five Diamonds' game. The world has changed significantly in the past three decades since the Reagan era. The Cold War ended with the Soviet Union collapsed, but Russia is going through a rejuvenation fully taking advantage of the mess in Middle East caused by the U.S. intervention. China has risen not only economically but diplomatically on the world stage. Other than Japan and the U.S., the developed countries, like U.K. Germany, France ..., all adopted a realist foreign policy embracing China's rise and her vision in global economic development. Why does the U.S. stick with an outdated or legacy China policy? In addition, Russia seems to be taking side with China.

So it is clear that the 'Fifth Diamond', Trump needs, is a new and fair US-China relationship where the U.S. will work with China and cultivate a friendly relation rather than target China and stimulate an arms race. Trump is correct to say that we need to bring jobs back to the U.S. and get our finance in order. This objective can be accomplished far easier by collaborating with China who is tuning her economy to a consumption driven economy. China needs hi-tech consumer goods not hi-tech weapons, why agitate China to invest in military development rather than assist China to elevate the standard of living of her billion people. In today's global environment with nations mutually and closely interdependent, a nation is not a great nation because she has military might and uses it at will. A nation is respected only when she is genuinely able to help other developing countries to make economic gains. A smart helper can make economic gain as well. One can recall that the U.S. helping Europe with a Marshall Plan after WW II was greatly appreciated.

Defining and constructing a collaborative and productive US-China relation is the Fifth Diamond that Trump would need to make a bridge game. In a 'bridge game', communication is the key element, the object of the bridge game is to bid and make a game if possible. A bridge game is not like the poker game, in which the winner takes all. In a bridge game, everyone tries to play the best making the game enjoyable by all. Three No Trump is a game and Five Diamonds is also a game but one must accept what cards are dealt to one's hand and try to play the best game. Looking at the cards that are dealt to the parties of Republicans and Democrats, I venture to say that the Republicans have a chance to win the 2016 presidential election if Trump bids and plays a 'Five Diamond' game.

CHAPTER 19

Will The Warm UK-China Relation Be A Long-term One?

—ɷ—

ABSTRACT

WHEN CHINA ADVOCATED A PLAN of stimulating the economic development for the entire world by proposing 'the one belt and one road' (OBOR) vision, a collaborative infrastructure development program bridging Asia, Europe and Africa in joint commerce development, the U.K., despite of the U.S. displeasure, took the initiative to join the China created Asia Infrastructure Investment Bank (AIIB) to support the OBOR program. Observing the current activities between the two nations, it seems that the U.K. is forming a close bond with China. One wonders, is that a short-term foreign policy or a long-term diplomatic relation? In view of the fact that the U.K. just voted yes to 'Brexit' from EU, the title question deserves a review from a historical perspective.

—ɷ—

In politics, diplomacy, and foreign relations, most would agree that people and nations are realists with a short-term or a long-term view. Sure, there is always ideology at play in the domains of politics and foreign affairs, but in the timeline of history, vast number of political principals, inevitably, have yielded their principles and ideologies to reality, especially over a long time. In hindsight, history is a book of realist stories not a hypothetic theory. The case in point in this paper is the UK-China relations, its recent development and historical evolvement prompted the author to ask the title question, will the current warm UK-China relation be a long-term one? This question is of great interest and importance not only to the British and the Chinese but also to the Americans and the world citizens in view of the fact that the UK just voted yes to Brexit from EU.

The United Kingdom had a glorious history as an empire. As a nation the U.K. is not a typical democratic system; she maintains a royal crown yet she has contributed to democracy and capitalism in a significant way. As an empire the U.K. practiced colonialism zealously enabling her flag flying in sunshine twenty four hours a day (Perhaps I should say daylight, since the Sun does not seem to favor London). The British footprint or occupation was appearing all over the world, including all five continents and numerous isles in the four oceans. The U.K. is a realist in her evolution as a nation; she embraces democracy but remains as a royal kingdom to this day. She lost the entire North America yielding to the American Revolution which claimed independence from her. The fact that the British Empire did not move her palace to New York or Toronto in the eighteenth century might be interpreted as the natural result of a Royal government with limited vision. The royal family perhaps never entertained the idea of moving away from Buckingham Palace. The political figures as subjects of the Crown thought and behaved as smart short-term realists just to satisfy the ruling Crown. They never worried the day that the British isles would be the limiting factor in sustaining the empire.

China had been a great nation over several millennia. China had been called an empire only occasionally in her five thousand years of history simply because colonialism was never in the Chinese dictionary or on her emperors' minds until she became a colonial target of the Western powers led by the British Empire. Different from the continent of North America, China has had a rich culture and strong economy despite of the fact that China had no navy. The Ming emperors, Yongle (1402-1424), Hongxi (1424-1425) and Xuande (1425-1435) were pro-commerce to enrich their treasury. Emperor Yongle (Zhu Di) sent the famous 'Ambassador' Cheng He (1371-1435) sailing the world seven times with a fleet consisting of ships over 400 feet long dwarfing any ship in the world at that time. Cheng's disappointing report to the Emperors, that the rest of the world were culturally backward, had made the

Ming Court angry which made an edict to forbid ocean exploration to foreign land as a waste of the emperor's treasury. Most political figures in the Chinese dynasties behaved like realists with short-term views. All the maps and records of Ming Dynasty's ocean exploration were ordered to be burnt except a few were hidden and eventually passed on to the hands of foreigners. (reference Matteo Ricci, 1552-1610 and Michele Ruggieri, 1543-1607 and their writings)

The U.K.-China relation in the late 19th to early 20th century was a sad story for the Chinese. The British started the infamous Opium War forcing China to accept opium trade and to open her ports to the British merchants. As the victor of the Sino-British wars, the British Empire demanded not only huge amount of silver as reparation but also forced China to cede the Hong Kong island in perpetuity to her. Perpetuity was a very long time compared to Russia's 25 years of rights in control of Da Lian, a Chinese freeze free northern port (Port Arthur). This right was signed over to Japan (the Portsmouth Treaty, Russia also evacuated from China's Manchuria and recognized Korea to be Japan's territory of influence not China's protectorate) after Russia lost in the 1905 Russo-Japanese war. The 26th U.S. President, Theodore Roosevelt was the mediator for the Portsmouth Treaty and won the Nobel Peace Prize for balancing the Russian and Japanese powers in Asia at the expense of China. Roosevelt made a realist decision far from justice and fairness. China was too weak to alter any of the unequal treaties infringed on her sovereignty. Given Hong Kong to the U.K. was just one case demonstrating that in foreign relations strong nations are realists (never idealists) and weak nations have no voices nor rights. Fortunately, China survived the invasions and WW II, the U.K. made a realist decision to return Hong Kong back to China on July 1, 1997.

The U.K. is a declining empire ever since WW I and further damaged after WW II, but by her clever and realistic foreign policy allying with the rising superpower, the U.S., she remains on the center stage of the world. As a realist, the U.K. recognizes that the U.S. is the dominating player in world affairs. She acted as the strongest ally of the U.S., of course, without harming her own national interests. Being the ruler of Hong Kong over 150 years, the U.K. could not help but recognized the change of the Mainland

China, especially over the recent three decades. China had struggled to build the nation avoiding the control by the Soviet Union. She had experimented with communism and learned bitter lessons. She had embraced capitalism in planned steps and had risen to be the second largest economy in the world. It is clear to the U.K. that China is no longer an "Asian Patient" and China has grown mature enough to take a proper place on the world stage. The U.K. may not be the first (nor the only) West nation to appreciate China's transformation and continuous reform but she certainly appears to be the first to take a realist step to embrace China's rise. In contrast, the U.S. seems to wish away China's rise.

When China advocated a plan of stimulating the economic development for the entire world by proposing 'the one belt and one road' (OBOR) vision, a collaborative infrastructure development program bridging Asia, Europe and Africa in joint commerce development, the U.K., despite of the U.S. displeasure, took the initiative to join the China created Asia Infrastructure Investment Bank (AIIB) to support the OBOR program. Observing the current activities between the two nations, it seems that the U.K. is forming a close bond with China. One wonders whether that is a short-term foreign policy or a long-term diplomatic relation? China's President Xi Jinping visited the U.K. and received a royal "Royal Treatment" arousing the attention and envy of many heads of states. China has promised to invest $10B in U.K. and most recently the People's Bank of China announced plan to issue Chinese government sovereign debt in RMB in London. Do all these signal the beginning of a long-term warm relationship between China and UK forgetting the Opium Wars and colonization of Hong Kong? So far, the U.K. seems to be the beneficiary of that warm relationship. However, no one can say that the current warm UK-China relation will definitely last long but we can say that as realists both China and the U.K. currently seem to desire their warm relation to last long. The increased activities between UK and China (likewise between Germany and China) do beg the question why is the U.S. holding out a hostile policy towards China? The U.S. has always been a realist just like the U.K., must she choreograph an anti-China play to maintain her supreme position in the world? No, it does not look like a good realist play!

CHAPTER 20

Taiwan's Fate Not Dictated by Hegemony Theory

—◆—

ABSTRACT

JOHN MEARSHEINMER IS THE PROPONENT of Hegemony theory. He published a long essay, entitled, Say Goodbye To Taiwan, in National Interest (March-April 2014). His conclusion may very well be correct but his reasoning and arguments based on hegemony theory are questionable. This essay presents "Wang Dao" (a philosophy may be explained with modern language as soft power and rule-based foreign policy) versus "Ba Dao" (essentially the hegemony theory, ruling by power and preventing the rise of other hegemons) and their historical understanding by the Chinese. The Chinese people including many overseas Chinese firmly believe and expect reunification of Taiwan will occur under the "Wang Dao" philosophy. Chinese people are extremely patient towards political systems and political changes. Mainland China will not use force to reunify with Taiwan unless a foreign party is involved to spoil the natural "Wang Dao" reunification process.

—◆—

John Mearsheinmer is one of my favorite author and speaker on foreign relations. I like to follow Mr Mearsheimer's articles not because I always believe he was right about his conclusions rather I was always intrigued by his analyses and arguments about the international relations at hand. In fact, John advocates his theory of hegemony, which has a significant followers in the diplomatic and military circles in the United States and world wide, with a safe disclaimer: his hegemony theory can not predict future since future, not like past, is not a being and is not predictable. Nevertheless, John's analysis and carefully selected historical evidences are very powerful and intellectually stimulating, hence making his essays very interesting to read.

Recently Mr. Mearsheimer published a long essay, entitled, Say Goodbye To Taiwan, in a website (May 2016), www.chinausfriendship.com based on his old article published in National Interest (March-April 2014). The title of this article for sure will catch lots of eyeballs, but its content essentially contains his hegemony theory and uses Taiwan as a case study. Based on hegemony theory, he analyzes what the U.S. will do regarding China's desire to reunify with Taiwan and Taiwan's desire to maintain de facto independence. He assumes that China will continue to gain power and the U.S. will be reluctant to go to war against China on behalf of Taiwan. Then he concludes among the three options, 1. Developing nuclear deterrence, 2. Developing conventional military deterrence and 3. Adopting a version of Hong Kong Strategy; Taiwan has no choice but accepts option 3. In essence, Taiwan will be eventually reunified with Mainland China, just a matter of how far beyond a decade of time.

After reading this essay (unlike Mr. Mearsheimer's other essays), I do not necessarily disagree with John's conclusion, but I do beg for difference in John's arguments or analysis to reach his conclusion. Here I would like to offer my comments based on an oriental philosophy and historical facts. On the Mainland China-Taiwan reunification issue (to some degree the Korea reunification issue), the current situation is entirely created artificially, possibly partially promoted by the U.S. attributable to hegemony behavior Mearsheimer characterized, but not due to China following a hegemony theory. This is my main disagreement with Mearsheimer's arguments. I shall list my reasoning below.

I believe that in the Orient, particularly in China, the hegemony theory and behaviors are well understood, however, China through her several thousand years of history (experienced hegemony behavior as early as Chun Qiu and Zhan Guo eras, 771-221 BC), had developed a philosophy not to pursue hegemony but honor the "Wang Dao". In history, China has repeatedly adopted the "He Qing" policy to deal with the aggressors from the North (Marrying the Emperor's princess to the King of the aggressive northern state to avoid war which is always devastating to the people) rather than pursuing a hegemony strategy. China has also built the Great Wall (1100-223 BC) consuming enormous resources and man power for defense rather than resorting to military build-up to defend or conquer others. In Ming dynasty, after successfully dispatching "Zheng He" (1371 - 1435) to explore the world seven times (1405 through 1433) with a large fleet consisting of ships longer than 400 feet, the emperor after knowing that the rest of the world was far less developed than China had ordered destroying the big ships and forbid further exploration as waste of national treasury. In Qing dynasty (1644 - 1911), the ruler repeatedly swallowed the hegemony and colonial behaviors of the Western power and the Imperial Japan to the point that China was near annihilation. These historical evidences illustrate one thing that the Chinese people firmly prefer to "Wang Dao" which is the opposite of "Ba Dao" as the governance and nation building philosophy. This firm belief has a strong influence on Chinese political leaders.

Naturally, there were debates about the merits of "Wang Dao" (this philosophy may be explained with modern language as soft power and rule based foreign policy) versus "Ba Dao" (essentially the hegemony theory, ruling by power and preventing the rise of other hegemons), but the Chinese people and statesmen overwhelmingly preferred the "Wang Dao" philosophy. This philosophy may have caused China to be defeated militarily numerous times, but in Chinese history, the conquerors, such as the Mongols and Manchurians (when they were powerful and invaded and occupied China), gradually yielded to the Chinese "Wang Dao" philosophy. This philosophy gives Chinese tremendous tolerance to military invasion, but the greater the tolerance the greater the resolve in resistance, this was proven in WW II, while many Western countries quickly surrendered to Nazi military force, the Chinese was extremely resilient to the powerful and cruel Imperial Japanese Army. Despite of Japan's superior military force and determined objective to conquer China, the Chinese resisted for nearly a decade eventually defeating Japan. The nuclear bomb might have accelerated Japan's surrender, in fact, it was China who tied up Japan's huge army and exhausted it to eventual failure. Japan may deny it out of shame but it is the real truth.

Taiwan had a treacherous history as a part of China's sovereignty. Taiwan had been captured and ruled by foreign invaders a number of times, first by the Dutch (1624 - 1662) then by the Japanese (1895-1945). Post WW II, the anti-communism ideology artificially separated Taiwan from Mainland China again. Taiwan depended on the U.S. protection and the U.S. was viewing Taiwan as a strategic island as Mearsheimer pointed out, an unsinkable carrier right between the East and South China Sea. Whatever the political maneuver on the island, be it pro-independence or color revolution, I believe the fate of Taiwan is not in the hands of the U.S. nor Japan, simply because the Chinese people believes in their unwavering reunification principle. Politics, propaganda, even brain wash may change the mood of people (more likely the young people for a period of time), but the traditional culture including the "Wang Dao" philosophy has a tremendous staying power. Just like China eventually gave up communism and pursue her own governance system principally influenced by the "Wang Dao" philosophy, Taiwan would find a suitable democratic system compatible with her culture and tradition. No matter which political party is in control, the political leaders will accept the "Wang Dao" philosophy. The Japanese tried very hard to 'Japanize' the people in Taiwan for fifty years, but the people remain to be Chinese in culture and in tradition.

The Chinese people including many overseas Chinese firmly believe and expect reunification of Taiwan and mainland but there is no specific time table for it. In the "Wang Dao" philosophy, people are extremely patient towards political systems and political changes. Mainland China will not use force to reunify with Taiwan unless a foreign party is involved to spoil the natural reunification process. Taiwan will not declare independence and has no compelling reason to do so (nothing to gain and everything to lose). The people across the Taiwan Strait do have patience to observe the natural changes to embrace a mutually acceptable political system. During this wait-and-see process, there may be external political influence trying to terminate the process, but in today's fully developed communication environment, people can not be manipulated and fooled for long, the "Wang Dao" philosophy will eventually prevail over the hegemony theory. The hegemony behavior of the Western countries in the 19th and 20th century will eventually be diminishing in the 21st century simply because nuclear deterrence will render hegemony behavior not workable, a point Mr. Mearsheimer concedes. Human race will have no choice but accept "Wang Dao" philosophy and abandon hegemony theory to avoid the destruction of the human race. Taiwan will be reunified with Mainland China eventually, in agreement with Mearsheimer's conclusion but for a different reason.

CHAPTER 21

Connections of Government and Mafia in Japan

—ᴍ—

AN EMAIL WITH LINKS TO some organic reporting about Japan's Mafia, Yakuza, posted on Spitfirelist.com, opened my eyes on the title subject. Mafia in any country tends to maintain their activities in secrecy and out of the public's attention including the government. In the U.S. the FBI does a reasonable good job in monitoring Mafia activities and tries to bring Mafia bosses to justice whenever warranted. In Japan, Mafia also exists, but they are less known outside of Japan, yet the Japanese Mafia is an international underground organization. Yakuza is a transnational crime syndicate with far longer history than the American Mafia. We will make a comparison of Yakuza with American Mafia and discuss the connection of the Japanese government with Yakuza.

In the United States, the most notorious mafia is the Italian-American organized-crime network operating in large cities across the nation, notably New York and Chicago. The US Mafia is a secret organization which rose to power through success in many illegal and criminal ventures. In 1920s Prohibition era, the Mafia nearly monopolized the illicit liquor business and made fortunes. After Prohibition, the Mafia moved into other criminal but highly profitable activities from selling drugs to operating illegal gambling. American Mafia became well known by movies featuring the Mafia bosses such as Al Capone and John Gotti. These Mafia movies fascinated the public. The US legislature and government have established anti-racketeering laws to convict leading mobsters and to destroy their organizations; however, the Mafia is very skilled in 'corruption' – using money to corrupt law enforcement. Hence, the American Mafia has remained in existence today with presence in labor unions and a number of labor intensive industries. The Mafia has ability to launder their 'dirty' money from criminal activities through legitimate businesses.

The Japanese Mafia, known as Yakuza, has a much longer history than the US Mafia. Yakuza's origin started in the 17th century from peddling illicit and stolen goods as well as from operating gambling. The organized peddlers controlled allocation of stalls and offered protection for the stall commerce activities. The Japanese government eventually recognized the peddlers' organization and granted their leaders the right to carry the short Samurai sword (The long Samurai sword was the exclusive right of the nobility and the Samurai warriors). The gamblers had a lower social status than the peddlers since gambling was illegal. Most of the gambling houses ran loan sharking for gambling clients and kept their own security personnel. Over the years, the Yakuza has diversified their businesses, grown into a transnational organization and maintained the hierarchical structure of foster parent – foster child adopting a code of justice and duty where loyalty and respect is strictly observed. During WW II, the Yakuza organization declined as Japan was under military rule. Post war, Yakuza flourished and operated internationally now with an estimated membership over 100,000 in four major families with a large presence in the Japanese media and a strong influence in politics.

Unlike US Mafia, Yakuza did not start from liquor business. The Sake rice wine was the ceremonial element in building spiritual bonding between the foster parents and foster children relationship in the Japanese Mafia. All Mafia in the world tend to master similar criminal activities such as loan sharking, extortion, blackmail, prostitution, illegal gambling and drug trafficking with some legal or semi-legitimate businesses as a front. Thus mafia can penetrate and dominate certain industry, for example, American Mafia had been in control of the Garment industry when it was a labor intensive industry. Mafia has always been in the 'power and corrupt' business, trying very hard to establish ties with government officials partly for gaining power and partly for survival. Unfortunately there are always some government officials to be bought, falling 'in the pockets of the Mafia'.

The Japanese Mafia is no exception. Yakuza in Japan is a very sizable organization divided into four major families, Yamaguchi-gumi being the largest with members over 55,000, Sumiyoshi-kai over 20,000, Inagawa-kai over 15,000 and Aizukotetsu-kai over 7,000 in members. The Yamaguchi-gumi is headquartered in Kobe and directs criminal activities throughout Japan, Asia (formerly Japan occupied areas) and the United States. Yoshinori Watanabe (nicknamed Mr. Gorilla) was the fifth head of Yamaguchi-gumi (1989), an intelligent and aggressive boss, was credited with creating a 'pension plan' to take care of his retired employees to solidify and draw back exodus members and he also kept membership dues low. Through aggressive gang wars, he expanded the organization to become Japan's largest organized crime group; by 2004, the Yamaguchi-gumi headquarters were collecting $25 million per year in association dues. Watanabe was a folk hero in Kobe after organizing relief efforts and providing food, water, and essential supplies to the locals after the Great Hanshin Earthquake occurred in January of 1995. Ironically, this led to present day Yakuza's involvement in earthquake disaster relief and its connection with the nuclear industry.

A magnitude-9 earthquake shook northeastern Japan on 3-11-2011, unleashing a savage tsunami which caused a cooling system failure at the Fukushima Daiichi Nuclear Power Plant. The cooling failure caused a level-7 nuclear meltdown and release of radioactive materials. Tokyo Electric Power Company (TEPCO) admitted in July 2013 that about 300 tons of radioactive water continues to leak from the plant every day into the Pacific Ocean. Hours after the first shock waves hit, two of the largest crime groups went into action, opening their offices to those stranded in Tokyo, and shipping food, water, and blankets to the devastated areas in two-ton trucks and whatever vehicles they could get moving. The day after the earthquake the Inagawa-kai sent twenty-five four-ton trucks filled with paper diapers, instant ramen, batteries, flashlights, drinks, and the essentials of daily life to the Tohoku region. An executive in Sumiyoshi-kai, even offered refuge to members of the foreign community. The Yamaguchi-gumi, has also opened its offices across the country to the public and been sending truckloads of supplies quietly. Wouldn't you wonder why the mafia was so keen in doing philanthropy and civil duty?

The answer is that Yakuza has been serving 'the role of heroes' in the nuclear industry. Yakuza, is essentially dominating the nuclear industry in Japan in providing workers especially for nuclear clean up and trafficking nuclear waste. It is a challenge to find workers to work for nuclear industry especially for disaster clean up; typically they are homeless, debtors or former Yakuza. The restoration of a nuclear disaster is long term, 30 to 40 years. Yakuza is very keen to win those long-term lucrative restoration contracts. The transnational Yakuza has become a necessary evil in Japan's nuclear industry for disposing radiation contaminated materials in foreign land (and trafficking nuclear fuel for Plutonium production), just like Yakuza has been a necessary evil in Japanese politics in 'getting out the votes' and squelching or generating scandals for politicians. Yakuza has had a strong connection with the Japanese government, for example, post war, a Yakuza political fixer, Yoshio Kodama, was hired by CIA to play the role to keep Japan from going communist. He later put up the money to support the liberal Democratic Party (LDP). Kodama was prison cellmate of former Prime Minister, Nobusuke Kishi (1957-60, LDP), grandfather of current prime Minister, Abe Shinzo and LDP has dominated the Japanese government over 60 years. It is no surprise that one would hear that the minister of Justice was matchmaking for a Yakuza underboss' daughter or a finance minister had ties to the Yakuza. The connection of Japanese government and Mafia clearly exists.

CHAPTER 22

Will China Overtake the U.S. as the Superpower?

—ɯ—

ABSTRACT

FOREIGN AFFAIRS MAY/JUNE 2016 ISSUE, published a long essay, entitled, The Once and Future Superpower - Why China Won't Overtake the U.S., authored by Stephen G. Brooks and William C. Wohlforth, both professors at the Dartmouth College. The article argues that China can't overtake the U.S., but the question really has no meaning since whether China will or won't overtake the U.S. really depends on the US China policy. If the U.S. adopts a hostile targeting China strategy, it is almost certain that China will adopt an 'Overtake the U.S.' Strategy regardless whether she can or cannot overtake the U.S. In the contrary, if the U.S. adopts collaborative friendly China policy, China has no incentive to engage an arms race straining her economy. Pursuing a hostile China policy, the U.S. in the end will not be a respected superpower on the world stage after China and the U.S. mutually destroy each other with their nuclear arsenal. "Will China overtake the U.S. as the superpower" is a false question to ask in the consideration of US security

—ɯ—

In the Foreign Affairs May/June 2016 issue, there is a long essay, entitled, The Once and Future Superpower - Why China Won't Overtake the U.S., authored by Stephen G. Brooks and William C. Wohlforth, both professors at the Dartmouth College. Wohlforth and Brooks are seasoned authors on foreign affairs and the U.S.; a number of books, such as Lean Forward - In Defense of American Engagement (coauthored with G. John Ikenberry),

Reshaping the World Order - How Washington Should Reform International Institutions and American Primacy in Perspective are to their credit.

The Brooks and Wohlforth article in the current Foreign Affairs issue is adapted from their 2013 book, America Abroad: The United States' Global Role in the 21st Century with a little update. It is no surprise for Foreign Affairs to publish extraction of a book with some update, but I am surprised that Foreign Affairs has extracted such a long essay from Brooks and Wohlforth's old book under the new title, The Once and Future Superpower - Why China Won't Overtake the United States. This essay actually devoted many pages of arguments to Why China Can't Overtake the United States which in my opinion (and more importantly in many professional political analysts' view) has already been accepted.

Based on what we know about the superior hard and soft power the Unites States cumulated and possessed today, it does not seem to need such a big volume of space in Foreign Affairs to conclude that 'China Can't Overtake the U.S.'. In my opinion (but not necessarily in many U.S. Political analysts' views) Brooks and Wohlforth did not do justice to the Word WON'T in the title of their article. They did not explain, at least not adequately, why China won't overtake the United States. From observations in the past, China under the current leadership (and previous leaders for several decades) has conscientiously followed a strategy not to overtake the U.S. for many good reasons, but one is related to oriental political philosophy most western political analysts either ignored or simply did not know. For this reason, I will devote this paper to talk about the above referenced Foreign Affairs article.

One may find that there is a little illogical reasoning in 'in my opinion', that is if one (and China) believes that China can't overtake the U.S. then 'she won't overtake the U.S.' will be an obvious wise national strategy. So why there is any question whether China will or will not (won't) overtake the U.S.? Please bear with me; there is a significant subtlety in this question, in fact an important question. It is so important that I will state my concluding remarks first just in case the readers get confused and departs from reading any further.

What I would like to conclude and convince you in this article is that whether China can or can't and China will or won't overtake the U.S. really depends on the China policy of the U.S. This point is not made obvious in Brooks and Wohlforth's article.

If the U.S. adopts a hostile targeting China strategy, it is almost certain that China will not adopt a 'Won't overtake the U.S.' Strategy whether she can or cannot overtake the U.S. for several good reasons, but survival is the main and sufficient reason. China may not be able to change the status of 'can't overtake the U.S., but she will try and by all means try to diffuse 'the targeting China policy'. This resolution fortified by China's history and culture will resort to military measures to the point that an all out mutually destructive consequence may occur. (a decade long bitter war against Japan's invasion was a clear example) Of course, by mutual destruction, the U.S. will no longer be the superpower, whether China can or can't overtake the U.S.

Brooks and Wohlforth had offered a number of arguments to ascertain that China can't overtake the U.S., technology gap (Manufacturing limited to processing, intellectual properties and R&D), US global span of alliances, China's internal problems, China's lack of mature military-industry complex, deployment and use of sophisticated weapon systems as well as arguments stating that strong economic power does not translate into military power. They also cautioned the U.S. not to overreacting to the rising China in her assertive stand regarding reducing her vulnerability especially close to her peripheral sovereignty such as the South China Sea islands. They advised that the U.S. should make a more modest goal in defining the US core interest without diminishing 'the grand strategic maxim' so to avoid the temptations of misusing her superpower. However, they did not analyze the U.S. China Policy and its consequences from China's attitude and responses which of course depends on the US China policy and which will ultimately determine the outcome of world order.

Projecting the current US China policy, it sure will stimulate more and accelerated arms race. The signs had been there already but the U.S. had ignored them and continued a legacy strategy of targeting China. This will force China to compete with the U.S. military, perhaps wisely to accelerate her nuclear warhead ballistic missiles which is one of their military strength. Under such a strategy, whether she can or cannot overtake the U.S., the end result in either case is not beneficial to the U.S. So the strategic question is not China can or cannot overtake the U.S., it is will or will not the U.S. lead the China into a strategy that China aims at overtaking the U.S. in order to survive. My prediction is that China won't overtake the U.S. if the U.S. treats China as a friend not as an enemy. Treating China as an enemy, the 'can or can't overtake' question is irrelevant, because the U.S. in the end will not be a respected superpower on the world stage after mutual destruction taking place.

The Oriental political philosophy has a long history and deep rooted influence on Chinese people and their leaders. The famous Sun Tze, a strategist, wrote a concise and profound book (Sun Tze Bin Fa, a brief thirteen chapters) about wars, diplomacy, foreign relations and nation building. This book is taught in many places including the US WestPoint Military Academy. One of the key principles Sun emphasizes is that using military power to win or to settle things is the last resort for a nation to employ; use it only when everything else has failed. This principle alone (well supported by historical cases and logical reasoning) should be adequate to cast doubt on the merits of Hegemony Theory which was used to explain the occurrence of WW I, WW II and Cold War. The U.S. achieved her superpower position not because of atomic bombs but because of Marshall plan restoring Europe and a reconstruction plan to rebuild the demoralized and devastated Japan. Using military power to settle international problems only brought the world more problems as clearly evidenced by post Cold War events, Iraq etc. It is time for the U.S. to rethink what is a right US China policy in the 21st century. Brooks and Wohlforth's book, America Abroad: The United States' Global Role in the 21st Century (oxford Press 2013) and other US-China Relations books should be all updated with more content on the understanding of the U.S. and China through the oriental political philosophy to give a fair assessment on the question should the U.S. or China be concerned who will or will not overtake whom on the world stage and what should be their stage manners!

CHAPTER 23

Leadership Transition Must Occur on the World Stage

—⟋⟋⟋—

ABSTRACT

A TRANSFORMING WORLD MUST BE led by visionary world leaders and among them a leader of leaders. Under the United Nations architecture, a leader nation in the UN body or on the world stage not only has to be a great nation with strength having both economic and military power but also must have visionary leaders. The U.S. is the world leader at present but she must recognize the changing world is expecting an effective leader. Unfortunately, the political system in the United States, although being stable for centuries, seasoned in practicing democracy, and somewhat successful for many decades, but the leader the electoral system selects may not be able to deliver a right statesman fit to lead the world. China started as the weakest UN permanent security council nation state in 1971 but she has earned her credits to become a respected and effective UN member. As the world is globalizing and transforming, the world leader must transform and prepare to accept a leadership transition.

—⟋⟋⟋—

As human civilization is slowly formulating a globalized community, the world order is slowly changing accordingly. This transformation however slow must be led by the visionary world leaders and among them a leader of the leaders. Structurally, there is a United Nation with 193 member states, but the UN has been organized as an administrative body with its executive leadership guided by the UN Security Council, a body of fifteen members with five permanent members, China, France, the Soviet Union, the United Kingdom, the United

States with veto power. Under this structure, the de facto leadership for the world is essentially falling into one or two great nations of the UN permanent security council member states.

A leader nation in the UN body or on the world stage not only has to be a great nation with strength having both economic and military power. This leader state must have statesman leadership capable of not only leading a strong and powerful nation but also moving the world toward a peaceful and prosperous global community. The U.N. was established on October 24, 1945 after the ending of WW II. Since then, the United States and the Soviet Union have emerged as the two strongest nations, respectively pursuing a capitalistic and socialistic society polarizing the world with constant confrontations, a prolonged Cold War. Even though the two leading nations have embraced socialism and capitalism to a different degree, the rivalry persisted. In the end, the Soviet Union collapsed in 1990 under the burden of arms race and failed economic development.

Post Cold War, the United States has become the sole superpower, a de facto world leader. However, in the past quarter of century under the U.S. leadership, the world has not advanced toward a peaceful and prosperous path; contrarily, the world witnessed continuous wars and unrests in the Middle East and elsewhere, spreading worldwide threat of terrorism and recently the rising tension in the Asia Pacific as the United States initiated a 'Pivot to Asia Pacific' policy. Some international political analysts interpreted the current situation as the consequence of the rising China challenging the world leadership of the United States, but many more attributed the world problem to the poor leadership of the U.S.

In reality, as the world is undergoing globalization, a world leadership transformation and transition is necessary. In this process, the challenges lie in the fact that the leader must recognize that the member states in the world community have different governance systems adopting different ideology. It is a good thing that democracy as a method for reaching decisions has been gradually accepted by the world but democracy is not an ideology and cannot be promoted as a tool to target or replace any government or governance. Democracy has been accepted and practiced in large and small kingdoms (such as the United Kingdom, Sweden, Bhutan, etc. in various degree and form) as well as in post WWII reformed nations (such as Germany, Japan, South Korea, etc). Democracy as a method has also been practiced differently in different systems and institutions, for example, in business corporations, international non-government organizations and in the institutions established under the UN charter. The leadership for the world cannot be defined by neither military power nor economic power alone or created by one nation one vote election process. It has to be transformed and transitioned gradually to be effective in leading the world and to be accepted by the world.

The U.S. is the world leader at present but she must recognize the changing world is expecting an effective leader. The United States has the pre-requisites of a world leader, that is, a developed nation, a strong economy and a powerful military; however, the pre-requisites are necessary but not sufficient conditions to be an effective world leader. To lead the world, we need a statesman (or a team of statesmen) who not only can lead the United States to sustain her in the above mentioned pre-requisite conditions to be a world leading nation, but also can lead the world with convincing leadership, demonstrating the ability of understanding the world and providing a visionary blue print for the world development.

Unfortunately, the political system in the United States, although being stable for centuries and seasoned in practicing democracy, somewhat successfully, for many decades, but the leader the electoral system selects may not be able to deliver a right statesman fit to lead the world. Take the two presumptive presidential nominees, Donald Trump and Hillary Clinton, as examples, the former is a righteous and smart individual, who may be perfectly suited for getting the U.S. to be great again businesswise, but he may not have learned enough to understand and lead the world. The latter may be a well-experienced politician in the U.S. familiar with her political system but her motivation for power and lack of empathy for the developing world may not be fit to be a world leader either. Based on her adherence to the U.S. legacy in foreign policy, especially her China policy based on a biased view of China makes her a questionable world leader.

China is still considered a developing country even though the size of her economy is about to surpass that of the United States. The fact that China has risen both economically and diplomatically, amply indicates that the current Chinese leader (and his predecessors) has a clear grasp of the world from a developing country's point of view as well as from a great nation point of view. China started as the weakest UN permanent security council nation state in 1971 but she has earned her credits to become a respected and effective UN member. (The U.S. leadership should reflect on this!) China has openly declared that she desires to rise peacefully as a great nation and the facts are not far from that desire and the truth. However, the U.S. seems to be targeting China's rise as a threat and launches policies basically aimed to deter China 's rise. This approach (out of either insecurity or hegemony thoughts) itself is not what a true world leader should take. It is so obvious that if the U.S. would work with the fast developing China, it could be more productive for mutual benefits and for the World economy and development.

As the world is globalizing and transforming, the world leader must transform and prepare to accept a leadership transition. Military or nuclear power was never the effective deterrent tool or a slug hammer to control the world order. A genuine world leadership must have a broad and deep understanding of the developing world. An effective world leader must be able to offer a sincere win-win visionary development plan for the world. A true world leader must be able to rally the world and implement a solution to lead the world out of poverty and into peace and prosperity. Observing what the Chinese leader Xi Jinping has proposed, the 'One Belt and One Road' inter-national development plan linking Asia, Africa and Europe, one has to give him credit for playing a world leadership role. It is time for the U.S. think tanks to study the world leadership issue so that a sound advice can be developed to help our elected President to transition to a true and effective world leader.

CHAPTER 24

The Importance of Transparency in National Security, Core Interests and Foreign Policy

—⚊—

ABSTRACT

HISTORICALLY, GREAT NATIONS WITH STRONG economy and military strength play a dominating role in leading the world, to resolve geopolitical issues and to influence regional economical and political problems for maintaining a healthy global economy and a peaceful world. The existing and emerging powers, however, have their own perspectives of national security, core interests and foreign relations, therefore, often produce conflicts. As the world progressed continuously with advanced communication, manufacturing and technologies, a uni-polar leadership will be evolved into a mult-polar leadership as far as world order is concerned. In order to avoid regrettable war and to be an effective world leader, it is very important for a great nation in a multi-polar world to maintain transparency in national security, core interests and foreign policy. We urge the U.S. and China to conduct such a 'transparency' strategy through dialogs in order to gain trust, reduce tension and work collaboratively to maintain world order and achieve world peace and prosperity.

—⚊—

World order is maintained under interplay of properly balancing national security, core interests and foreign relations among nations. Historically, great nations with strong economy and military strength play a dominating role in leading the world, to resolve geopolitical issues and to influence regional economical and political problems for maintaining a healthy global economy and a peaceful world. In this process of managing world order, The fact that over 193 sovereign nations, multiple races and numerous cultures having social strata in wealth, societal classification in sex and gender and communal belief in different religions all exist on Earth Planet, it is understandable that maintaining world order is a very complex and extremely challenging task.

When continents are separated by vast oceans, the world is naturally divided in regions. When humans began to develop maritime technology and naval power, maritime trade became the economic force for great nations to expand and control the world. Great nations, focusing on their national (self) interest, often practice hegemony to expand their influence and to exert control over conquered land (nation) through colonialism. Such expansionism naturally causes competition and conflicts among great nations eventually leading to wars between great powers, spreading to nations leading to world wars. The WW I erupted in Europe and was mainly confined there but the WW II nearly spread over all continents lasting years.

Post WW II, two great nations had emerged creating a 'bi-polar' world divided by ideology: capitalism, valuing individual freedom especially economic freedom, versus communism valuing communal equality especially favoring a socialistic system. This confrontation essentially had divided the world into two camps, one led by the U.S. and her allies including the NATO countries and the other led by the Soviet Union and her allies including the Warsaw pact. The bi-polar world did not erupt into another world war largely because the two leading countries each had piled up significant amount of nuclear arsenal with devastating power which had deterred each other to wage war. The situation of 'détente' could not last forever because the continuous arms race required a continuous strong economy to sustain. Ultimately, the Soviet Union collapsed under the pressure of her failing economy. The world then transitioned to a 'uni-polar' world with the U.S. being the strongest superpower, economically and militarily.

As the 'uni-polar' leader post Cold War, the U.S. indeed tried to be the world police to maintain world order. However, the world has advanced further in science, technology, manufacturing, infrastructure and transportation as well as communication and the media creating an inter-dependent but far more complex global world. The leadership required to manage this new world order must expect the existence and/or the emergence of other great nations and be prepared to deal with a world transitioning from a uni-polar to a bi-polar and to a multi-polar world. The rise of China and the rejuvenating Russia are two competing great nations; Brazil, India and South Africa are also rising economic powers joining the existing G-7, Canada, France, Germany, Italy, Japan, the United Kingdom and the United States. The U.S. as the leader of G-7 had no choice but to welcome and deal with the fast developing BRICS.

As the world progressed continuously with advanced communication, manufacturing and technologies, the emerging great nations naturally not only rise in economic power but also exert influence on the world stage. During this progress, unfortunately, arms race has been continued non-stop since the ending of the Cold War. The U.S. either failed to discourage arms race or naively believed that her unmatchable military strength will remain unmatched and be effective in keeping the ever more complex world in order. In reality, not only great nations such as Russia, India and China now possess nuclear weapons even small nations like Iran and North Korea desire to gain nuclear arsenal and become members of exclusive nuclear club as a bargaining tool. So in the multi-polar world, proliferation of nuclear weapon is a serious problem which will further neutralize the U.S. military power as a deterrent force to act the role of the world police. The world events in the past decades showed us how ineffective it was to resolve world issues using military force. To avoid a devastating nuclear war, the best we can hope is that all nuclear powered nations will refrain from using nuclear weapon, and gradually and ultimately transform the whole world into a no-nuclear world as President Obama has proposed.

Observing the current world events, one cannot help but worry about the U.S. foreign policy. The U.S. seems to be still adhering to a 'uni-polar' world model and trying very hard to maintain world order as the sole superpower without accepting the fact that the world has transitioned to a multi-polar world. In such a world, economic and military power may be necessary pre-requisite for a nation to play a world leader role but they are not sufficient condition. Today's world leadership requires political power, that is political wisdom, political knowledge and political skills backed by economic and mili-tary strength, to deal with world problems. The leaders in the great nations are created in different ways through different trainings. The U.S. is proud to have the most open and democratic political system to create her national lead-ers. Unfortunately, the US election process is corrupted by money; the leaders elected are great fund raisers, media manipulators and political orators with little honest evaluation on their political power to deal with foreign policy and world issues. Even candidates with administrative and foreign relation experi-ence are not scrutinized on the basis of their ability and integrity as a world political leader and on the basis of having a clear vision of the multi-polar world.

The Russian leader, Putin, and the Chinese leader, Xi Jinping, have risen to their supreme political positions with a very different scrutiny. Their 'career' experiences speak volume of their political wisdom, knowledge and skills. Whether is Russia's rapid annexation of Crimea or China's long-term 'one belt one road' vision of world co-development plan, we can see the skillful play of their political power. In contrast, Clinton-Obama's Pivot to Asia policy of fuzzy objective and inconsistent implementation creates more tension and little purpose. Obama's visiting Hiroshima is another political mistake, negat-ing history, dishonoring our war heroes and simply playing into the hands of the Japanese Right Wing politicians. Obama's visit reminds the world that the U.S. was the one throwing the first atomic bomb without understanding the feelings of all Asian countries invaded and brutalized by the Japanese imperial army.

The current South China Sea (SCS) saga is clearly orchestrated by the U.S. The tension and visibility are raised but for what purpose? If the purpose is curtailing Chin's rise, the effect is opposite. An arms race stimulated in Asia Pacific only leads to war. However, so far one thing the U.S. and China had done correctly regarding SCS was that they both appreciated the importance of transparency in declaring great nation's actions – a necessary behavior to show a nation's wisdom in world politics. Even though the U.S. cannot articulate and justify her agitation and intervention in S.C.S, at least she has given ample advance notice about whatever military maneuver she will make. Likewise China has given ample explanation whatever reaction or counter move she will make. It is this transparency that has kept the fuse from igniting. However, the lack of clarity and transparency on what and why the US pivot to Asia Pacific matters to her national security and core interests and the inconsistency of US foreign policy regarding China, Japan and Asia do not make the U.S. an effective world leader. In world politics, if you want war, you keep secret plans, if you want peace, you make the foreign policy transparent.

In order to avoid regrettable war and to be an effective world leader, it is very important for a great nation in a multi-polar world to maintain transparency in national security, core interests and foreign policy. We urge the U.S. and China to conduct such a 'transparency' strategy through dialogs in order to gain trust, reduce tension and work collaboratively to maintain world order and achieve world peace and prosperity.

CHAPTER 25

The U.S. Legislative Process and the Asia-Pacific Maritime Security Bill

—ᨇ—

ABSTRACT

THE UNITED STATES HAS A unique legislative process to enact laws for the US federated states to obey as well as a means of making diplomatic declaration to the foreign states to understand the U.S. As a nation of immigrants, citizens stratified with wide gap of wealth and its constituent states having geopolitical differences, many domestic issues as well as some foreign policies, have become controversial dividing the U.S. When comes to foreign policy, the Congress plays a critical counter balancing role to the executive branch. The Congress may introduce a legislative bill to oppose/denounce or to support/enhance the executive branch's policy. Recently, U.S. Senators Cory Gardner (R-CO), Ben Cardin (D-MD), Robert Menendez (D-N.J.), and Brian Schatz (D-Hawaii) drafted legislation, the United States Policy on Asia-Pacific Maritime Security, to enhance American maritime capacity and leadership and to increase support to American allies in the Asia-Pacific region. This essay comments on this legislation's contradictory facts and its ill effects on US-China relations and urges fellow Americans to express their opinions to their legislators.

—ᨇ—

The legislative process in the two chambers (Senate and House) of the U.S. Congress is one unique democratic method of introducing laws for the US federated states (governments, military, corporations and citizens) to obey as well as a means of making diplomatic declaration to the foreign states to understand the U.S. foreign policy, supposedly fairly representing people's views. In both situations, the language of the legislative content may vary depending on the legislators in each chamber who represent and interpret their constituents' views on the legislative matter at hand. As the United States is principally a two-party system, Republicans and Democrats (some independents and a few minority party followers), the above legislative process is usually initiated by legislative members of one party and endorsed by one or both and/or other parties. (*the executive branch may initiate legislation through the Congress but usually via its party) The proposed legislative bill get passed by one chamber and modified by the other chamber after the bill was presented, reviewed and debated in one or both chambers. This legislative process works most of the time when a legislative matter is not a controversial or politically divisive issue facing the nation.

Unavoidably, as a nation of immigrants, citizens stratified with wide gap of wealth and its constituent states having geopolitical differences, many issues such as social welfare, taxation reform, immigration and labor, healthcare, and other domestic issues including abortion, gun control, environment, gay marriage as well as some foreign policies have become controversial issues dividing the U.S. As a democratic country, lobbying during legislative process is permitted by law; however, the lobbying activities directed through media or targeted at Congress members require financing. This lobbying effort has become controlled by the money hands (wealthy class) over the years that corrupt the legislative process; worse, the same money hands can influence the election process to elect the legislative representatives to do their favored bidding.

The power of the legislated law or foreign policy declaration depends very much on the language in the legislative bill whether it contains mandates supported by funding appropriation or not. One of the problems in the legislative laws in the U.S. is that sometimes mandates contained in the legislations are not adequately appropriated with funds to be executed. This phenomenon, 'unfunded mandate' happens widely in both federal and state laws, acutely in the domain of education and social welfare and more seriously when governments run a budget deficit and/or when Congress and executive branch have sharp political differences. Often the budget appropriation is used by the two branches of government to force or sabotage the mandates contained in the legislations. This governmental malfunction can be easily understood by citizens on education mandates such as forcing a national standard onto states, or on healthcare mandates or labor laws, etc. etc.

When the executive branch or the legislative chamber is initiating a foreign policy declaration, it is usually desirable to solicit and solidify the nation's position on a particular foreign policy matter. Through a transparent legislative process consisting of initiating a bill, conducting extensive dialogue in the public as well as holding serious hearings and debates in the chambers, hopefully a genuine consensus may be reached and a justified declaration drafted to express the U.S. position on a foreign policy issue. Usually, this type of foreign policy declaration has a significant impact on the security and/or core interests of the U.S. Examples of such declarative legislation in the past include declaring wars, human rights, trade agreements and foreign policies, for example, the Taiwan Relations Act following President Carter's formal recognition of the People's Republic of China and the sanction bill against Russia and Russian individuals after Russia annexed Crimea.

When comes to foreign policy, the Congress plays a critical counter balancing role to the executive branch. The Congress may introduce a legislative bill to oppose/denounce or to support/enhance the executive branch's policy. The New Cuban policy is one example which was adopted unilaterally by the executive branch and might be opposed by Congress. When Obama re-established relation with Cuba in December 2014, Senator Bob Menendez from New Jersey (D) and Senator Marco Rubio from Florida (R) (both descendants of Cuban immigrants) expressed opposition, they may choose to introduce a bill to limit or slow down the US-Cuba diplomatic relation but that may not be feasible during the 113th Congress (1/2013-1/2015) because an override of Obama's veto on an opposition bill from Congress may not be possible, hence, Congress may have to wait after the 2016 election. On the other hand, the United States Policy on Asia-Pacific Maritime Security Initiative drafted in the Congress, is an example that Congress is trying to enhance the executive branch's current policy. The Congress may hope to get the bill passed in the 114th Congress (1/2015-1/2017). This bill is not only significant from the US-China relationship point of view but also important for American citizens (especially the Chinese Americans) to exercise their influence on the outcome of the bill.

U.S. Senators Cory Gardner (R-CO), Chairman of the Senate Foreign Relations East Asia Subcommittee, Ben Cardin (D-MD), Ranking Member of both the Senate Foreign Relations Committee (SFRC) and the SFRC East Asia Subcommittee, Robert Menendez (D-N.J.), a senior member of the SFRC, and Brian Schatz (D-Hawaii) drafted a legislation on 4-27-2016, entitled, the United States Policy on Asia-Pacific Maritime Security, to enhance American maritime capacity and leadership and to increase support to American allies in the Asia-Pacific region. This 22-page draft bill proposed by the heavyweight senators from SFRC is obviously a support bill to endorse the administration's current policy. After examining the bill, one may conclude that the main objectives of the bill are fourfold: 1. Declare the U.S. as a power in Asia Pacific with desire to support her allies in the East and South China Sea (S.C.S.) in maintaining maritime security. 2. Authorize the State and Defense departments to provide Foreign Military Financing Assistance and International Military and Educational Training to Asia Pacific countries for maritime security capability building and domain awareness in S.C.S. 3. Authorize appropriations of $7.5M for the State Department's Southeast Asia Maritime Law Enforcement Initiative and allocate funds for the assistance and training programs up to $75M in fiscal year 2017 and $100 M for year 2018-2021. 4. Revise Military Sales Status for the Philippines and authorize the transfer of excess defense articles. This bill is loaded with reporting (to Congress Appropriation Committees) requirements on timetable and milestones suggesting a lack of clear outlook for this maritime security initiative.

When the legislators were interviewed, Senator Gardner stated: "China's ongoing reclamation activities and militarization of the South China Sea threatens regional stability and represents a clear and fundamental challenge to the international law." Senator Cardin said: "China is of course not unique in its actions, which have complicated efforts to resolve conflicting claims diplomatically or legally, but the quantity, scope, and scale of its activities have a quality all their own." Senator Schatz said: "China's ongoing action to unilaterally redraw the region's maritime borders exacerbates the risks of misperceptions and conflict." Senator Henendez said: "With this legislation, we offer this new way forward: challenge the Government of China on its destabilizing policies in the region, assert legal and rightful international authority over maritime boundaries, and send a signal to our friends and allies in the region that the international community – led by the United States – will no longer tolerate China's efforts to militarize its foreign policy."

Just based on the above statements alone, one can detect the underlying contradictory facts regarding the S.C.S. situation. First, China's well engineered reclamation effort was a reaction to the reclamation activities started long before by "other" countries. Second, the U.S. Pivot to Asia policy including moving naval forces to AP is more like 'militarizing' foreign policy than China's reactionary efforts shifting lighthouse construction to missile deployment. This U.S. Maritime Security Initiative further enhances her efforts in "militarizing" her foreign policy through weapon sales and transfer of defense articles. In view of the rising tension in S.C.S. as an American citizen, shouldn't we examine the facts carefully? Shouldn't we speak up and influence our legislative process? Write to your Congressmen and Senators – why are we driving ourselves to war with China?

CHAPTER 26

Tibet and Tibetans We Come to Understand

—◊◊◊—

ABSTRACT

BEAUTIFUL TIBET IS A MYSTERY land of snow. Its secluded traditional religious-politic-economic system and community was slow in responding to a fast changing world in the past century. A recent book (2015 Random House ISBN 978-81-8400-387-1) written by Gyalo Thondup, older brother of the current 14th Dalai Lama, offered a chronological story of Tibet over the last eight decades of time detailing the process of Dalai Lama selection by reincarnation search, life experience of the holiness and his family and the governance of Tibet people by the ruling cabinet of the Dalai Lama. This commentary essay reviews the history of Tibet and facts and lessons learned from Gyalo's book. The author then offers discussions and comments about the Dalai Lama's life experience and his government in exile and suggests it is time to terminate his near six decade exile and return home to help the Tibet people.

—◊◊◊—

To most people in the world, Tibet remains a mysterious land of snows having beautiful high mountains and being a pilgrimage holy place of religion. The Himalayan peaks kept most parts of Tibet difficult to reach and numerous world mountaineers dreaming to visit. To Chinese, Tibet is a part of the vast Western China, remote and unique in culture representing four principal minorities and Han immigrants (Tibetans, Huis, Manchus, Mongolians, and Hans); However, the population really include aborigines and several generation of the old immigrants throughout several millennia as early as Tang

(618-907), Yuan (1271-1368), Qing (1644-1911) dynasties as well as in the recent twenty and twenty first centuries. Prior to and during WW II, many Chinese (Hans, Huis, Manchus and Mongolians) were forced to migrate to Southwest China to escape or retreat from the Western and Japanese invasion in the North, East and South of China. Thus, Tibet being far and high out of the human path remained secluded and insulated from the past and current events. Tibet is too complex a story to understand even by the people who lived there, partly because of its thousands of years history not being recorded in writing as completely as the Hans of China and partly because of Tibet being a secluded religious community which had a religion controlled political and economic system, naturally or deliberately, insulated from the external world.

Only a few books were written about Tibet and some are tinted by political bias. Tibet is never a simple human rights case like (Africans) or (American Indians). Tibet is a huge territory scantly populated enjoying a de facto independence without understanding what independence really means in the modern world. The Tibetans are very ignorant and naive about political affairs; even the learned monks and elites in the political ruling class were not aware of the significance of the western colonization of her neighbor India and turmoil happening in the continent of China. To the Tibetans, the following dates of 10-10-1911, collapse of Qing Dynasty and beginning of the Republic of China, 7-7-1937, the open invasion of Japanese in China, 9-2-1945, the surrender of Japan and the ending of WW II, 8-15-1947, independence of India, 10-1-1949, establishment of the People's Republic China and 1-1-1979, the recognition of China by the U.S. and 3-11-1990, the collapse of the Soviet Union seem to have very little meaning, while reincarnation test is used to find leader succession creating a vulnerable political system for decades idling for the chosen child to grow up.

In 2015, a book, entitled, The Noodle Maker of Kalimpong, was published by Gyalo Thondup and assisted by Anne F. Thurston. The significance of this book about Tibet is not only because Gyalo Thondup is the elder brother of the 14th Dalai Lama, the spiritual and political leader of Tibet selected by 'reincarnation' after the 13th Dalai Lama's death, but also because Gyalo

Thondup, with his entire family, devoted all their lives to take care of the 14th Dalai Lama before and after the Holiness reached 15 years old, actually taking over the administrative power from the caretaker Reting Regent. Among five male siblings, Gaylo is the only one who did not become a monk. He studied in Nanking and in the U.S. but was not a diligent student admitted by himself. Nevertheless he was groomed to serve the 14th Dalai Lama. Gyalo's book is an autobiography reflecting his honest nature as a Tibetan illustrating his and Dalai Lama's life long experiences with chronological detail. More importantly, not to be misled by the title, this book described the inner workings of the reincarnation search and the Reting Regent government structure as well as the grooming process of the Dalai Lama from infant to maturity age to assume the spiritual and political leadership assisted by a cabinet of advisors. Thurston was honest to say: "political rule by incarnation is an almost certain guarantee of bad government".

Through Gyalo's book, we can learn that the unique religious practice in Tibet has controlled the Tibetans lives in an unfair social political system for generations. The monks and elites had the power and wealth but the people, devoted believers, remained poor peasants generation after generation. Gyalo might have recognized that Tibet needed reform but the ministers surrounded the Dalai Lama apparently clanged to traditions insisting on keeping the system as true independence. Failing to respect the written history of where Tibetans came from and consisting of (for example Chinese Wencheng Princess, 628-680, Tang Dynasty, married King of Tibet) and failing to understand the meaning of separation of politics and religion and ideologies prevailing in the contemporary world (Sun Yat San's Three Principles and Mao's Words on Revolution) sowed the seeds for disaster when demanding the maintenance of Tibet's traditional religious-politico-economic system.

When Gyalo was only a young man (his brother 14th Dalai Lama 2 years younger), he served as a leading figure and spokesperson for Tibet but he was powerless to do anything by himself. In hindsight, we see that the Reting Regent was stubborn and ignorant to understand the British selfish foreign policy towards India (and Tibet and China). Even Gyalo himself was naive to understand the intrigue politics of the Chinese political parties, CCP and KMT from 1911 to 1949 and beyond. Gyalo and his cabinet colleagues were not in the league of Indian Prime Minister Nehru thus could only hopelessly accept Nehru's decisions and change of hearts toying the Tibet independence issue. Gyalo was also ignorant about the US-China and US-Taiwan relations, naively believing that the CIA (the U.S.) was sincerely helping Tibet to achieve independence rather than simply creating problems in China's backyard, a strategy based on anti-communism and legacy of Korean War.

Perhaps because of his innocence, naivety, and likable personality, Gyalo as a spokesperson for Dalai Lama was presented with many opportunities to have direct contacts with world leaders, besides Americans and Indians, Gyalo maintained contact with both Chiang Kai-Shek (KMT) and Zhu De and Mao Tse Dong and later Deng Xiaoping (CCP) but never was effective in producing any meaningful negotiation to obtain any real commitment from either side to maintain Tibet's antiquated religious and political system. The Tibetans including Gyalo and Dalai Lama just did not understand these leaders' views of Chinese history and nation building. In 1949, when CCP won the struggle against KMT and established the People's Republic of China, Tibet was invited to attend the celebration but Tibet representatives failed to negotiate an autonomous region status for Tibet which was most likely acceptable to CCP at that time, a long historical practice throughout Chinese history. Insisting on maintaining existing political system and the indecision to accept Mao's proposal, eventually invited the Chinese troops. The wishful thinking that India and the U.S. even Russia would sincerely fight for Tibet was again naive.

Dalai Lama's exile and maintaining an exile government in India which offered no assistance made no sense. Inconsistency and lack of skills in diplomatic protocols messed up a number of opportunities to reach a meaningful agreement with CCP as Gyalo admitted and explained in several chapters of his book. Eventually, the Dalai Lama had made compromises yielding political claims such as let the Chinese Central Government have the foreign policy responsibility over Tibet. This would produce a workable system under China's one nation multiple systems policy designed to deal with Hong Kong, Tibet and Taiwan issues. When 10th Panchen Lama died (1989), Dalai Lama should have accepted the CCP's invitation to preside at his memorial service as the Tibetans' leader. Afraid of being kidnapped is not a justifiable excuse knowing that the 10th Panchen Lama had been outspoken in fighting for Tibet's benefits while living in China. Gyalo was right to say that was an opportunity lost.

The 14th Dalai Lama was born in 1935 and anointed in 1939. It is understandable that in the early part of Dalai Lama's life, he was an inexperienced youth basically influenced by bad advices from his senior conservative monks. Now Dalai Lama is 81, living outside of Tibet since 1959, what is the excuse not to return to Tibet to focus on restoring and maintaining the Tibet culture, language and religion since the entire China (including Tibet) has been restoring from the culture revolution. Witnessing the changes in the world, religiously (Catholicism, Christianity, Islamism) and politically (WW II, Cold War, Rise of China), it would be wise to bury the past (mistakes made by all parties) and go back to the highest monastery in the world to do something for the people of Tibet and for the peace of China and the world.

CHAPTER 27

The Right to Speak and the Art/Effect of Diplomatic Speech - 2016 IISS Shangri-La Dialogue

—ɱ—

ABSTRACT

IT IS ALWAYS MORE DESIRABLE to rely on dialogue and international forum to settle world issues than resorting to military forces. However, the right to speak cannot be obtained easily or arbitrarily; more likely it has to be earned by credits or deeds. In world politics, the powerful nations tend to control the right to speak and then follow with diplomatic effective speeches to accomplish their goals. Not every nation is skilled in this art to acquire the right to speak and making effective speech. The recent IISS Shangri-La Dialogue and the South China Sea tension are used as an exemplary case to discuss this important diplomacy. The U.S. orchestrated a set of presentations addressing the security issue in Asia and through Secretary of Defense Ashton Carter's speech declaring the U.S. as the security provider in Asia. This speech seems to be effective at the meeting putting China on the defensive, but whether this speech and the U.S. strategy would be effective in the long run is very questionable.

—ɱ—

Whether it is to accomplish a goal or to promote a cause, one must first have the right to speak. Depending on what is the matter at hand, one may want the right to speak in a conference room addressing the audience captured there or one may need the right to speak on a world stage declaring to the media covering the world. However, the right to speak cannot be obtained easily or arbitrarily; more likely it has to be earned by credits or deeds. In world politics, the powerful nations tend to control the right to speak. The U.S. as the super-power has been able to control the right to speak on various issues through numerous venues. The U.S. earned that right by being the largest economy in the world and having the mightiest military power on Earth. Other nations, not only the big nations like China, India and Russia but also the smaller nations even the city nation, Singapore, do want and need the right to speak as well.

As the title of this paper suggests, obtaining the right to speak is one issue and making the speech effective is another. This space is devoted to discuss the two issues using recent events. I hope that nations will devote their energy to seek the right to speak and make their diplomatic speech effective so that world problems can be solved and world progress can be made through dia-logues and speeches rather than by military confrontation and wars. As an optimist, I believe that if we global citizens can better understand the intrigue of the art of seeking the right to speak and the art of making diplomatic speech effective, we will be in a better position to sift out the good diplomatic speech through the rhetoric and to use our influence helping nations to settle their international disputes and conflicts peacefully.

Let's use the 2016 IISS Shangri-La Dialogue and the South China Sea (S.C.S.) issue as an exemplary case to discuss the subject issues. The Shangri-La Dialogue (SLD) is an intergovernmental security forum, held annually by an 'independent' think tank and attended by defense ministers, permanent heads of ministries and military chiefs of 28 Asia–Pacific states. The forum has been held in Shangri-La hotel Singapore since 2002. IISS is a British research insti-tute in the area of international affairs headquartered in London since 1997. It was founded in 1958 initially focused on nuclear deterrence and arms con-trol and is rated among top ten think tanks in the world today. IISS describes itself as a primary source of accurate, objective information on international strategic issues for politicians and diplomats, foreign affairs analysts, interna-tional business, economists, the military, defense commentators, journalists, academics and the informed public. The Institute claims no allegiance to any government or to any political or other organization but it does have strong establishment links with former US and British government officials among its members. The CEO of IISS since 1933, Dr. John Chipman, is responsible for the growth and contribution of IISS as a think tank. SLD is thus an important international forum that the world pays attention to.

The two-day conference of IISS focuses on security issues concerning the Asia Pacific. From the agenda, it seems that the U.S. has obtained her full right to speak at the 2016 SLD by having Dr. Ashton Carter, Secretary of Defense as the speaker of the first plenary session in a prime time slot of 9-10AM on Saturday on the subject of Meeting, Asia's Complex Security Challenges. He is followed by the Ministers of Defense of India, Japan and Malaysia in the 2nd plenary session with a 30min speech each addressing the topic of Managing Military Competition in Asia. The speakers of the 3rd plenary consist of Minister or Secretary of Defense of Indonesia, South Korea and UK discussing Making Defense Policies in Uncertain Times. This collection of presentations provides the main threads of discourse for the conference. The next six parallel sessions after lunch divide the attention among North Korea Threat, Military Development, Irregular Migration, Jihad Terrorism, S.C.S. Tension and Cyber Security. The 4th and 5th plenary sessions on Sunday Morning focus on Challenges on Conflict Resolution and Pursuing Common Security Objective. China in this 2016 SLD did get two speaking slots related to S.C.S. issue. Major General Yao Yunzhu a military scholar spoke in the afternoon SCS session and fielded more than a dozen questions whereas Admiral Sun Jianguo spoke in the Sunday 4th plenary session and offered China's position regarding resolving conflicts. China seems to be put in a defensive position in the SLD.

Why do I as an observer feel that the U.S. has successfully orchestrated the diplomatic events in the past few years and enabled Dr. Carter to deliver an effective diplomatic speech at the SLD while leaving China in a defensive position? I am offering below an analysis as a token to draw Americans and Chinese people's attention to ponder on the importance of earning the right to speak on the world stage and effectively delivering a diplomatic speech to accomplish a strategic objective without resorting to war. In fact, this kind of thought was originated from Sun Tze, the most famous strategist, he said, "To win without engaging a war is the best military strategy." Apparently, in Asia and the S.C.S. case, the U.S. has applied this strategy.

The announcing of the U.S. Pivot to Asia policy in 2011 is a strategic shift probably motivated by a host of considerations, i. Failure and burden in the Middle East, ii. Threat from the new leader in North Korea, iii. Success of China in cultivating economic and diplomatic relations with Asian countries especially ASEAN, and iv. Improved bilateral US-China relation requiring some leverage. Strategically, this policy was pushed through two fronts: The Economic front via Trans Pacific Partnership (TPP) to make the U.S. a principal player and investor in Asian economy and the Security front through military alliances to make the U.S. appearing as a security provider in Asia. The progress of these two fronts were not smooth by any means, however, they certainly caused China to feel uneasy.

The rise of China on the other hand has made the U.S. uneasy as well. Forcing the U.S. to deal with China more seriously as China gains international influence through her bilateral economic relationship with many countries in the world. Diplomatically, China has gained her right to speak in many important international forums such as Asia Pacific Economic Cooperation (APEC), ASEAN Regional Forum (ARF), Boao Forum, etc. to the point that the U.S. was pushed to the side. Since Hu Jiantao and Xi Jinping visited the U.S., the U.S. had found ways to have direct dialogue with China but feeling that China's rise and assertiveness are threatening the existing world order, namely the U.S. world leadership. As a result, the U.S. is accelerating the above mentioned strategy to maintain her world leadership. On the economic front, the U.S. is making limited progress hence she is now placing more emphasis on the security front.

The U.S. does not want to have a war in Asia especially directly against China but strategically she needs to create some leverage in Asia to reverse the tide of being pushed to the sideline by China. The recent events in Asia Pacific relating to US-China relations can be traced to this strategy. Declaring neutrality in territorial dispute (avoid real military conflict) and yet condoning Japan to break the promise of tabling the dispute on Diaoyu Islands with China, to strengthen the US-Japan Mutual Defense Treaty and to revise Japan's Pacifist constitution all intended to but did not raise the tension in East China Sea enough. Then the U.S. raised the freedom of navigation flag and moved the focus to S.C.S., again, by declaring neutrality in territorial dispute but encouraging the Philippines and others to heighten the disputes with China in S.C.S. In order to create the need for the U.S. to be a security provider, she has to stir up security issues. Surprisingly, a few historically disputed rocks and the created "Freedom of Navigation" issue accompanied with military exercises (RIMPAC etc) worked to some extent to raise the security concern of ASEAN countries even Australia and India. The bilateral, trilateral and multi-lateral military alliances the U.S. and Japan cultivated in Asia Pacific are evidences of that. Thus the U.S. has successfully created a security scenario and turned around and earned the right to speak on security issues of Asia Pacific and acted as Asia's security provider.

The U.S. Secretary of Defense chose the IISS SLD as the venue to deliver his AP security speech, entitled Meeting Asia's Complex Security Challenges. Is it an effective diplomatic speech? Yes, Dr. Carter's speech is effective for the time being but questionable in the future. His speech praises the Asian countries for their developments and appeases the Asian political and military leaders with their forward-thinking ability; he creates the key phrases or code words, "principled security network" and "principled future" to lead the audience to think what the U.S. has done in Asia and S.C.S. as principled but leaving the principle unexplained for audience to interpret as they please. China of course views the US actions as unprincipled. Dr. Carter uses "self-isolation" to describe China and to vindicate the U.S. actions as never intended to be targeting China nor isolating China. He applauds the bi-lateral, tri-lateral and multi-lateral military alliances as means for enhancing Asia security. It may sound logical in his speech for the time being, but it is doubtful they will stand the test of time.

Judging on the speech made by the Chinese delegates at SLD, they are defensive and not prepared for the orchestrated agenda and various speeches.

Yao Yunzhu correctly questioned the code words, "principled" and "self isolation" but offered no rebuttal. Sun Jianguo's four point proposal, peace, tolerance, dialogue and local security structure appeared to be toothless and did not challenge the key issue, why the U.S. or who is the security provider of Asia? Is it the one who sells and provides more weapons and signs more military alliances or the one who proposes and invests in collaborative development in Asia. Contrasting TPP and RIMNPAC to One Belt One Road and AIIB, one should wonder which policy enhances Asia security? I think Carter might be right about Asian leaders being forward-thinking, and I believe, the Asian leaders may be temporarily flashed by the orchestrated speeches at the IISS meeting but through many private meetings and follow-up discussions, the Asian leaders will return to their wisdom and senses. China of course will have to work hard to clarify the code word "principle" for Asia and demonstrate that China is not "isolated" plus explain what exactly a local security structure means for the benefit of the local Asian countries.

IISS SLD is just one international forum. It is good that big and small nations are using the right to speak and try to make effective speeches to resolve international problems than using military force. Every country and its citizens should understand and appreciate the art of gaining the right to speak in a world forum and the art of making effective diplomatic speeches on world stage.

CHAPTER 28

Are We Addressing the U.S.-China Confrontation Correctly?

—⚏—

ABSTRACT

THE U.S.-CHINA RELATION IS A delicate one, partly due to mutual dependence calling for collaboration and partly caused by competition leading to mutual distrust. Lately the latter factor seems to be rapidly heading towards serious confrontations. As concerned citizens we observe that the official interactions and media spin between the two countries exhibit complications, confusions and contradictions. We should ask ourselves, are we addressing the US-China confrontation correctly. In this paper we probe this question on both military confrontation and economic confrontation.

—⚏—

Let's first leave the truthfulness and sincerity aside, on the surface, the U.S. is clearly targeting China and claiming China as a threat to the U.S.; whereas China is claiming no intention to challenge or replace the US world leadership but China is becoming more assertive in her diplomatic dealings. Unfortunately, despite of opening channels for dialogue, the US-China relations seem to be rapidly heading towards serious confrontations intermixed on two fronts, one on military involving defense strategy, weapon development and alliances and the other on economy entailing economic model, trade and investment as well as currency policy. What concerns the global citizens of course including American and Chinese citizens is that are we addressing the US-China confrontation correctly? As we citizens observe the official interactions and media spin between the U.S. and China, we see complications, confusions, contradictions and counter actions based on counter actions (C4) without engaging an honest reflection on assumptions, motives, and causality principle (AMCP). (*C4AMCP is created to draw the military officials' attention. Please read on.)

Previously, I have discussed the military confrontation issue following the publication of an article, The Once and Future Superpower – Why China Won't Overtake the U.S. (Foreign Affairs May/June/2016), by Stephen G. Brooks and William C. Wohlforth, professors at Dartmouth. That article's main point is that the U.S. is militarily superior and China will not overtake the U.S. at least decades away even if she goes all out to try. My opinion is that it is wrong for U.S. to provoke China into a military competition; whatever outcome; it is not beneficial to the U.S. A nation's continued successful military development is contingent on a strong economy of that nation. The collapse of the British Empire and the Soviet Union are clear evidence in the history to back this conclusion. While China is rising more rapidly economically comparing to other nations, it is a bad strategy to provoke China to divert her resources into military spending. Some may say that China has been increasing her military budget steadily over the past decade, but has anyone asked why? A country, with many thousands miles of coast line and bordering 14 nations (some historically hostile) plus a century of foreign bullying and invasions in her history, deserves to have a defense capability, doesn't she? At present, China's defense budget, proportional to her GDP, is less than a quarter of the U.S. defense budget and is peaked due to a slower economic growth. Why shouldn't the U.S. pursue a strategy to limit each other's military spending instead of engaging in an arms race?

Recently a congressional paper entitled, China Naval Modernization: Implications for U.S. Navy Capabilities – Background and Issues for Congress, by Ronald O'Rourke, Specialist in Naval Affairs, was published by Congressional Research Services dated May 31, 2016. This paper investigated China's Navy Plan in detail and raised issues for the Congress to consider backing a US Navy plan to counter China's Anti-Access/Area-Denial plan (A2/AD) and her Anti-Ship Ballistic Missile (ASBM), submarines and command and control, communications, computers, intelligence and reconnaissance (C4ISR). The details of the Chinese naval plan, just like the acronym names implied, are defense and not offense military strategy. Why should our Congress be encouraged to increase military spending so we could break China's defense? What is the logic? Don't we understand the Causality Principle? If someone is building a strong shield, must we build a stronger spear to pierce the shield to prove that we have the strongest spear? After examining this and other reports about China's military strategy, it is easy to come to the conclusion; China is reducing her military size (reducing 300,000 personnel) to reduce cost but is increasing technology content especially in communication to deal with modern warfare like that occurred in the Middle East. I think this should be clear to our Congress; the military confrontation with China is not an issue if the U.S. does not create that issue; and we should never provoke China to develop spears from shields!

On the other hand, the U.S.-China economic confrontation is real, but it is not an issue to be solved by arms race or a military solution. Another recent article in Foreign Affairs (March/April 2016), entitled, Can China's Companies Conquer the World?, by Pankaj Ghemawat (Global Professor of Management and Strategy at New York University) and Thomas Hout (Lecturer at Middlebury Institute of International Studies, Tufts University and University of Hong Kong) is very relevant to the topic of economic confrontation. Ghemawat and Hout essentially argue that GDP number is not the measure of the real strength of economic power. Even China's GDP surpasses the U.S. (in their estimate not until 2028), but the real economic strength is in the corporations underneath the economy. They claim that strong macroeconomic data do not tell the economic story, citing that from 1990 to 2013, as the Chinese GDP grew at roughly 10 percent annually, the stock market barely moved. They attribute the real strength of economy lies in the real world of corporations and industries that actually create growth and wealth. Then they venture to characterize the differences between Chinese and US corporations and industries and claim that the U.S. is leading in design and R&D as well as 'capital goods' and high-tech manufacturing. (*capital goods are goods used to produce other goods)

The above paper sounded more like a morale boosting article for US businesses and industries than an objective economics thesis analyzing two economic models, the U.S. vis-à-vis China. It seems to me some of the observations and deductions are little out-dated and confined in a nationalistic view rather than a global view. Since the US-China economic confrontation (or any global competition) is not avoidable, perhaps, it makes sense for economists to examine the business models in the global context. It is true under free capitalism the U.S. (and Western) corporations and industries (claimed in the above article) are leading in the global economy. However, the transformation of global business models does not guarantee that the US corporations remain to be US owned forever nor US industries can remain their leadership as seen in auto and solar industries. The U.S. must cultivate her business environment to entice the corporations and industries to remain in the U.S. and yet be competitive enough globally.

Conversely, China's growth has been accelerated by state planning and propelled largely by state-owned corporations. As China engages more into the global markets and opening her domestic market for competitors from multi-national corporations, she also faces a challenge to transform her business environment to enable her state-owned corporation to evolve into a free enterprise to compete in the free markets without government subsidies or strings attached. Observing recent business activities, it shows that China is eager but gingerly in executing her economic transformation, internally through upgrading industries to higher technology content and externally through investment abroad to gain leverage to expand globally. Contrasting the two economies, it appears that the U.S. and China have a lot to be gained if they collaborate in their economic development to find win-win cooperation rather than scheming to exclude each other in trade, investment and technology development.

In US-China Relations, if both countries can realize that military confrontation bears no good fruit and economic confrontation is natural and unavoidable, then it would make good sense that two countries channel their energy to a business transformation process and develop a collaborative relationship to cultivate win-win projects and supplement each other with the other's unique strength.

CHAPTER 29

Accepting Multi-Polar World Order
Is Inevitable And Beneficial

—⋙—

ABSTRACT

WORLD ORDER IS BASED ON the balance of three elements, economic activities and strength, military power and distribution and political system and leadership. Historically, the world has never been a uni-polar world led by one single superpower. Post WW II, the U.S. has emerged as a superpower leading the capitalist world in confrontation with a communist bloc led by the Soviet Union. As the Soviet Union collapsed after more than four decades of Cold War confrontation, the U.S. had become the sole superpower seemingly treating the world as a uni-polar world. However, many large nations such as Brazil, China, Germany, Japan and India have rapidly advanced their economy under their own evolving political systems (except Japan being fostered by the U.S.); even small nations such as Singapore, Vietnam, and South Korea, have also made outstanding economic progress having varying military strength and different political governing systems. Thus a multi-polar world order is inevitable and the U.S. must accept it.

—⋙—

World order is based on the balance of three elements, economic activities and strength, military power and distribution and political system and leadership. Historically, the world has never been a uni-polar world led by one single superpower. Throughout conflicts and battles, the world has endured millennia of wars with rise and fall of powerful nations or empires led by one or two of the above three elements but never all of the three. Hence, the world has never really functioned under a uni-polar leadership even though from time to time nations rise into a superpower status economically or militarily.

WW II was a long fierce war on Earth extended more than a decade in some regions. Following WW II, the U.S. and the Soviet emerged as superpowers militarily when most other warring nations were devastated and weakened by the war. The U.S. was able to rebuild her economy to be the largest in the world with a commanding position to help other nations to develop their economy. The U.S., benefitted from a democratic political system and a capitalistic economic system, was promoting 'democracy' erroneously in my opinion as an ideology rather than a methodology of decision making to assist political leaders and their governing systems to enact and execute policies for the benefits of their people. With her strong economy, the U.S. was able to win the Cold War against the Soviet Union, making the U.S. as the sole superpower in the world to this date.

Since the ending of the Cold War in 1990, the U.S. is strategically leading the world as a uni-polar world even though there is no unique political system recognized by the world. The U.S. governing system is by no means perfect (from the point of view of other nations) and the UN structure is by no means effective in resolving international issues. In the meantime, many large nations such as Brazil, China, Germany, Japan and India have rapidly advanced their economy under their own evolving political systems except Japan being fostered by the U.S. Small nations with varying military strength and political governing systems, such as Singapore, Vietnam, and South Korea, have also made outstanding economic progress. Despite of the uni-polar approach by the U.S. subordinated by Japan, the third largest world economy, the world is still stubbornly acting as a multi-polar world with China and India rising as great nations and economies and Russia, not only remaining as a strong military power but also evolving economically with serious reform.

Recently, Professor Yan Xue Tong, Dean of School of International Studies in Tsinghua University, in an interview by Global Times (5-3-2016) commented on the very issue of how the US-China relation will become in the evolving multi-polar world. He discussed that the shrinking gap between the U.S. and China in economy as well as in military strength will inevitably lead into conflicts damping cooperation between the two nations. Besides economical competition, the U.S. and China face a number of issues such as unification of Taiwan and Mainland China, North Korea nuclear threat, and freedom of navigation in the South China Sea. Although the seriousness of the issues are more attributed to US attitude and actions than those of China's, Professor Yan's view is that the U.S. and China will not engage in direct war even though the conflicts will continue and get more complicated.

While I tend to agree with Professor Yan's diagnosis and prediction on the US-China relation regarding their current conflicts, I do believe that we need to analyze the US-China relations in a bigger context of how the two great nations will live with each other in a multi-polar world. Most importantly, we need to understand why the two countries should not pursue a uni-polar world strategy and must objectively accept the inevitable multi-polar world in which the two great nations can play a complimentary role for mutual benefits and world prosperity and peace. Only through objective analysis, can these two countries reach understanding and bar emotional decisions as often being uttered during the U.S. presidential election campaigns or the Chinese leadership transition. I also agree with Prof. Yan's conclusion that after a new US President taking office into the second year, the new leader will most likely come to a more rational attitude towards the US-China relation.

As the world is evolving into a multi-polar world, we must recognize a few things. First, no country has a given right to be a world leader. The U.S. earned her superpower position with the victory against the Axis nations and by her post WW II Marshall Plan to restore Europe and her effort to rebuild a devastated Japan. This success may make the U.S. to appear as the sole superpower in the world, but in reality, it is more cultivating a multi-polar world. The U.S. must objectively accept that consequence. Otherwise, she has to deviously destroy any rising economy or country to keep herself as an empire. The latter strategy would never succeed as borne out by the collapse of many empires in human history. The collapse of the Soviet Union in final analysis is due to her own problems in conducting a faulty economic system and a corrupt political system imposed on a compulsory collected states. In an objective analysis, the U.S. cannot view the winning of the Cold War as the success of trying to build a uni-polar world with the U.S. being the de-facto leader.

Secondly, post Cold War, the world order has not become more orderly, rather, it has become more complicated. It is obvious that many global issues whether they are economic problems or security issues require collective deliberations and decision making; G7 and G20 as well as APEC, ASEAN, etc are clear examples that the world is a multi-polar structure and world issues must be resolved by multi-polar leadership. Looking back to the history of the U.S., the U.S. foreign policy has advocated the Monroe doctrine (in America) to keep the foreign powers away while in America the U.S. more or less practiced 'cow-boy behavior' policies (Guns settled any land disputes or issues). Going forward and beyond WW II and Cold War, 'cow-boy behavior' justice doesn't work. The U.S. must accept objectively the realities presented to her by the multi-polar world.

From the world perspective, the evolution of a multi-polar world to maturity is a blessing to mankind. In this process, multi-cultures and different governing systems will be tolerated and accepted, the human race stands to gain and be enriched. With a balance of power among multiple great nations, the world issues will be most likely be settled with more not less justice. The small nations have a choice to align themselves to one of the world leaders based on their assessment of a beneficial relationship. Prof. Yan pointed out that China may have to pay more attention to her relationship with neighboring small countries than to great powers in the world. This certainly is a logical policy based on a multi-polar world environment.

In a mature multi-polar world, going forward, each nation small or big may align itself economically with a great nation and militarily with another great nation and yet develop a unique political system of its own without rigidly identifying with another great nation. World issues will be settled through dialogues and discussions with participation of multiple relevant great nations.

CHAPTER 30

Comment on The End of Eras: Donald Trump and the TPP - The E.R. Podcast

—ɯ—

ABSTRACT

PODCAST CAN BE MORE INTERESTING and easily followed than reading a lengthy essay written with dry grammatically correct paragraphs with little emotional content. The E.R. podcast contains enough thought provoking vocabularies such as racist, arsonist, extortionist to characterize Donald Trump and many colorful words such as crab, shit and pooh to describe foreign policy issues and the current administration's deeds. However, the discussion in Rothkopf's podcast fails to convince audience that Donald Trump will not win the 2016 presidential election nor he will be unfit to an institution with ample safeguard to protect the nation. The country needs a change from the 'target China' legacy policy to enter into a genuine global economic integration strategy that will benefit the world.

—ɯ—

The podcast episode of June 27th, 2016, Foreign Policy's The Editor's Roundtable (The E.R.) caught my attention because its title, The End of Eras: Donald Trump and the TPP. FP's editor David Rothkopf hosted the podcast with Kori Schake and Dan De Luce (FP) and David Sanger (NY Times national security correspondent) in a free style conversation focusing on Donald Trump and foreign policy. Although the panelists jokingly commented that this podcast had only 11 listeners induced by receiving a free mug, nevertheless, this episode was well advertised on FP hoping to reach republican supporters of Donald Trump, the presumptive 2016 Republican presidential nominee. Podcast can be more interesting and easilier followed than reading a lengthy essay written with dry grammatically correct paragraphs with little emotional content. It is the emotional flavor of the podcast that sometimes makes it effective. Elites invited into a podcast are granted the right to speak in the public media.

The above E.R. podcast contains enough thought provoking vocabularies such as racist, arsonist, extortionist to characterize Donald Trump and many colorful words such as crab, shit and pooh to describe foreign policy issues and the current administration's deeds. I did listen through the 40 minutes discussion just to get the point about TPP at the end, but I was not impressed with their negative comments about Trump and ill supported conclusion that Hilary Clinton will be a better Commander-in-Chief in the Oval Office. They started off with Rothkopf's question to Sanger why did Trump love Sanger (NY Times) better than other mainstream media even though Sanger's interview with Trump was damning to Trump? Sanger had no answer other than saying that Trump thought all media were bad to him and NY Times had not been bad enough yet. They basically set the mood to be bad to Trump and hoping to influence Republican elites to be bad to Trump.

They later went into a contradictory discussion, on the one hand, Trump as a realtor had little experience with foreign policies and on the other hand, the U.S. institutions would have sufficient safeguards to prevent the Commander-in-Chief to act in a lunatic manner. They commented that the Congress would provide check and balance and the military chiefs would not obey unlawful orders. When Rothkopf asked the panelists to name names who had openly discredited Donald Trump to be a qualified U.S. President, they came up only with Paul Ryan who would support Trump but had objections on Trump's positions on some issues. In contrast, they pointed out that John McCain did not oppose Donald Trump's candidacy and a group of people would serve the Trump administration on the basis that they could limit the possible damages (Trump might cause) and the controversial issues.

The discussion turned into Rothkopf's presumption that Hillary will enter the White House, with generous comments that she would do a better job in foreign policies. But other panelists did not echo with endorsing statements. As an audience I am especially disappointed that this group of media elites had casted their discussion to convince Trump's supporters, especially 'the elites' in their view, to dump Trump but yet offered little convincing arguments on specific foreign policy. They have mentioned a bunch of issues, Middle East, Ukraine, Russia, North Korea and Asia Infrastructure Investment Bank (AIIB) that the Obama administration had handled badly; on these issues, Rothkopf had used the colorful language (crab, shit and pooh) to describe the current administration's performance on these issues. How can one expect a better performance from foreign policy point of view from a Clinton II administration following an Obama legacy?

The podcast finally focused on the TPP question near the end, the issue is whether it will be ratified by the Congress. They fairly stated that Trump, Sanders even Hilary Clinton were not favoring any free trade agreement. They commented that as candidates no one is favoring free trade agreement (election issue) until they get into the White House (facing the reality). They cited Bill Clinton administration's effort to get China into the WTO and jokingly commented that Bill Clinton said he would campaign against his own trade policy. TPP took a long time to reach a consensus among the twelve Pacific Rim countries who signed on 2-4-2016, but whether it will be ratified by the U.S. Congress or not is still a big question. Obama is facing an opposition with his own party thus relying on the Republicans to pass the bill. Since the current Congress is not likely to ratify TPP, it looks like that the TPP decision will have to be delayed until the new administration and the next Congress.

The U.S. Government considers the TPP a companion agreement to the proposed Transatlantic Trade and Investment Partnership (TTIP), a broadly similar agreement between the U.S. and the European Union. TTIP is under ongoing negotiations with three main areas: market access, specific regulation, and broader rules and principles and modes of cooperation. The negotiations are not expected to be finished till 2019 or 2020. Now with the U.K voted to exit from the EU, the TTIP negotiations will be complicated. The Brexit vote is also saying no to TTIP. Since TPP excludes China, it has the advantages of bringing Pacific Rim nations closer to the U.S. giving the U.S. more influence on future rules for the global economy. On the other hand, there are plenty of criticism including impact on employment loss to the U.S., violation of international human rights and division of trading zones in competition of economic integration.

China has been brilliantly successful in conducting bi-lateral trade agreements with her key trading partners while keeping economic integration in mind. China's AIIB proposal and One Belt and One Road (OBOR) program to link Asia, Africa and Europe together appears to be a visionary foreign policy. FP's The E.R. Roundtable acknowledged the difficulty of getting TPP ratified. They talked about the possibility for Hillary Clinton to take a vacation after winning the presidential election and let Obama get TPP passed during the brief time window after the presidential election and before she taking office in 2017. Of course, this is based on a wishful thinking that Donald Trump will not win the election and the Republican Congress will help Obama in voting for TPP ratification. However, the presidential election is still four months away, I will not be as optimistic as David Rothkopf to wish Donald Trump away from the White House. The 2016 presidential election does not seem to be an election to be easily iron cast by media elites. The country needs a change from the 'target China' legacy policy and take up a realistic foreign policy with genuine global economic integration in mind. Donald Trump's campaign trail so far has shown that the hostility of mainstream media towards Donald has not been able to trump him in the primary elections. Come November, Donald Trump may just trump into the White House!

CHAPTER 31

'Soft Landing' Makes Great Sense in the Sino-Philippine SCS Dispute

—ɷ—

Abstract

On 6-30-2016, a new president was inaugurated in the Philippines. President Rodrigo Duterte can be considered as a post WW II generation. Duterte entered his presidential campaign in late 2015, the 70th anniversary of WW II; there was not much mainstream TV coverage in the U.S. on Duterte's election victory and campaign, even less news coverage on the Philippines war history. Duterte is not a typical politician; he has a unique political career and possesses a 'Trump like character' as a presidential campaigner. In this column, I present a brief review of the modern history of the Philippines, a detailed description of Duterte as the Philippines' new leader and a comment on his "soft landing" remark regarding settlement of the Sino-Philippine South China Sea (SCS) dispute.

—ɷ—

On June 30th, the 16th President of the Philippines, Rodrigo Duterte was inaugurated. Rodrigo "Rody" Roa Duterte was born on March 28, 1945, the year the Imperial Japan surrendered to the Allies and a year before the real independence of the Philippines was granted by the U.S. Therefore, President Duterte can be considered as a post WW II generation. Duterte entered his presidential campaign in late 2015, the 70th anniversary of WW II. There was not much mainstream TV coverage in the U.S. on Duterte's election victory and campaign, even less news coverage on the Philippines war history. However, on the Internet, there is a lot of information on the Philippine's modern history and Duterte's personal story which American citizens seem to be ignorant. Duterte is not a typical politician; he has a unique political career and possesses a 'Trump like character' as a presidential campaigner. In this paper, I would like to make a brief review of the modern history of the Philippines, a detailed description of Duterte as the Philippines' new leader and a comment on his "soft landing" remark regarding settlement of the Sino-Philippine South China Sea (SCS) dispute.

The modern history of the Philippines suffered from colonial power like China had but as a small country the Philippines was fully occupied by the Spanish in the 19th century. China as a big nation, although maintained independence, was victimized by the invasion of seven Western nations and the Imperial Japan. In 1897, a 28 year old Emilio Aguinaldo started a revolution in the Philippines against the Spanish rule but failed and exiled to Hong Kong. In April, 1898, the Spanish-American war broke out, the U.S. won the war and settled with Spain by the Paris Treaty which allowed the U.S. to annex the Philippines as the U.S. territory (The treaty was ratified by the U.S. Senate on 2/6/1899). Aguinaldo returned to the Philippines and tried to gain independence by convening an assembly and drew up a constitution but his effort faced the resistance of the U.S. resulting in a guerrilla war against the U.S. On March 23, 1901, Aguinaldo was tricked and captured by the U.S. troops, a size of 65000. Aguinaldo pleaded allegiance to the U.S. but the rebels fought on. In the end, after the infamous Massacre of Samar, a retaliation to the insurrection, the U.S. General Jacob Smith directed the Samar Island Massacre by killing all men above 10 years old. Although Jacob Smith was court-martialed and forced to retire, the U.S. took over the administration of the Philippines in 1902. The U.S. rule lasted untill 1935 when she approved "the Common Wealth of the Philippines" and finally granted the real full independence to the Philippines on 7/4/1946 after the end of WW II. In 1962, Philippines changed her National Day from July 4th to June 12th commemorating the Philippine Declaration of Independence from Spain on June 12, 1898.

The Republic of Philippines has a democratic government having three interdependent branches, the legislative, the executive and the judicial; a system similar to that of the U.S. Corruption has been a pervasive, long-standing problem in the Philippine government. (Philippine improved her ranking in Transparency International Corruption Perception Index from 105 to 94 in 2013) President Ferdinan Marcos and his wife Imelda (1972-1986) practiced corruption on a grand scale. Former President Joseph Estrada was impeached for corruption in 2000 and convicted on 9-12-2007. Former President Gloria Arroyo was impeached several times since 2006 for electoral fraud and other political crimes and on 10-5-2007, she was impeached for corruption (Arroyo pardoned Estrada on 10-25-2007). President Benigno Aquino won the presidency in 2010 on a good government platform to combat corruption. During 2010, the government convicted 42 officials in 125 corruption cases including House Representative and university president. The public perceived that there were serious corruption in the Philippine National Police (PNP) and in the nation's prison system. The Philippines Presidential Election in 2016 was hard fought but Duterte won in a decisive vote of 16.6M, 6.6M more than his closest rival, former Interior Secretary Mar Roxas who was backed by Aquino. This landslide margin certainly cemented Duterte's leadership for a six-year term of the Presidency.

Rodrigo Duterte came from a political family with his father Vincente Duterte served as the Mayor of Davao, Ceba and governor of Davao Province and his mother Soledad Roa served as a civil leader. He was first appointed Vice Mayor of Davao City in 1986 at age 0f 41. He served to term limit until 1998 then ran for Congressman of the 1st district of Davao City. In 2001, he ran for Mayor again and got elected, then re-elected in 2004 and 2007, served a total of seven terms (service of 22 years). Duterte was urged to run for the Philippine presidency numerous times and offered job as the Secretary of Interior four times but he rejected them. He was reluctant to run for Presidency in 2015 considering his age (71 if elected) but eventually he formally signed election filing on 12/8/2015. He is known for his straight forward and tough languages in his speeches; hence, Duterte has been compared to Trump, the US presumptive Republican Presidential Nominee on anti-media and rough language. Apparently, the Filipino voters loved his 'Trump like character'; one wonders whether the majority of American voters in November would likewise vote for Trump.

Duterte is a unique public servant who not only has made a number of significant achievements but also has demonstrated his strong 'righteous' character and conservative philosophy with little concern of 'political correctness' similar to Trump's behavior. He is especially known for his stance against drug crime and earned a nickname, "the punisher", for taking tough actions against drug dealers. He is also a strong human rights fighter for minorities as well as philanthropic in his deeds of opening drug rehab clinics and offering P1200/month to addicts to kick the habit as well as offering aids to typhoon and earthquake victims in Philippines. He has won international awards for his mayoral administration running a large urban city. He has reduced Davao City crime rate drastically and established the first free call 9-1-1 in his city. Through executive orders, he imposed comprehensive anti-smoking ordinance, ordered all shopping malls and commercial centers to install high-end closed circuit TV cameras at all entrances and exits. Duterte has passed the city's Women Development Code to uphold the rights and dignity of women, the first and only code in the Philippines.

On the inauguration day, Duterte convened his first cabinet meeting, enacting a number of initiatives: establishing a 24-hour complaint office, De-congesting Aquino International Airport, eliminating airport privileged treatment for cabinet members, studying healthcare models (Cuba system), stopping online gambling and evaluating the implication of arbitration court ruling regarding the SCS dispute with China. After the inauguration in a press meeting, Duterte expressed his desire of a "soft landing" on the SCS issue, a most constructive official statement on the Sino-Philippine SCS Dispute from the Philippines. As we observe the current developments in the SCS, it is clear that the SCS tension has been artificially raised under the banner of "Freedom of Navigation". In reality, there was no navigation problem, no pirate activities nor shipping incidences. Over half of the world commerce (China, Japan, South Korea, India, Singapore, etc) transport their goods through South and East China Sea without accidents or navigation problems. Why can't any SCS dispute be resolved through bi-lateral negotiations? China has denied the arbitration court's jurisdiction on the Sino-Philippine SCS dispute. A friendly Sino-Philippine relation is definitely beneficial to both countries, since each is treating reform and fighting corruption as top priority while maintaining a healthy economic growth. President Duterte as a mandated new leader has an excellent opportunity to navigate the SCS issue into a "soft landing" so that both countries can focus on their own domestic issues. We wish him success.

CHAPTER 32

Is Taiwan a ticking time bomb for the United States?

—w—

ABSTRACT

TED GALEN CARPENTER, A SENIOR fellow of Cato Institute, wrote, on July 6, an article with an alarming title, America Should Step Back from the Taiwan Time Bomb. Carpenter regarded the recent 'Missile Misfiring' incidence as another step in the deterioration of relations between Beijing and Taipei since the successful winning of the presidency and legislature in Taiwan by the Democratic Progressive Party. These recent events may be interpreted as having damaging effect on the cross-strait relations but whether or not Taiwan Strait can be characterized as a ticking time bomb is questionable. Americans will not fight and die for Taiwan's fake ideology battle, especially when it has all the signs of right-wing Japanese imperialist notions. The U.S. will let no one, neither Japan nor Taiwan, hijack her U.S. China policy as she realizes that the US-China relationship is so critical to her future as well as to the world economy and peace. Eventually the American people with better understanding of the historical facts about Taiwan, South China Sea and China will steer the US China policy back to a mutually beneficial path.

—w—

Triggered by the 'Missile Misfiring' incidence happened in Taiwan Strait, Ted Galen Carpenter, a senior fellow of Cato Institute, wrote, on July 6, an article with an alarming title, America Should Step Back from the Taiwan Time Bomb. The misfiring of the supersonic Hsiung-Feng III (means brave wind

III) anti-ship missile flew only 45 miles within mid-line of the strait hitting a fishing trawler registered with Taiwan and killing its skipper and injured three crew men. The incident has not raised much reaction from Mainland China but caused a political storm in Taiwan, ranging from criticism of the military training and discipline to speculated political motives behind a possible orchestrated accident.

Carpenter regarded this incidence as another step in the deterioration of relations between Beijing and Taipei since the successful winning of the presidency and legislature in Taiwan by the Democratic Progressive Party (DPP). China's Taiwan Affairs Office of the State Council did make a statement about the incident, "(it) caused severe impact at a time when the Mainland has repeatedly emphasized development of peaceful cross-strait relations." Carpenter pointed out even though Tsai Ying-Wen was not as strident as Chen Shui-Bian in open advocacy of independence for Taiwan, but she embarked on an extremely conciliatory policy towards Japan. Indeed, she is seemingly following the directive of Lee Deng-Hui, the former Taiwan President born by a Japanese parent, to resist Mainland China by leaning towards Japan. After Tsai's inauguration, Taiwan for the first time held a memorial service for the victims of the Tiananmen student protest which is a sore spot now openly admitted by the CCP. These recent events may be interpreted as having damaging effect on the cross-strait relations. But whether or not Taiwan Strait can be characterized as a ticking time bomb is questionable.

Based on the 1979 Taiwan Relations Act passed by the U.S. Congress, the United States has a real, however loosely defined, obligation to defend Taiwan if she is attacked. This is the fundamental reason for Carpenter to write his warning article that Taiwan is a time bomb and the U.S. needs to re-evaluate her Taiwan policy in view of the above incidents that are occurring. Carpenter was right to point out that if the fishing trawler was a Mainlander's boat or worse a Mainland naval vessel, the reaction of the Mainland would not be a mild one. However, Taiwan-Strait may be a time bomb, but in my view, it is not a ticking time bomb since its fuse lead is controlled by a two-step ignition switch, one in the hands of Mainland China and another in the hands of the U.S. Carpenter's concern is well taken, but neither Mainland China nor the U.S. has the intention of throwing the ignition switch yet. Therefore the Taiwan-Strait bomb is not ticking from both the U.S. and Mainland China's point of view.

Let's agree with Carpenter for a moment that the Taiwan-Strait is a time bomb. We may ask the Question: Who has set the time for the bomb to explode? I venture to say that neither Mainland China nor the United States is the one setting the time. In fact, based on 'the joint Shanghai Communiqué' announced in 1972, the United States recognized the one and only China and expected a unification process without a specific time table for the Mainland and Taiwan. Since Mainland China has not set a time table for 'unification' with Taiwan, thus, Taiwan-Strait is never considered as a time bomb as far as China and the U.S. are concerned. However, Carpenter's concern is not entirely groundless based on the events happening in the past decade. Taiwan's democracy is seriously challenged, not from Mainland China rather from Taiwan's internal changes. The current Taiwan-Strait situation can be described with a biological metaphor - growth of a tumor turning to be cancerous. Cancer is like a time bomb and its explosion is unpredictable. The only effective treatment for cancer is to find the causes of its growth and then remove or suppress the causes. Conversely, if the cancerous cells are fed with stimulating fuel, then an explosion in the Taiwan-Strait is not only possible but unavoidable.

The anti-Mainland China attitude and policy are the fuel feeding the growth of cancerous cells in Taiwan. What the Americans, the Mainland Chinese and the Taiwan people should ask is a question: while Mainland China is embracing capitalism and trying government reform making concrete progress for the people and the economy, (by the way, it is for the people world-wide and for the benefit of the global economy), why does the DPP of Taiwan conduct a 'hate' government in the name of democracy? A small group of people in DPP hate history, hate mainlanders, hate veterans, even smear the Chinese culture and inheritance and distort Taiwan's history, brainwash the youth and create hatred among Taiwan's residents. Why? Don't they know they are feeding the cancer and they are ticking the time bomb?

Mainland China has offered Taiwan trade favors, privileged status for Taiwan residents to enter the Mainland and do business there, as well as breathing space on the world stage; and they have not applied any real military threat to Taiwan for decades. Why does the DPP still paint Mainland China as a brutal regime? Are the Hong Kong people worse off than 20 years ago? Are the Tibet people worse off than 20, 30, 50, or 70 years ago? No, they are not. Chinese people world-wide are cheering for the change and transformation of China and they are trying to stop the Cold War mentality of the world - no hatred, no jealousy, no discrimination but embracing collaboration and co-prosperity. China has a long history which has shown that the Chinese people are not war mongers. Chinese has absorbed aggressors, for example, the Mongolians and the Manchurians and cultivated them into Chinese with their peace loving Chinese culture.

American citizens may not have paid enough attention to the Chinese history, but they are not stupid to ignore the facts if presented to them. An Anti-China strategy may be pushed by Japan to woo the U.S. and her 'Pivot to Asia Pacific' policy but the U.S. is clearly weighing all the pros and cons and carefully balancing her geopolitical interests. The U.S. military industrial complex may be leaning towards a legacy foreign policy, but the debate on the right China policy is still going on. China has been growing too fast and she realizes that the fast economic growth is not sustainable. For self interests, the U.S., of course, would rather see China to grow at a moderate non-threatening rate. So in reality, the U.S. and China really do not have an irreconcilable conflict. Therefore, there is no reason for the U.S. or China to turn on the ignition switch of the Taiwan-Strait bomb, so dramatically characterized by Carpenter.

No, Americans will not fight and die for Taiwan's fake ideology battle, especially when it has all the signs of right-wing Japanese imperialist notions: denying and white washing war history and justifying Japan's invasion and colonization of Taiwan. The current South China Sea saga will be only a temporary distraction to China for slowing down China's fast rise. The U.S. will let no one, neither Japan nor Taiwan; hijack her U.S. China policy as she realizes that the US-China relationship is so critical to her future as well as to the world economy. Eventually the American people with better understanding of the historical facts about Taiwan, South China Sea and China will steer the US China policy back to a mutually beneficial path!

CHAPTER 33

Recipe for World Politics – Old Cold War to New Cold War

—⟋⟍—

ABSTRACT

COLD WAR WAS A RECIPE for world politics created post WW II. The globe is symbolically divided into two hemispheres each being brushed with a secret sauce - NATO pact and Warsaw pact respectively. The Cold War recipe of world politics was practiced by two giant adversary chefs. The Cold War took 45 years to end (from 1945 to 1990) but the result is far from satisfactory. Even though Warsaw was dissolved and NATO gained strength, the world is still full of problems. It is crucially important that the U.S. must adjust the recipe and accept the reality in dealing with today's world. We must point out that targeting China and rekindle the Cold War recipe is not a safe solution. The current US China policy makes us looking like bad guys, opposing cooperation and stirring up conflicts and troubles.

—⟋⟍—

Cold War was a recipe for world politics created post WW II. It was principally invented by the U.S. and co-invented by the Soviet Union, a strategy and a process propelled by a strong ideological conflict, namely capitalism versus communism. The recipe calls for placing the globe in a baking oven, adding fuel to increase oven temperature - an arms race and economic aid activities to broil the global economy and cause turbulence as well. The globe is symbolically divided into two hemispheres each being brushed with a secret sauce - NATO pact and Warsaw pact respectively. The Cold War recipe of world politics was practiced by two giant adversary chefs - the U.S. dabbing the NATO and the

Soviet Union contriving the Warsaw. The two chefs were adventurous but not very creative. They focused on controlling the fuel (managing arms race and economic aid but not genuine global development) and continuously adding more ingredients into their sauce recipe and courting assistant chefs. The NATO chef recruited Britain, France (Guest Chef, not always willing to take orders from the principal chef) and West Germany as assistant chefs as well as accepted Japan as a apprentice chef (eager to learn and practice the recipe). The Warsaw Chef recruited Czechoslovak, East Germany, Hungary and Poland as assistant chefs as the opposing camp.

It turns out baking a globe into a harmonious world requires patience. The history bore out, the Cold War took 45 years to end (from 1945 to 1990) but the result is far from satisfactory. The ending of the Cold War could be clearly attributed to the brilliant strategy that the U.S. successfully solicited a critical guest chef - namely China in 1972. Chef Nixon went to China in 1972 and humbly recognized China's long history of dealing with world politics (as well as her variety of cuisines) under dominating as well as under treacherous conditions, especially in dealing with the Russian chefs. China had embraced communism and had been friend with Russia but realized it was not a right cup of tea for China. Ever since China collaborated with the U.S. in the cooking or baking contest, the Cold War became an effective 'simmering' process - low heat for arms race and a 'stir-fry' process – stimulating economy revealing a sharp contrast. In the end, the Soviet Union collapsed, the U.S. became the sole super power and China had a taste of successful economic development.

Since the 90's, the world is under the leadership of the Super US Chef. Even though Warsaw was dissolved and NATO gained strength, the world is still full of problems. The United States did assume the role of the world police but the world is sick with lots of patients and not all patients are criminals. What the world needs is careful diagnoses and prescription drugs to strengthen its immune system. Unfortunately, the U.S. opted for surgical solutions and invasive interventions. Not only the world is not cured but it is also wakened; the world problems spread with no end in sight. This is seen in Africa and Middle East. Now the US Chef pivots to Asia, to find new medicine? No. It appears that the U.S. is repeating the old Cold War recipe which has worked and made the U.S. a super power. This time around, the new target of the new war is China who has risen economically to be the world's second largest economy. It appears that the U.S. is soliciting Japan as her assistant chef for the new Cold War. Will the next Cold War be the U.S. and Japan against China? Japan may see her being an assistant chef in the New Cold War as an opportunity for her to restore her Imperial glory, but what will the U.S. gain by using this new Cold War Recipe? If the recipe worked, Japan would become a far more dangerous chef than China threatening the U.S.; if the recipe failed, the U.S. would lose her world leadership for good. The irony is that the U.S. seems to be pushing towards the latter likelihood.

It is crucially important that the U.S. must adjust the recipe and accept the facts in dealing with today's world. We must point out that targeting China and rekindle the old Cold War recipe is not a safe solution. Firstly, targeting China is not going to wish away the problems in the Middle East nor the slow decay of the European Union. They are not caused by China. Secondly, the military strength is no longer effective in settling world disputes and foreign affairs as proven by the numerous wars the U.S. had engaged in, in the past decades. The world economy not only has redistributed but more importantly the future economic growth is favoring China who practices collaborative economic development than invasive intervention. The NATO recipe against Russia has not worked wonders after the ending of Cold War and its effectiveness to Middle East problems is entirely futile. Now the U.K. voted to exit EU, its implication is obvious. The U.K. sees a brighter future in joining a collaborative economic development group than sticking around in a disintegrating EU; so she chose to join Asia Infrastructure Investment Bank (AIIB).

There is more evidence to prove that the U.S. must change her world politics recipe. On June 24, 2016, India and Pakistan joined and attended the Shanghai Cooperation Organization (SCO) summit which showed that even archenemy India and Pakistan were willing to join the international organization stressing cooperation. This cooperation organization was founded in 2001 in Shanghai by the leaders of Shanghai Five, China, Kazakhstan,

Kyrgyz Republic, Russian Federation and Tajikistan (Shanghai Five formed in 1996) and Uzbekistan (then renamed as SCO in 2001). In July 10, 2015, the Beijing based SCO decided to admit India and Pakistan as full members. If the U.S. wanted to pivot to Asia, why isn't she trying to join the organization rather than flexing naval muscles in the South China Sea? Another recent event worth noting is the Russian President Putin's visit to Beijing signing as many as 30 agreements and announcements with China. The more significant ones relevant to our discussion are i. Global security strategy and stability, ii. Collaboration in network security and development, and iii. promotion of international law. The closer Russia and China get the less sense for the U.S. to conduct a new Cold War recipe against China.

Some political analysts have already said that the 21st century is the Asian century meaning that there is more positive energy coming from Asia. As an American citizen, who pays attention to foreign affairs, one cannot help wonder why is the U.S. repeating a Cold War recipe targeting China rather than cooperating with China? It makes us looking like bad guys, opposing cooperation and stirring up conflicts and troubles. The international view (over 70 nations) on the arbitration court's verdict on the South China Sea is that the US-Japan-Philippine orchestrated the saga, a rigged court issuing a ridiculous verdict even calling Taiping Island with residents, fresh water, hospital, school and post office not an island but a piece of submerged rock during high tide, clearly and purposely contradicting truth. The Republic of China has control over Taiping Island since the end of WW II, with the help of the U.S. navy giving ROC battle ships (Taiping is the name of one of the ships) and Taiwan is still an ally of the U.S. What is our State department doing? Is jealousy of China's rise making our IQ dropping to zero? We recognize one China, we honor cross-strait reunification by a peaceful process and yet we intentionally create needless hostility by acting recklessly. If the phony verdict stands, thousands of fishermen in Taiwan will lose their livelihood. Why do we do it? Do we really want to turn Taiping Island into a US military base against China?

CHAPTER 34

Hiroshima and South China Sea - Truth Be Told and Justice Be Served to Correct the Military Culture

—◊◊◊—

ABSTRACT

AS THE FIRST SITTING PRESIDENT, Obama visited Hiroshima and delivered a message which Japanese atomic bomb survivors regarded as an apology. But many Americans especially war veterans thought it was a wrong gesture. Hiroshima led to the Japanese surrender and the International Military Tribunal for the Far East. Jerry Delaney wrote an article about the injustice the tribunal did to the war crimes and pointed out its serious consequences – suppression of war crimes committed certified a dangerous military/war culture which is still practiced by the U.S. today. The author echoes this concern and relates to the Japanese right-wing behavior in the past, WW II, as well as in the present, South China Sea tension.

—◊◊◊—

Hiroshima and South China Sea (SCS) are two key words representing two events occurring 71 years apart, what is the connection? On May 27, 2016, as the first sitting president, Obama visited Hiroshima and delivered a message that Japanese atomic bomb survivors regarded as an apology. But many Americans especially war veterans thought it was a wrong gesture. In the same month, I came across a long essay in Foreign Policy written by freelance writer Jerry Delaney, entitled Hiroshima, My Father and the Lie of U.S. Innocence (5-9-2016, FP). Delaney was born in 1932 in Montana and he moved to Tokyo at age of sixteen with his father, Thomas Ronald Delaney (Creighton University, school of law, 1930). His father served as a prosecutor for the International Military Tribunal for the Far East (IMTFE). Thomas Delaney, respected as a truth teller, never talked about the trial. Jerry wondered why; he did some research and found out why.

Jerry Delaney's article moved me by his candid writing and his courage of speaking up about why his father was mute for more than four decades about the tribunal, a significant milestone of Thomas Delaney (The library of Creighton University has a collection of Tokyo Trial papers donated by Thomas in 1985, http://culibraries.creighton.edu/tokyopapers)Through Jerry's research work, he not only found out the truth about why the U.S. (Through General Douglas MacArthur and US Chief Prosecutor Joseph Keenan) suppressed some serious war crime charges and refused to hear testimonies in the trial but also pointed out that such suppression certified and encouraged a dangerous military/war culture which is still practiced by the U.S. today. Recently, an international arbitration court, although far less prominent than the Tokyo Tribunal, nevertheless, grabbed the media headlines worldwide by its ridiculous verdict claiming Taiping and others in the South China Sea (SCS) not islands but rocks (though Taiping has fresh water, residents, school, airport and post office) and denying the historical sea sovereignty line (drawn as 9 dash line recorded by many international maps) with a single purpose: to prevent the Mainland China and Taiwan from claiming sovereignty over these islands and their rightful exclusive economic zone (EEZ). Since this arbitration court has no jurisdiction over sovereignty issues, naturally both Mainland China and Taiwan rejected this illegal verdict. Today we live in a far more vocal world, thus the global citizens have begun questioning and condemning this rigged arbitration court.

During WW II, the allies (Chinese first and Americans last) had realized that the Imperial Army of Japan were trained as brutal warriors who would rather fight to death than surrender. They had indiscriminately bombed China and mercilessly massacred over 18 million Chinese civilians. They had used Kamikaze pilots to attack American naval vessels (Japan promoted that as 'A Honor' to die with the American ship, but it is 'A Horror' for American soldiers). Therefore, the air raids to Japan's homeland and the use of atomic bomb had become the only hope to end the devastating war sooner, even though Japan was losing momentum drastically in her dream of conquering China. It was true that the casualties in Hiroshima and Nagasaki by atomic bomb reached close to 150,000. The devastating air raid on Tokyo in March 1945 involved 334 B-29 bombers dropping 2000 tons of bombs in 4 square mile area killing nearly 100,000 Japanese civilians and the overall air raids to 66 cities killed one million Japanese. These atrocious casualties no doubt contributed to the statistics of the Asian part of WW II, a war started by the Imperial Japan and devastated many Asian countries.

The IMTFE, popularly known as Tokyo Trial or Tokyo War Crime Tribunal, was convened to try the leaders of the Empire of Japan on April 26, 1946. The Tokyo Trial was essentially a U.S. enterprise as the other allies were busy curing their war wounds. On January 19, 1946, MacArthur issued a special proclamation ordering the establishment of IMTFE and approved the Charter of IMTFE (CIMTFE). CIMTFE generally followed the Nuremberg Trial as far as how the tribunal should be formed, crimes to be considered and court procedures to be followed. On April 25, some amendments in the original Rules of Procedure of IMTFE were adopted. Then MacArthur appointed 12 judges.

The Tribunal became a wholly US owned and was dictated by Gen. Douglas MacArthur and Chief Prosecutor Joseph Keenan. In Keenan's opening remarks, he reduced the complexity and nuances of Japan's war crimes to a morality play – Japanese leaders' guilt of plot of conquest, stated from Delaney's article. The most chilling infamous unit 731 of Japanese Imperial Army in Harbin, China experimented with bacteriological agents on 3000 human subjects and injected civilians and prisoners of war with anthrax pathogens or cyanide compounds to test for efficacy, yet the Japanese commander Lt. Gen. Shiro Ishi received immunity, why? The court refused to hear testimonies on Japan's unmistakable violation of human rights of colonial subjects in Korea and in Taiwan and in the occupied regions, Philippines and Burma. There were no charges on the crime of systemically forcing thousands of women of Chinese, Duchess, Koreans and Philippines to be sex slaves, called "Comfort Women" for the Japanese Imperial Army. Sadly, the most atrocious massacre, the Nanking Massacre, was not brought to justice in the Tribunal either. The Japanese Emperor Hirohito should never be exempted from the Tribunal. In the end only 25 were tried and the verdict was 7 hanged, 15 sentenced to prison, 2 died during trial and one sent to psychiatric hospital, a far cry for justice for the twenty million innocent people murdered by the Japanese Imperial Army.

Delaney questioned the motive and justification of the U.S. (MacArthur et al) suppressing many of the Japanese war crime charges in the IMTFE for concerns of Japan bringing counter charges to the US air raids in Japan. Even for purpose of protecting the U.S. military or maintaining the innocence of the U.S. in WW II, the consequence is serious as pointed out by Delaney and mentioned above. To clarify his point further, such suppression of war crimes (to be brought to justice) certified a dangerous military/war culture: the purity of intentions masks the savage effects of military actions, a culture that nourishes those toxic strains of exceptionalism and righteousness that run deep in the U.S. history. Perhaps this culture already exists in the Japanese Bushido and runs deeper in Japan's right wing military as exhibited by its desire to restore the pre-war Japanese military glory, to exonerate war criminals and to deny war crimes such as Nanking massacre and comfort women. Delaney further says such a culture is a vigilante culture: innocence gives rise to righteousness, righteousness to arrogance and arrogance to ruthlessness. It remains as the present day culture of war. Indeed, more vividly, the current Japanese administration appears to be applying this culture and justifying her old war culture.

Although there is no war happening yet in the SCS, the events (behaviors of naval and diplomatic confrontations) leading to today's tension in SCS do seem to support Delaney's description of military culture above. Ignorance and denial of history (innocence) leads to false claims and territory squatting (righteousness) then to military exercises and demand of freedom of navigation (arrogance) and possibly leading to naval battles of carriers, ships, submarines, planes and missiles (ruthlessness) if countries there do not exercise diplomatic constraint. Hopefully China with her thousands of years of history would understand this type of military culture and with her rising diplomatic status could diffuse the SCS tension and lead neighbors back to the negotiation table. Ultimately a bi-laterally negotiated practical solution is more useful than any unenforceable verdict issued by a rigged court.

CHAPTER 35

What is the Impact of Brexit to Everyone?

—◊—

ABSTRACT

52% OF UK VOTERS (OVER 33 millions had their say) passed the "Brexit" referendum, Though completion of Brexit may take two years, UK's 'leave' vote still came as a shock and created a serious impact at least initially on financial markets throughout the world in terms of stock prices and currency exchange rates. In the weeks after the Brexit vote, world leaders and political analysts have begun to offer comments on the Brexit impact from both political and economical point of views. While so many news reports, interviews and opinions relating to the impact of Brexit are circulating in the mainstream and organic media, it is prudent to do a summary review on the 'impact' issue from an impactee's perspective.

—◊—

On June 23rd, 2016, 52% of UK voters (over 33 millions had their say) passed the "Brexit" referendum, that is, they want to leave the 28-member European Union. On July 9th, the British government rejected a petition signed by more than 4 million people calling for a new poll on whether Britain should stay or leave EU. The petition was actually started by a 'leave' voter worrying that the first poll might turn out to be a 'stay' vote. So the rejection is a right decision thus Brexit is certain. The UK Prime Minister David Cameron has said he will resign in October and let a new PM to carry through the Brexit. The negotiation procedure to leave EU may take two years according to Article 50 of the Lisbon Treaty which says that a member state seeking to leave the EU has two-years to complete negotiations to withdraw and define its post-exit relationship with the union.

Though completion of Brexit may take two years, UK's 'leave' vote still came as a shock and created a serious impact at least initially on financial markets throughout the world in terms of stock prices and currency exchange rates. In the weeks after the Brexit vote, world leaders and political analysts have begun to offer comments on the Brexit impact from both political and economical point of views. The political concerns are national security, military development and spending as well as UK's role in NATO and relationship with the U.S. The economic concerns are Britain's economy, trade relations with EU members and other large trading partners such as the U.S. and China. Naturally, the impact of Brexit is perceived and will be felt differently by the U.K. vis-à-vis the EU and the other countries in the world, such as China, India and Russia. While so many news reports, interviews and opinions relating to the impact of Brexit are circulating in the mainstream and organic media, it is prudent to do a summary review on the 'impact' issue from an impactee's perspective. Surely, different impact may be felt immediately and possibly very differently in the long run by everyone.

The immediate impact of Brexit on UK is seen in the sharp drop of UK real estate values as well as her sterling exchange rate. Since the yes vote of 52% is not a super majority, it can be expected the debate on Brexit's pro and con would be continuing and the speculation of its long-term effect is churning many Britons' mind. Cameron's resignation and the selection of a new PM most likely a person well schooled on the EU matter will dominate the British political scene.(*Theresa May, a parliament member since 1997 will be sworn in on 9/2) It is interesting to point out quotes from Barclays Bank that Europe would be worse affected by EU than by UK and the U.K. might become a 'safe' haven for investors. Brexit will open a Pandora box for the crisis laden EU. As EU politics turns for worse, Brexit may lead to Grexit, Itexit, etc. However, there also exists views that the impact of Brexit through trade and investment would be most severe for UK than for EU in the long run considering regulatory divergence over time which will affect trade volume and investment attraction. These opposing views are certainly dependent on the political situation of future EU and UK.

While Brexit had a sharp impact on the UK real estate, its effect on the U.S. real estate market is minimal. In fact, perhaps indirectly because the concern of Brexit, the FED did not increase the interest rate in 2016 and Brexit causes more investors to buy US treasury bills driving interest rate down. This helps mortgage interest staying low beneficial to the housing market. The 401K investors did see a drop of their investment value due to Brexit, but likely to be a transient effect. Since the exchange rate of the pound versus the dollar dropped after the Brexit vote, it makes UK a cheaper vacation spot hence may draw more American tourists this summer. Americans have always been a large part of UK tourism. Overall, the impact of Brexit is incredibly modest for the U.S.

China is another country very much concerned about the possible Brexit mostly for economic reasons. UK only accounts for 2.6% of China's exports so economists expect the trade impact of Brexit on China limited. However, China values Sino-EU relations both economically and politically; a strong EU is in the national interests of China. Hence China like the U.S. did not want to see UK leaving EU. UK-China relationship has entered into a golden era with trade agreement and cross investments. While the U.K. is eyeing China's money and market, China sees the U.K. as a springboard and liaison to EU in her long-term strategic view of forming a strong Sino-EU relationship. China has established a RMB exchange center in London, with UK exiting EU, China is likely to establish another exchange center in the European Continent. Brexit definitely disappoints China though not as much as it disappoints the U.S., since she depends on the U.K. as a loyal strong national security partner and a major supporter of NATO. In the long run, Brexit will burden China and the U.S. diplomatically in their triangular relationship with EU for losing an effective liaison.

Post Brexit vote, President Obama's administration could not help being disappointed but Obama stressed that the US-UK strong "special relationship" will endure. In China, some would say that Brexit will draw UK closer to China creating a 'booming' mutual relations; new cooperation opportunities in various sectors, especially military, infrastructure and high-tech, will spring up in the post-Brexit period which will boost UK's trade with China already being the number two among EU members. Without pressure from EU member countries, the UK-China free trade agreement (FTA) may enter into high gear. Overall, the Chinese public (so is American public) has not shown a strong interest in Brexit as can be seen on Sina Weibo (similar to Twitter) in China, the hashtag of "Brexit" garnered 2.3 million views and 631 comments (6-18-2016 data) in comparison with 260 million views and 110,000 comments under the hashtag of "the US election" at the same time.

The impact of Brexit on EU, however, can never be overstated. There was no hiding the concern in the EU media as well as behind the scenes as the Brexit shockwaves rippled through the EU. The European Union was created on November 1, 1993 as a political and economic union between European countries. Prior to Brexit, EU has 28 member countries, being a body that has been vital to American foreign policy initiatives over the past two decades. The impact of Brexit on UK is perhaps best summarized by the former British Ambassador to the U.S., Sir Peter Westmacott: "Britain would be less influential in the world, in EU, in NATO and the Security Council and a less significant ally for the U.S. and others. The U.K. has to paddle harder to get a place at the table." Whereas the impact of Brexit on everyone else in the long run may be netted out as 'Everyone will get used to the Brexit and everyone must face the changes and reality dealing with nationalism versus globalism.'.

CHAPTER 36

From the Republican Convention Projecting
to the November Presidential Election

—⚒—

ABSTRACT

THE REPUBLICAN CONVENTION WAS HELD from July 18 to 21 a week earlier than the Democratic Convention (held from July 25-28). The GOP convention was fully covered by C-Span TV truly from Gavel to Gavel without interruptions of paid 'talking heads' as done on other TV channels. While the convention is in recess, C-Span opens three 'call in' phone lines for Republicans, Democrats and Independents to call the station and express their opinions on what is happening in the convention, how do they feel, and who will they vote for in the coming November Presidential election? After following the four-day GOP convention, I have learned a number of things which I would like to share with my readers while they are still fresh on my mind. I hope I will learn something at the next week's Democrat Convention as well to report them to you.

—⚒—

The Republican Convention was held at the Quicken Loans Stadium in Cleveland, Ohio from July 18 to 21 and the Democratic Convention will be held at the Wells Fargo Center, the Philadelphia Convention Center from July 25-28. This article was written after the GOP convention and before the Democrat convention simply because there were enough significant events taken place at the GOP convention fully covered by C-Span TV truly from Gavel to Gavel without interruptions of the paid 'talking heads' as done on other TV channels. In addition, while the convention is in recess, C-Span opens three 'call in' phone lines for Republicans,

Democrats and Independents to call the station and express their opinions on what is happening in the convention, how do they feel, and who will they vote for in the coming November Presidential election? These callers spoke their minds and certainly revealed the real sentiments of the voters than the 'talking heads' on the other mainstream media, which often carry their bias.

After following the four-day GOP convention, I have learned a number of things which I would like to share with my readers while they are still fresh on my mind. I hope I will learn something at next week's Democrat Convention as well to report them to you.

The GOP convention was a gathering of about fifty thousand people. Due to the long primary process with 17 presidential candidates, it is expected that the Republic Delegates were somewhat divided even in disarray going into the convention. One noticeable fact is that despite of the pledge the 17 candidates signed to support the final winner or presumptuous nominee, only Ben Carson, Chris Christie, Ted Cruz, Rick Perry and Scott Walker attended the convention. Marco Rubio sent in a video speech endorsing Trump and Carson, Christie, Perry and Walker made a warm endorsement speech but Ted Cruz delivered a 'campaign' speech advocating a conservative position but did not openly endorse Trump. Obviously, this gives the left leaning media opportunity to create negative sensational headlines and plenty of ammunition to make attempts to drive a wedge into the GOP unity. However, the GOP convention floor had shown a strong unity as they entered into the main events after they got over the convention rules. They paid attention to the speakers and responded warmly to the endorsement speeches by the governors, senators, house representatives and other public officials. The convention delegates responded warmly and enthusiastically to the endorsements by Ben Carson, Paul Ryan, Rick Perry, and Scott Walker and they even booed Ted Cruz when they did not hear him making an endorsement. This will have a bad impact on Cruz's political future rather than Trump's winning of the election.

The Trump family have done a superb job in their speeches to show that they are a decent, intelligent, hard working and loving family who genuinely love Donald and support his bid for the White House because they truly believe that Donald Trump will make the country safe and great again. The Trump campaign slogans, "we will make America work, safe, great, first, winning, rich again." were effectively worked into the four-day convention agenda as well as rhythmically into the inspiring speeches throughout the convention. After listening to the call-ins on C-Span in four days, one cannot help but coming to the following conclusion: the Republican Party is far more united in the rank and file than you would be led to believe otherwise, and they are fired up by Trump. The GOP party machinery is apparently oiled with continued successful fund raisings in the remaining days. The hard core Democrat is not likely to switch even those who supported Sanders and bitter about Hillary. However, there are some wavering Democrats who have openly come forward to say that they will vote for Trump mainly for the following reasons: Hillary's dishonesty (lies), lack of accountability and not trustworthy. The presentations about Benghazi, email abuse and the victims' testimonies at the GOP convention certainly left a deep impression on Democrats and Republicans alike.

Trump's acceptance speech was the longest ever in the history of GOP presidential nominee's acceptance speech, one hour and six minutes long which forced all major TV channels to delay their night news or regular programs. His speech of course increased the TV ratings. His speech netted out all aspects of issues, safety and security: intelligence gathering and law and order, prison crime, immigrants, border wall and security; economy: budget and trade agreements, jobs, wages and mother and children; foreign policy: Middle East and ISIS, working with Israel, protection of LBGTQ, pay us for protection; work: employment opportunities, reduce taxes, American citizen first; rhetoric: China currency manipulation and Mexico unfair trade and defense spending for rich Japan, but he opposes TPP and NAFTA and prefers bilateral trade negotiations as China does. His speech brought repeated cheers, an apparent success in uniting the party. His rhetoric cries more like to get fair deals than wage wars and threats.

Perhaps, Donald Trump's pick of Mike Pence as his VP running mate is the most significant decision not recognized by the political pundits in the media.

In my opinion, though Pence is not an exciting speaker or a well known name, Trump must have picked him for the win of the White House for the following two main reasons: One, Pence is a Christian, conservative and Republican in that order as he himself proclaims, which is what Trump needs to draw the conservative, attract the religious and unite the Republicans. The second, more importantly, Trump selected Pence because Pence is a good friend of Paul Ryan, Speaker of the House. It is a smarter move than picking Paul Ryan himself for VP if Trump is confident to win the White House. Trump needs Ryan to be on his side and in the House when he wins the Presidency; picking Pence, likely consulted with Ryan, Trump made a brilliant choice. After all, the VP is the key liaison to the Congress.

Democrats' convention is coming up next week. Hillary is busy making responses to Trump's convention already. The biggest news this weekend of course is that Hillary has picked Senator of Virginia, Tim Kaine as her VP running mate. Hillary's official line for her pick is that Kaine is beloved by his staff and Senate colleagues and he, with foreign policy experience. could step in as President. His background, however, is a past supporter of NAFTA and PTT and more so he is not a liberal stalwart to draw Sanders' supporters. Kaine is a Catholic attended a predominated black church for two decades and he speaks Spanish fluently, strength for attracting black and Latino minority votes. One contrast should be pointed out is that Hillary is pro-abortion and Kaine has been anti-abortion but now Kaine is shifting his position. Was he forced to shift because of the VP pick? It would be interesting to watch when Mike Pence a strong anti-abortion GOP VP candidate facing off Tim Kaine a recently "converted" pro-abortion Democrat VP candidate to debate this moral issue as a matter of personal integrity and belief.

CHAPTER 37

From the Democrat's Convention Projecting
to the November Presidential Election

—ɯ—

ABSTRACT

THE DEMOCRATS HAD THE ADVANTAGE of having the three-day weekend to respond to the Republicans' convention platform and their rally speeches, but a bombshell news about the embarrassing email leak (DNC officials played an unfair game against Presidential candidate Bernie Sanders) almost derailed the convention. In the end, The Democratic Convention was successfully concluded with Hillary Clinton accepting the Nomination. In her acceptance speech she made a lot of promises to every diverse group of Americans to respect their rights and solve their problems all achievable by raising taxes on the Wall Street and the rich 1% of the populace. Since Donald Trump believes in the opposite, reducing taxes to pump the economy then solve the problems, we the voters must demand a serious debate between the two candidates outlining the specifics of his/her first 100 days in office.

—ɯ—

The Democrat's convention at the Wells Fargo Convention Center in Philadelphia started on July 25th at the heels of the Republican's convention ended on July 21st at the Quicken Loans Stadium in Cleveland. The Democrats had the advantage of having the three-day weekend to respond to the Republicans' convention platform and their rally speeches. However, the highlights captured the media over the weekend and the following Monday were these two specific events.

The first was Hillary's timed announcement of her pick of Tim Kaine, Senator from Virginia as her running mate. The second which created a bomb-shell news was the resignation of Debbie Wasserman Schultz, the Democratic National Committee chairwoman, in the eve of the Democratic Convention, due to an embarrassing email leak published in WikiLeaks. Apparently, the DNC mail server was allegedly hacked by Russian hackers who released the damaging email revealing that the Democratic National Committee (DNC) officials had played an unfair game against Presidential candidate Bernie Sanders. The Hillary campaign manager, Robby Mook, immediately suggested that the Russian hackers breaking into DNC's server had Russian government involvement and the hacking was intended to help Hillary's opponent Donald Trump. This suggestion seems to be Mook's desperate tactics of damage con-trol. Naturally, the Trump camp was furious and rejected this allegation. Over the weekend, the DNC did come to a quick decision that Wasserman had to resign and step down from the Democrat convention chair duties as well.

Despite of the email leak surprise, the Democratic Convention was opened on 7/25 as planned with Ohio Representative Marcia Fudge as the perma-nent Democratic Convention Chair and with DNC Vice Chairwoman Donna Brazile to serve as the interim DNC chair through the election period. Brazile being a CNN political commentator had to suspend her contract with CNN and to remain on CNN programs without pay. This move might be prompted by the sudden turn of events, but it did not smell Kosher for CNN or DNC. I was glad that I could watch the two conventions on C-Span without subjecting myself to the bombardment of "Expert" opinions from the talking heads in the other TV channels.

The rank and file Republicans' claim of Trump's successful bid for the Presidential nomination is due to the fact that he started a movement, an anti-establishment movement, speaking the truth to the people and the peo-ple rewarded him with primary votes. In the end, Trump succeeded in win-ning against the party establishment. The sign of unity at the Republican Convention indeed suggests that the people is fed up with political talk, whether it is disguised in correctness or it is veiled with lies. On the other hand, the Sanders campaign is also an anti-establishment movement. With Bernie's liberal ideas, the movement may be considered as a revolution just as Sanders himself intoned. Unfortunately, this movement met the resistance of the Democratic Party establishment as evidenced by the leaked emails. In addition, Hillary is a very seasoned insider of the establishment, hence Sanders failed to win the primary against her, principally due to the DNC machinery (and the super delegates) stacked against him.

In the first day of the Democratic Convention including the satellite pre-convention meetings, there was apparent anger among the large number of Sanders' supporters. Their emotions were clearly vented through the loud boos given to any speaker who did not carefully craft their speech to woo the Sanders' agenda and supporters. There were many short speeches given by individuals who support Hillary. Elizabeth Warren, Bernie Sanders and Michelle Obama were the key speakers on the first day. Warren gave more sharp attacks on Trump than endorsing statements to Hillary. Sanders' speech repeating many of his winning lines used on his campaign trail was very well delivered and cheered enthusiastically by his supporters. He strategically kept his endorsement of Hillary towards the end of his speech which of course was what Hillary desperately needed. The sideline interviews conducted by media plainly showed that the Sanders supporters felt cheated and they were forced to support a candidate they really did not like or trust. It was clear that Sanders tried and perhaps succeeded in influencing Hillary on the Democratic platform, for example on the free tuition for public colleges. Michelle Obama gave a warm endorsing speech citing Hillary's accomplishments especially her devotion to children's education.

The second day continues with a number of caucuses and a string of speakers before and after the roll call of delegates, which is just like the one in the Republican convention, a tradition the delegates enjoyed to perform and the public was interested to watch on television. Bernie Sanders' supporters showed far more emotions than Ted Cruz's supporters in their respective convention. Even though Sanders lost the nomination to Hillary but he had won the roll calls of 16 States plus the group of Democrats from abroad. Sanders gracefully made a motion to suspend the convention rule to accept Hillary's nomination by acclamation. The day included a video from former President Jimmy Carter and was ended with the highlight speech by President Bill Clinton who offered some intimate stories about his college days courting Hillary in addition to characterizing her as one of the most qualified President and Commander-in-Chief. The crowd loved it. The mood of the delegates was also soothed by some beautiful music performances shown by video during the convention.

The third day had more caucuses and more speakers representing the wide diversification of American societies covering ethnic and racial groups, disabled, youth, labor, veterans, LBGT, faith, etc, etc as well as individuals with stories to tell related to social issues such as victims of violence crimes. Many speakers had been worked with or helped by Hillary. Vice President Joe Biden and President Barak Obama's endorsement speeches were excellent but together with Hillary's acceptance speech on the fourth day, they seem to be too eager in patting each other's back. The 4th day included more public officials' endorsements which intended to show that they were all with her – Hillary. Chelsea gave the introductory speech on her mom, it was very touching and smoothly delivered but in comparison with Ivanka's introduction of her father, Donald Trump, both speeches could get an A. Perhaps the real difference could only be found by measuring the number of 'online clicks' on their speeches. My guess is that Chelsea may get more clicks but Ivanka will get longer viewing time.

Hillary commented on Trump's acceptance speech being too negative and pessimistic about the U.S. problems with no specific solutions. It is true that Trump had been hitting the nails on the head regarding American problems, domestic economy, social ills and global relations. He offered few specifics other than boldly claimed that he could fix them. Hillary, in her acceptance speech, focused more on attacking Trump than giving specific problem solvers herself. She made a lot of promises to every American belonging to every diverse minority group that she will fix all their problems (wages, jobs, free education, infrastructures, healthcare, ...) and defend all their rights (except second amendment). Then she promised that she could accomplish all that by taxing the Wall Street and the top 1% rich Americans. Thus, the crux of the matter between Donald Trump and Hillary Clinton seems to be that DT believes in lowering taxes to pump the economy then deal with the other problems whereas HC believes in raising taxes to solve all problems. These beliefs seem to be too simple to be effective, judging by the deeds of the current and past administrations. No, we can't let the parties blame each other or use the grid lock as an excuse. The leader must produce results by working across aisles. Before the November election, the voters should demand serious answers from DT and HC issue by issue? Who are the appointees of the cabinet and Supreme Court? What proposals will be submitted to the Congress in the first 100 days? What votes are needed to pass them? Make the Presidential debates interactive with the American public 'call ins' and develop solid mandates on the President's proposals. Together we will be strong and let America to be great again!

CHAPTER 38

Can Taiwan Practice An Honest Democracy Leading to a Successful Reunification? - Taiping Island a Test Case

—m—

ABSTRACT

THE VICTORY OF THE DEMOCRATIC Progressive Party (DPP) in this year Taiwan's presidential election is one basic cause and consequence for cooling off the cross-strait cooperative pro-business economic development path and flaring up a wishful but dangerous anti-Mainland thinking and false independence movement. When it comes to taking a defending position in Taiping Island and SCS, the people of Taiwan have spoken. But they must be clear and leave no room for politicians to be vague or to play word game. The answer to the title question is yes; Taiwan must and can practice an honest democracy to pursue a successful reunification policy to benefit the people! The people in Taiwan should never let politicians hijack opinion surveys and democracy!

—m—

Following the U.S. 'Pivot to Asia' policy and the rising tension in the South China Sea (SCS), the 'Cross-Strait' has once again become a hot spot moving away from a 'peaceful gradual Chinese internal reunification' agenda towards an 'impossible treacherous false independence' path. Of course, the victory of the Democratic Progressive Party (DPP) in this year's presidential election is one basic cause and consequence for cooling off the cross-strait cooperative pro-business economic development path (the previous Administration, Ma Ying-Jeou (KMT) had cultivated with Mainland in the past eight years) and flaring up a wishful but dangerous anti-Mainland China thinking and false independence movement (the current leader Tsai Ing-Wen (DPP) coyly promoted 'independence' ever since she took office).

The most significant and distinct ideological difference between the KMT and DPP is the following: The KMT recognizes one China and the official agreement reached by the two cross-strait administrations in 1992, commonly referred to as 1992 Mutual Understanding. The U.S. has long committed since 1970's to the recognition of one China thus the U.S. has been in agreement with KMT in maintaining a warm and progressive Cross-Strait relation. Whereas, the DPP is purposefully trying to walk away from the 1992 Mutual Understanding to pursue an independence attempt which is aggressively promoted by a faction in DPP insisting on keeping 'Taiwan Independence' in the DPP party platform as an objective. The U.S. is not sure whether or not such a direction will lead to a beneficial outcome to the U.S. in the name of world peace. Hence, the U.S. is studying the situation and the DPP behavior carefully under the still evolving China Policy.

The Taiwan issue is a clear one for the Mainland China, that is, Taiwan must be reunited with the mother land, sooner or later, slower or faster in pace, but never can be denied by any internal entity or any external country including the U.S., Japan or the entire United Nations. In fact, the Taiwan issue is rather clear to most countries in the world. However, the issue is surprisingly unclear in Taiwan existing as a fundamental problem facing the people of Taiwan and a serious challenge to the Taiwan governing administration. Unfortunately, the people was long misled by politicians through misinterpretation of history (even by whitewashing their textbooks to confuse the young generations) and through manipulation of democracy (by lies and fact twisting of policy issues, 政策, and people's wishes, 民意, via media). The people in Taiwan was easily gullible but we must remember: you can fool some people some of the time, even most of the time, but you can't fool all the people all the time! Thus to the title question, I believe the answer is yes and let me explain.

Reviewing the international events, especially concerning the U.S. - China relations, the U.S. seems to be conducting a China Policy in a classroom, that is, it is a case in study; consequently, China's US policy is in a seminar style, that is, debate, argue and interpret the U.S. China Policy then issue responsive statements. As a result, the two nations engage in occasional hot rhetoric but in reality both sides wish to find mutually acceptable compromises. Since going to war is mutually destructive and unacceptable, no matter how inevitable hawks of each side chant. People in Taiwan must understand this dynamics and be realistic in cultivating a beneficial Cross-Strait policy.

The 'Pivot to Asia' policy is fundamental to the U.S., a correct one from the viewpoint of the U.S. interests and her necessary decision in retreating from the Middle East problems and EU turmoil. However, a correct policy does not guarantee a correct execution particularly when the case is still under study, namely, the rise of China is very dynamic and ongoing, its threat may be over exaggerated or even be elevated by the U.S. herself. The U.S. diplomatic and military moves in the East China Sea now shifting to the SCS have clearly supported my 'classroom' theory and China's corresponding counter actions fitted my 'seminar' metaphor. Hopefully, the think tanks of both sides will engage in more dialogue to complete the classroom and seminar activities into a for-credit case-study course so that others like Taiwan can take such a course and earn credits in the school of geopolitics.

Taiwan politicians and party politics have a false notion that Taiwan has a choice between (A) Relying on the U.S. and U.S. protégé Japan to pursue an independence movement and (B) Yielding to Mainland China to take the reunification path. In fact, the U.S. and Japan do not want to have a truly independent Taiwan, world politics tell us that a truly independent country cannot be controlled easily by another. That is why endless regime changes occur in small countries if they have geopolitical importance. From the purpose of control and influence, often supporting independence does not really mean supporting the establishment of a truly independent entity. Taiwan must understand this, moving towards independence means choosing to be controlled by your supporters. On the other hand, leaning towards reunification does not mean the total loss of identity, especially, when the mainland China is seeking to define her identity as well. Hong Kong is a living example, her former quasi-independent colonial state yields no better welfare than her present status receiving billions of investment. The longest ocean bridge linking Hong Kong, Macao and Zhu Jiang is a huge investment from Mainland to secure Hong Kong's future competitive position.

Singapore is often used as an example of shinning small independent nation. Is it? Singapore is situated between two large Muslim countries, Malaysia and Indonesia. Singapore has an overwhelming ethnic Chinese population but she is too far from China. She had no choice but relying on the U.S. for security, essentially turning herself as a US military base. Lee Kuan Yew was smart to play world politics; so long China's goods came through Singapore port without problem, China would let Singapore to use China to gain diplomatic leverage. Before China became strong enough, Singapore had no choice but to pick the U.S. for protection. Even though the U.S. regarded Lee as a dictator, there was no need for regime change or making Singapore a truly democratic nation so long she sides with the U.S. Taiwan is in an entirely different situation, Taiwan, in close proximity to Mainland, exports largely to the Mainland. Singapore, as a transfer port might diminish in value if other transfer routes to China could be used as substitute. Singapore's significance as a military base for the U.S. would then diminish accordingly. However, Taiwan will remain forever as a strategic land for China's security; the people in Taiwan must appreciate their Chinese heritage and geopolitical value to the Mainland.

The ridiculous ruling of the arbitration court declaring Taiping Island as a rock not an island is really a good test case for people's will in Taiwan and the real intension of the Tsai administration. The U.S. or Japan will never take the welfare of Taiwan people, especially Taiwan's fishermen, into their hearts. Taiping Island saga proves that Taiwan cannot defend her sovereignty nor ocean rights by just taking a pro-US or pro-Japan stand. The Tsai administration cannot negotiate with Japan on Taiwan's fishing rights (can't even defend the existing agreement Ma administration had scored) is evidence enough for her wrong Cross-Strait policy. In contrast, by aligning with Mainland China, which values Taiwan's strategic importance forever, and by acting as a 'to be reunified' Chinese people, Taiwan can stand up and have a voice in any negotiation on the world stage. Taiwan voters must understand this political reality.

People in Taiwan have enjoyed democracy for several decades; naturally, people in Taiwan have concerns whether they will lose their democracy if united with the Mainland. From an analyst viewpoint, Taiwan's democracy is as good as the people's intelligence and as valuable as it is perceived as true democracy. The likelihood of Taiwan's democracy being hijacked by party politicians is real and Taiping Island is a proven test. Tsai in her Washington Post interview on July 21, 2016, by Lally Waymouth, cited many times 'the will of the people' (民意) as her basis for her policies. Is that really true? When it comes to taking a defending position in Taiping Island and SCS, the people of Taiwan have spoken but they must be clear and leave no room for politicians to be vague or to play word game. Judging on the current development in Taiwan's political affairs, the dropping of performance rating of the Tsai administration, and the boiling emotions of citizens regarding defending Taiwan's rights (such as the Taiping Island status), one is hopeful that Taiwan's people do understand the importance of the Cross-Strait relationship and its dynamics discussed above.

So to answer the title question, the answer is yes! Taiwan must and can practice an honest democracy to pursue a successful reunification policy to benefit the people!

CHAPTER 39

Understanding of China's World
Development Program, OBOR

—⚏—

ABSTRACT

CHINA'S ONE BELT AND ONE Road program (OBOR) is an ambitious under-taking but it has not been well understood by the world, not only the people in America and Australia, but also the people in the three continents, Asia, Europe and Africa. In this paper we explain why so and most importantly we offer a description of OBOR, its historical origination, its economical signifi-cance and its future prospect gauging on its current momentum and recep-tion by the world. Proposals like OBOR bear people's welfare in mind; in the Chinese political philosophy, people extend to all people under the Heaven. One salient point, China must make and convince the world, is that OBOR is a win-win global development plan not a hegemony scheme to gain national power as a few nay-sayers claimed. The OBOR investment is no different from any good infrastructure bond investment. The risk involved will quickly diminish as many countries are getting on board. The OBOR program is too attractive to be sabotaged by anyone.

—⚏—

China's One Belt and One Road program (OBOR) is an ambitious undertak-ing but it has not been well understood by the world, not only the people in America and Australia, but also the people in the other three continents, Asia, Europe and Africa, where OBOR passes through. It has an impact on one third of the world's GDP, and the welfare of 65% of the world's total population. The OBOR concept was first revealed by the Chinese leader, Xi Jin Ping, at Kazakhstan in 2013. With today's advanced communication infrastructure, one would imagine that such a visionary undertaking would have received world-wide attention reaching every person every corner of the Earth. Surprisingly, it isn't so; many people have never heard of the acronym, OBOR, even two years after its announcement.

The above situation is somewhat unusual to such a major global program. Perhaps it has caught every country by surprise thus ill prepared to take a position on it. In this paper we explain why so and most importantly we offer a description of OBOR, its historical origination, its economical significance and its future prospect gauging on its current momentum and reception by the world. Naturally, the few intellectual elites on the world stage paying attention to international affairs have learned about OBOR, however, few of the few have engaged in communicating this amazing concept to the public in plain folks language. This lacking in mass communication in most countries obviously contributed to the mystic status of OBOR which could only be blamed on China for not doing an adequate PR work on OBOR and on some countries' lack of diligence in explaining OBOR to their citizens. There was also the possibility that a few nations might consider OBOR a threatening program and thus deliberately suppressing its news and messages. Hopefully, we will succeed to dispel that notion here.

On the positive side, there are international entities already engaged in studies and dialogues on OBOR. For example, the internationally recognized consulting firm, McKinsey & Company, has recently offered a podcast on the OBOR subject (hosted by Cecilia Ma Zecha, McKinsey Publishing Singapore) after her guests, Kevin Sneader, Chairman of McKinsey Asia, and Joe Ngai, Managing Sr. Partner in McKinsey Hong Kong, participated in a Hong Kong OBOR Summit where many ASEAN delegates attended. This podcast emphasized the magnitude and potential impact of OBOR as a significant trade platform across three continents and linking South China Sea, South Pacific, and Indian Ocean to Red Sea. It is no surprise coming from McKinsey that they probed many valid questions and implementation issues and urged international corporations and governments to take earnest studies of OBOR and what it may impact them economically and business wise if OBOR indeed took off.

OBOR Consists of two components, the One Belt, a land based "Silk Road Economic Belt" (SREB), inspired by the ancient Chinese Silk Road (used in 130 BCE to 1453 CE, Han Dynasty) a trade road linking Asia and Europe and an ocean based route "Maritime Silk Road" (MSR), which was inspired by the famous "Zheng He Voyages", a seven time ocean exploration in the Ming Dynasty (1371-1435) reaching as far as Indian Ocean and North Pacific Ocean. These historical accomplishments served as the basis and offered the confidence for modern China to offer these ambitious undertaking as global collaborative development programs for stimulating the world economy and advancing the welfare of global citizens. A modern version of the silk trading roads naturally requires tremendous amounts of investments in modernizing the physical infrastructure, roads, bridges, ports and canals, as well as upgrading the digital communication facilities to support the finance, banking and trading endeavors. As rightly pointed out by McKinsey, the establishment of Asia Infrastructure Investment Bank (AIIB*) and the New Development Bank (BRICS) exhibited the early accomplishment of the OROR program. (*The chronological account of the establishment of AIIB was described in an article in Understanding the US and China, pp 65-69, 2016, ISBN: 0977159442.)

Although not explicitly mentioned in OBOR, the history of the post-WW II Marshall Plan proposed by the U.S. to help restore Europe's economy, had a profound impression on the Chinese. Thanks to Marshall Plan, the Western Europe was quickly revived in the world economy. Similarly, In Asia, Japan was benefitted tremendously by the 'Occupation and Reconstruction of Japan' plan, whereas Mainland China, although an ally of the U.S., was treated as an enemy after the war hence never received any assistance from the West. It took a lot longer for China than Japan to rise up in her economic development. This historical background had not only taught the Chinese a lesson but also served as inspiration desiring to offer her development experience to her neighbors by proposing OBOR, in spirit, modeling after the Marshall Plan.

Unfortunately, the U.S., driven by her exceptionalism, did not gain the same inspiration that Marshall Plan has impressed on the Chinese. The U.S. China policy has been rooted in the Cold War legacy, viewed communism as a forever unchangeable evil. The U.S. state department has never seriously investigated the Chinese experience with communism under the deeply entrenched Chinese philosophy (including the political philosophy). China may have had the desire to implement a pure communist society prescribed by Marx in the 50's but she had learned her lesson through bad experiments since the 60's and 70's to realize that she needed her own system compatible with her traditional political philosophy: People's welfare must dictate the political policies but political policies must be delicately implemented and managed by a representative system derived from people's political power. This representative system is not one person one vote which cannot be completely implemented on every level even in the democratic system of the U.S. China currently conducts her political reform under one dominant party (CCP) with her political platform shaped with people's power (People's Congress) in an unique way. Proposals like OBOR bear people's welfare in mind; in the Chinese political philosophy, people extend to all people under the Heaven. One salient point, China must make and convince the world is that OBOR is a win-win global development plan not a hegemony scheme to gain national power as a few naysayers claimed.

On today's global economy, many nations including the U.S. and China are heavily engaged in debt-financing, that is, borrowing money to finance programs which can yield returns in the long run. China's OBOR must be viewed as such, not as an imperialist program. China's old silk roads were never meant to be imperial road to expansion. China's modern silk roads do not bear that trait either. Any country opposing OBOR either does not understand its historical background and source of inspirations or is jealous of its potential impact. In reality, OBOR is a program that will benefit every country and every person on earth. OBOR is no doubt a visionary program offering a common dream to more than half of the world population. China is in the right position to lead the effort. China is smart to kick off both SREB and MSR in the same time, since they are complimentary to each other and they serve as mutual insurance to each other to warrant China's initial $100B investment.

In my opinion, from private investor's point of view, the OBOR investment is no different from any good AAA infrastructure bond investment. The risk involved will quickly diminish as many countries are getting on board. The OBOR program is too attractive to be sabotaged by anyone. One good advice McKinsey should have made in its podcast is to encourage Japan and the U.S. to take a positive stand to gain benefits rather than taking a negative position giving no one any benefit.

CHAPTER 40

Condition for US China Cooperation
Leading to Better World (I and II)

—ⲱ—

Abstract

IF THE U.S. AND CHINA could cooperate, it would produce mutual benefits and lead to a better world. However, meaningful US China cooperation could not happen unless the two countries develop a good relationship. Thus under what condition will the U.S. and China maintain a good relationship is a ket question. Among a broad range of issues in US China relations spanning across economy (commerce, investment and finance), national security (military, diplomacy and international affairs), industrial relation (technology, manufacturing, and market sharing) and cultural understanding (history, arts, communication, tourism and social behavior), the key issue that will dictate the US-China relation is the Cross-Strait relation or reunification (CSR). CSR has never been a Chinese domestic issue as it should be but a critical foreign affair troubling the US China relation and hindering their opportunity for close cooperation. Removing the CSR issue will shed the historical 'China' baggage the U.S. carried since the turn of 20th century, WWII, recognition of one independent China, Cold War and beyond. With the CSR dangling and influencing the U.S. China policy, the U.S. has not been able to carve out a clear-cut foreign policy towards China leading to mutual benefits and world prosperity. In order to remove this obstacle, understanding and solving the problems of CSR are essential.

CONDITION FOR US CHINA COOPERATION LEADING TO BETTER WORLD – PART I

Among think tank analysts or common citizens, no one would reject the statement that if the U.S. and China could cooperate rather than fight against each other, the world would be much better off. However, among the opinions on prognosis of the future of US-China relations, there are clearly two camps. The Hawks seem to target China as the archenemy of the U.S. and believe in eventual war resulting from their irresolvable conflicts. The Doves seem to wish a friendly relation between the U.S. and China but have no clues why is their relation moving on a bumpy roller coaster yo-yoing from friendly gestures to hostility by their government's conducts and handling of current events. The two great nations seem to be preparing war. Yet it is obvious that cooperation between the U.S. and China will lead to mutual benefits and better world and confrontation to mutual destruction and world disaster. Therefore, it is desirable to understand: Under what condition the U.S. and China can fully cooperate and resolve conflicts. Many in both camps have criticized the current US policies and mishaps, but offer little wisdom on how to reach the goal for mutual trust and cooperation.

Nations always have conflicts, but great powers have unavoidable competitions in many areas and more complex conflicts of interests. The U.S. and China naturally have a broad range of issues in their relations spanning across economy (commerce, investment and finance), national security (military, diplomacy and international affairs), industrial relation (technology, manufacturing, and market sharing) and cultural understanding (history, arts, communication, tourism, and social behavior). In this essay we venture to claim that solving the Cross-Strait Reunification (CSR) issue is the most important of all conditions for building a sound US-China relation which will lead to mutual benefits and a better world. We discuss below why the CSR issue will dictate the US-China relation, what is the logic and reasons for this claim and how we may achieve the condition for better relation and cooperation.

The CSR issue has never been treated as a Chinese domestic issue as it should be. Instead of leaving the CSR as China's internal problem, the U.S.

considers the CSR issue her problem, elevating it as an international issue; thus, the US-China relation could not be maintained in a friendly manner. Presumably that the U.S. adopted such an approach with her national interests in mind, but that is a debatable point between the hawk and dove camps on China. What is clear though, two nations could not have a normal relationship if one nation does not respect the sovereignty of the other nation. Take Canada and Mexico, the two US neighbors, as examples. If the U.S. did not respect Canada's sovereignty over Quebec and treated Quebec's historical independence movement as her own problem and concern, would the U.S. and Canada have a nice and normal relationship? If the U.S. would send all the Mexican immigrants in the U.S. back to Mexico to establish a separate sovereign entity there, would Mexico and the U.S. maintain a friendly relation? The answers are sure no. The CSR issue is similar to the above hypothetical US-Canada and US-Mexico issues; why should the U.S. let the CSR spoil her relationship with China? What are the real national interest and the justification for the U.S. to interfere in the CSR issue?

The CSR issue has been a thorny issue for at least 71 years ever since the ending of the WW II. The CSR issue is actually more than a century old from a modern Chinese history perspective. In fact, the CSR has been an ancient Chinese sovereignty issue for several centuries. Taiwan was part of the ancient China (since the 15th century or earlier) from the traditional sovereignty point of view (discovery, occupation by residents of traders, farmers and/or fisherman and evidences such as documents, maps and other physical artifacts). However, the specific historical facts are not understood by the global citizens, including Americans. China's traditional sovereignty had been violated by the colonial invaders from the West (Dutch, British, Spanish, Portuguese, French, Germany, American, etc.) in the 19th and early 20th centuries. China was also a victim to the imperial invaders, Russia and Japan. China was the chief victim in Asia among her neighbors, Okinawa, the Philippines, Malaysia, Indonesia, Singapore, Indo-China and India. Taiwan unfortunately had a treacherous historical background being captured by the Dutch and recovered (1621-1641, Portuguese landed in 1517 and called it Formosa) then captured by the Japanese (1895-1945) and returned to China in 1945 after Japan was defeated and surrendered in WW II. China started her revolution seeking to establish a republic state but never completed it (from toppling the Qing dynasty to forming a republic nation, in 1911). Japan's intervention with invasions (the first Sino-Japan War, 1894-5 through the second Sino-Japan War, 1937-45, included the horrible 1937 Nanking Massacre) had thwarted the Chinese revolution throughout the entire 20th century resulting in a fractured China.

Post WW II, China was divided and intervened again by her two war allies turned into post-war rivals, the U.S. (supporting the KMT) and the Soviet Union (supporting the CCP). The ideological confrontation between the U.S. and the Soviet Union influenced China's unification and development and created the CSR problem existing up until today. Hindsight after the CCP embraced and abandoned the Soviet style communism and the KMT relinquished her authoritative governance to a two party democracy (KMT vs. DPP), the CSR should be a Chinese domestic issue rather than a legacy problem from the Cold War. The Cold War had ended in 1990. Taiwan and the Mainland each had gone through drastic experiences of successful economical development and advancement. Now the mainland China has become the world's second largest economy and Taiwan's economy has become an integral part of China's economy. So why should the CSR remain an American business at all, under her One China Policy established since 1979?

CONDITION FOR US CHINA COOPERATION LEADING TO BETTER WORLD – PART II

The CSR issue can be looked at from a geopolitical point of view. Taiwan, with her surrounding small islands situated in the Pacific Ocean, has a vital geopolitical importance to the Mainland China which can be easily understood. But why Taiwan is geopolitically important to others in the Pacific Ocean and beyond is bewildering, except (in one hegemony theory) someone intends to control Taiwan to contain China. Some countries may be concerned that the reunification may impact upon their national interests, but where is the justification of that concern? Some neighboring countries of China and the U.S. may assume that China may be an imperial invader; but historical evidence has shown otherwise. China will defend her sovereignty bitterly but she has not invaded her neighbors or anyone elsewhere. Based on the sovereignty argument discussed above, the CSR issue is a Chinese domestic issue, no one should interfere. Any interference would produce serious confrontation and destroy a normal cooperative relation. Assuming China to be an imperial invader is a false reasoning for interfering in the CSR issue; China has never been an aggressive invader or an eager meddler in international affairs. China had not taken any aggressive steps or adopted an urgent time table in resolving the CSR issue giving no one any reason to interfere with China's CSR issue. If anyone did interfere, it would give China and the world the impression that there was an evil motive of thwarting China's reunification. Unfortunately, the U.S. seems to have become the crucial factor in the solution of CSR.

The 'China fear' or 'targeting China' are really false policies if the goal is world peace and global prosperity. Economically, a stable and growing economy in China and in the U.S. will bring and assure global prosperity. By taking on an illegitimate sovereignty interference like CSR to suppress China's growth can hardly be justified without being viewed as a trouble maker against China. There was no justification in creating the Taiwan Relation Act after the U.S. and China announced the joint Shanghai Communiqué which clearly spelled out the necessity of peaceful reunification. Unfortunately, the Taiwan Relation Act, although not binding the U.S. government, has been misused to turn CSR into an international issue and Taiwan a hotspot in Asia. A few neighbors of China are apparently following the US lead regarding CSR. With China's increasingly more transparent diplomacy and open collaborative global economical development programs, she is likely to allay those fears. The recent East China Sea and South China Sea turbulence are extensions of the false policies. They only strengthen China's resolve in settling the CSR problem with anxiety, possibly from no time table to a planned time table.

From the Cold War legacy, democracy and human rights were used as justification by the U.S. for intervention even regime change in foreign countries. But the results were not good; more wars were created and more social disasters resulted in the Middle East and Europe. Asia was spared until now;

the 'pivot to Asia' seemed to create conflicts among nations and tension in the region. Hopefully, Asians can learn from the history and war events happened elsewhere and become smart enough to avoid being pushed into chaotic situations. The CSR issue can be examined also internally in Taiwan from human rights and democracy point of view. The internal complexities come from Taiwan's political struggle between political parties is a direct result out of her self-developed democracy and value system on human rights. One unfortunate phenomenon in Taiwan politics is that somehow politicians representing a small fraction of people in Taiwan can influence the majority through the faulty legislative system and the manipulative media. This phenomenon is exhibited in the social and national issues that have even been called out by the well-respected aging Buddhist, Xing Yun Da Shi. Taiwan's politics has also twisted human rights of the aborigines, mainlanders and various factions of earlier settlers in Taiwan creating frictions among citizens. These internal complexities could be clarified eventually if external intervention from other countries would stop meddling.

These internal complexities may also be compounded by people in Mainland China, due to their lack of understanding and sensitivity of the psychological changes of Taiwan people under their own value system. Conversely the Taiwan people under the external influence may have also misunderstood the psychological feelings of the Mainland people in their view of the CSR issue. The external influence from the U.S. may be represented by the China Relation Act and her inconsistent China policy but the external influence from Japan is her continued wishful thinking to have Taiwan as a part of Japan. Unfortunately this Japanese influence was deeply implanted in Taiwan through Lee Deng Hui, Taiwan's President (1988-2000, born and educated under Japanese occupied Taiwan) who turns out to be a deep mole (expelled by KMT in 2001 for launching a Taiwan independence party opposing reunification) for Japan with a hidden agenda in opposing reunification and pushing Taiwan to be a part of Japan - an amazing political traitor story in modern China. Lee had also successfully cultivated his protégés, Chen Shui Bian (President 2001-2008) and the current President Tsai Ying Wen (2016-).

There were some Taiwan residents granted Japanese citizenship during Japan occupation and some Japanese remained in Taiwan after Japan surrendered at the end of WW II. Though a minority, they have been the source of Taiwan's internal complexities. They were impressed by Japan's rapid recovery with the U.S.post WW II "Occupation and Reconstruction" Plan (the Marshall Plan of the East) when Taiwan was in a very difficult economic situation, hence they have kept a strong pro-Japan sentiment. Similar to the sentiments of Japan's right-wing faction represented by descendents of WW II participants in Japan (for example, Abe Shinzo, grandson of a charged WW II criminal), they deny and whitewash WW II history and brainwash young generations by revising textbooks. This internal problem expanded so fast in the past two decades was largely due to the deep mole, Lee Deng Hui and his proteges. The majority especially the young generations must understand and wake up from the decade long China bashing plot. The CS people in Taiwan and the Mainland both have a responsibility to tell the facts and truth to deal with this internal complexity to foster reunification. Will the truth prevail? It is very likely, since the world has begun to reexamine the history of WW II through commemorating the end of WW II. Based on the ancient and modern Chinese history, Taiwan should be and will be eventually reunified with the Mainland.

After recognizing the internal and external problems of CSR, we can discuss what solution is there for solving the CSR issue. The 'external intervention' was the main impediment of realizing CSR; the motives behind intervention were evil aimed against a United Single China. No question that both Mainland and Taiwan must resist the external intervention. Without the external intervention, the internal complexities can be simplified and dealt with in time. Lee Deng Hui is now 94 years old, his generation and deceitful influence will wear off soon. With global open internet and free communication, the younger generations will have opportunities to receive true facts and history despite of the current DPP administration's independence push. The interaction of CS economic development and the creation of CS job opportunities will tighten CS relation and eventually cultivate a right condition for reunification. It makes great sense for the U.S. to stay away from interfering with CSR and focus on US China cooperation.

The solution for the CSR issue is actually quite straight forward, that is, to tell the truth about history, the WW II history and the ancient Taiwan history. The truth will reverse the white wash and misunderstanding of history which had generated mistrust, induced Japan to militarize again, and caused the U.S. and China to turn from allies to adversaries. The U.S. must reflect on The Marshall Plan and the Occupation and Reconstruction Plan where the U.S. offered genuine help to Europe and Japan and derived mutual benefits. The U.S. can draw lessons from that history and appreciate that offering of genuine help to China will yield mutual benefits as well. By adopting a strategy to raise the standard of living of the 1.3 billion Chinese through a cooperative plan, the U.S. will not only develop a genuine friendly relationship with China and her people but also a thriving US economy. The U.S. will gain benefits as she did post WW II in rebuilding Europe and Japan. By truly recognizing one China and removing the CSR issue, the U.S. can direct the Taiwan Relation Act to help reunification instead of impeding it (for example, stop selling arms to Taiwan to avoid an arms race). The U.S. should formulate a China policy based on the following logic: I. CSR is China's sovereignty issue and China's own internal problem, II. Truly honoring one China with no interference on CSR will lead to a friendly US-China relationship, III. A better US-China relationship will lead to genuine cooperation, and IV. US China cooperation will benefit not only the U.S. and China but also the entire world!

CHAPTER 41

Americans Should Understand What Spoils
A Friendly US-China Relation

—⁗—

ABSTRACT

THE BASIS FOR A FRIENDLY relation is trust, everyone agrees. So what is preventing us to build trust or what is destroying trust is the crucial matter in the US-China relation. Reviewing the history and geopolitical relation between US and China versus the close neighbors of the U.S., one can point out that respecting a country's sovereignty is fundamental in building trust and creating friendly relation. Even though the recent South China Sea saga touches on sovereignty issue, the real crux of the matter in the US-China relations is Taiwan and the Cross Strait Reunification (CSR) issue. Taking a position to impede CSR and provoking China to enter in arms race is the main reason for mistrust between the U.S. and China; ultimately they damage the U.S. national security. American citizens should understand this and urge their government to revise an outdated China policy.

—⁗—

Hi, Doc, how was your China trip? Did you see our carriers in the South China Sea (SCS)? Will the U.S. start a war with China soon?

Hi, Joe, I was nowhere near SCS, I will tell you, China will not start a war and the U.S. won't have a war, so long as the American citizens understand what troubles the US-China relation.

Hey, Doc, You told me before that if the U.S. and China would have a friendly relation, then they could cooperate; it would be better off for all of

199

us and the world. But, if China kept threatening the US security, how can we have a friendly relation?

Joe, do you feel threatened? Are you preparing for war? I am not. When Americans understand the crux of the matter in the US-China relation, there won't be any war. American citizens want peace and prosperity not war.

Doctor Wordman, You are right, but tell me, what prevents a good US-China relation?!

The above conversation took place at a gymnasium, Dr. Wordman gave Joe the following conclusion and story over 30 minutes of walking on the tread mill.

Joe, The crux of the matter in building a good US-China relation is really up to us. The basis for a friendly relation is trust, everyone agrees. So what is preventing us to build trust or what is destroying trust is the crucial matter in the US-China relation. Let me first tell you a bit of history, geopolitics and current events then come to the core question, why US and China won't trust each other?

First, let's look at our two close neighbors, Canada and Mexico. We maintain a pretty friendly relation with them. How? Very simple, we respect their sovereignty. For Canada, we don't consider their 'Quebec Independence' issue our problem; we don't interfere in their racial, language and ethnic issues. We let the Canadians handle their own domestic problems. Trade, business competition, investment, border management, immigration, etc do not impact seriously the US-Canada friendly relation.

Mexico likewise, we had wars but we now respect Mexico's sovereignty. We do not send Mexican immigrants back to Mexico or to build an independent buffer State between us. Again, trade issue, immigrants, border security, even drug traffic do not impact seriously the basic US-Mexico relation. Internally, we might have different opinions regarding trade agreements with Mexico, but we don't send carriers to Gulf of Mexico to make threats.

Now, let's look at China. The reason we don't have trust to build a friendly relation is because we don't respect China's sovereignty. So long as the U.S. interferes in China's sovereignty, we cannot build trust. Trade and technology competition, mutual cyber snooping and border conflict (we don't have borders other than giant ocean) should not seriously impact our relation. So what is the crucial sovereignty issue spoiling our mutual trust? No, it is not the tiny islands in the SCS; it is Taiwan.

Taiwan is the crux of the matter. The U.S. signed the Shanghai Communiqué in 1971 recognizing one China and supporting a peaceful reunification between Taiwan and the Mainland, known as the Cross Strait Reunification (CSR). But instead of treating the CSR as China's domestic issue, the U.S. persistently interferes in the CSR with a motive not so honorable. The U.S. ignores China's repeated declaration that China would allow two or multiple political systems to coexist in China. The tiny Hong Kong is the living example, Hong Kong was returned to China by the U.K. in 1997; it has been transforming from a British controlled colonial island to a democratic governance with her security in trust with Mainland China. Hong Kong not only continues thrusting as a free port and an international finance center but also earning envy as a conduit bridging Mainland with the rest of the world.

Intentionally or not, keeping the CSR unsettled over four decades is a bad foreign policy preventing US and China having a trusting relationship. The history of US-China relation is a twisted one. It started in 19th century while the U.S. was one of the Western powers (UK, France, Spain, Portugal, Germany) invaded China's sovereignty. But the Americans were better regarded by the Chinese people because the Chinese revolutionary leader, the founding father of the Chinese Republic, Dr. Sun Yat Sen, was educated in Hawaii, the United States (Lolani Elementary school (1879-1882) and the Punahou high school (1883) where President Obama graduated in 1979). Many American friends of Dr. Sun helped him in his revolution endeavor.

Sun Yat Sen founded the KMT. After a dozen years, the revolution toppled the Qing Dynasty and established the Republic of China. But the Chinese revolution was never completed due to the ambitious and merciless Japanese invasion and China's internal turmoil. Japan won the first Sino-Japan war (1894-95) and occupied Taiwan. Japan continued her aggression in Northern China which led to the second Sino-Japan war in 1937. While the U.S. supported the KMT, Russia supported the Chinese Communist Party (CCP) during the war. Japan eventually failed in her dream of conquering China. Japanese army was stuck in Mainland China for eight years facing fierce Chinese resistance. Finally, Japan was exhausted and surrendered in 1945 after the U.S. dropped the atomic bombs ending the WW II.

Post WW II, while the U.S. was focusing on the occupation and reconstruction of Japan, the CCP with Russian support won the Chinese internal war. The CCP captured the entire Mainland and the KMT government retreated to Taiwan. Partly out of feeling sorry and partly out of her 'solemn quest of stopping communism', the U.S. stood behind KMT and protected Taiwan from CCP's attempt of liberating Taiwan. As time went on, the CCP parted way from the Soviet style communism which prompted Nixon and Kissinger to open up to China leading to the eventual recognition of one China and the support of a peaceful CSR. However, the U.S. did not take seriously China's pledge of one nation multiple political systems. Instead of promoting a peaceful CSR, the U.S. continued to arm Taiwan under the anti-communist theme. The unsettlement of CSR is the crux of the matter in a rocky US-China relation. Using Taiwan as a part of island chain to curtail China is adding insult to injury, turning disrespect of China's sovereignty to targeting China as an enemy.

Targeting China as a pure Communist country is an outdated concept. Curtailing China's rise is either an insecure excuse or a devious hegemony objective. In either case it brings no honor to the U.S. nor peace and prosperity to the world. China is thousands of miles away from the U.S. compared to Canada and Mexico as next door neighbors, China poses no threat to the U.S. while we maintain the strongest military forces on this planet. Taking a position to impede CSR and provoking China to enter in arms race actually damage the U.S. national security. China's slow but steady political reform should be recognized and pushing China to ally with Russia should be avoided. Encouraging Japan to rearm and deny WW II history is a bad policy. American citizens should understand 'genuinely to honor one China and encourage a peaceful CSR' will create a stable China with whom the U.S. can cooperate to create mutual benefits and world prosperity.

CHAPTER 42

Diagnosis and Solution of Cross-Straight Reunification Issue

—〜〜—

ABSTRACT

THE CROSS STRAIT REUNIFICATION (CSR) issue has existed over seven decades. Both Mainland China and Taiwan have experienced social political transformation and rapid economic development. The reason that the CSR was not settled could be attributed to external interferences and Taiwan's internal complications. However, the time has come for the world to realize that there is no fundamental reason to impede the CSR. The unsettlement of CSR is the basic reason preventing the U.S. and Japan to have a friendly normal relation with China. It should be clear to global citizens that when the CSR is resolved, the US-China relation will become more of a cooperative one rather than a confrontational one, thus leading to mutual benefits and world prosperity.

—〜〜—

The cross-strait reunification (CSR) problem is like a social psychological disease when it is viewed as a Chinese internal sovereignty issue. Because the different historical development happened in Mainland and Taiwan over the past century or so, the people on two sides of the strait have a different identification with the history. The majorities of people in Taiwan maintain an emotional attachment to the Chinese heritage but face a political reality that Taiwan has evolved in a different political system with continued external influences. Due to Taiwan's geopolitical importance, the external influence had been persistent since the ending of WW II. When Japan was defeated and surrendered in 1945, Taiwan was supposedly officially returned to 'China', but China was divided by its civil war that eventually created the cross-strait reunification issue. The CSR issue existed over seven decades and is the critical element impeding a normal relation between the U.S. and China. Why the CSR problem has not been resolved is a question many global citizens, especially 1.3 billion Chinese, 4 million Chinese Americans and possibly all 322 million Americans ought to understand. When the CSR is resolved peacefully, the U.S. and China can have a friendlier cooperative relation creating mutual benefits and world peace.

Let's first clarify why CSR has become a social psychological disease. CSR has a complex background from geopolitical and historical perspectives. Geopolitically, the beautiful island Taiwan (formerly Formosa) along with her surrounding small islands are situated in the Pacific Ocean and has a vital geopolitical importance to the Mainland. Taiwan is geopolitically important to others in the Pacific Ocean and beyond only because these 'others' do not wish to see the CSR completed; in the worst case these 'others' wish to use Taiwan to curtail the rise of China. These 'others' include the neighbors of Mainland China and Taiwan as well as counyries at the other end of the Pacific Ocean and the Indian ocean. These external views have been the major impedance to a peaceful CSR.

Historically, Taiwan was part of the ancient China (1300 or earlier) from a traditional definition of sovereignty - based on discovery, occupation (such as residents of traders, farmers and/or fisherman) and evidential claims (such as documents, maps and other physical objects like monuments). But as a big nation, China's traditional sovereignty unfortunately had often been violated by aggressive invaders as clearly seen in modern history through the colonial occupation by the Western power (Dutch, British, Spanish, Portuguese, French, Germany, American, etc.) and the imperial invasion by Russia and Japan. Sadly, China was the chief victim in Asia among Okinawa, Philippines, Malaysia, Indonesia, Indo-China, Singapore, etc similar to India and Africa. Taiwan unfortunately had a long treacherous historical background being first captured by the Dutch and recovered (1621-1641) then captured by the

Japanese (1895-1945) and returned to China in 1945 after Japan was defeated in WW II. China had a late wakening to the revolutions first occurred in Europe and America; her revolution, though succeeded in toppling the corrupt Qing dynasty, had never been smoothly completed like the U.S. did in forming a Republic nation due to the external interferences. Most devastating is the fact that Japan was anxiously and greedily eyeing to conquer the entire China. China after repeatedly losing sovereignty to Japan's aggression had finally broken out to engage an all-out war against the Imperial Japan in 1937. The bitter battles and cruel Japanese war crimes (including the infamous Nanking Massacre) continued until Japan was exhausted and brought down by the final 'straw' – the American atomic bomb.

Post WW II, China was struggling to complete her revolution to establish a modern republic. This struggle unfortunately was interfered again by her two war allies, the U.S. and the Soviet Union, who turned into post war rivals each supporting a faction, KMT and CCP respectively. Though the two political entities all desired to reunify China as one China but their leaders were pulled apart by their personal political ambitions. The 'external intervention' term was an appropriate description of the Soviet Union's and the United States' support of the CCP and the KMT simply because their motives and objectives were far from achieving a unified China. Had they really honored one unified China, they would have left the Chinese alone to complete their revolution however their own way.

The divided China in many ways like two Guinea pigs as two Germanys, two Koreas, two Vietnams and others were in the post WW II world arena where the Cold War confrontation was orchestrated by the two rivalry camps, NATO and Warsaw. The Cold War confrontation was more focused in Europe for more than four decades eventually resulted in the collapse of the Soviet Union in 1990 leaving the U.S. being the sole super power. But the Cold War did not really end as the confrontation continued and shifted to the Middle East and today pivoted to Asia. It is under the current world politics, the CSR issue remains unsettled and exhibits complexities, in addition to external interventions with added internal complexities.

The principal external influence on CSR can be represented by the Taiwan Relation Act passed by the U.S. Congress as resentment to Carter Administration's formal recognition of the People's Republic of China with sovereignty over Taiwan and the wishful thinking of Japan to get Taiwan to be a part of Japan. Since the Shanghai Communiqué signed by the U.S. and China (2-28-1972) and the Joint Communiqué signed between Japan and China (9-29-1972) both clearly stated that the U.S. and Japan both recognize only one China under the PRC government and expect a peaceful reunification of Mainland China and Taiwan, the CSR should be regarded as China's domestic issue without any ambiguity.

Both Taiwan and Mainland China went through political transformation and rapid economic development. The reunification should have naturally taken place except the above described external interferences and an internal complication. A pro-Japan politician, Lee Deng Hui, with Japanese ancestry and close tie to the right-wing faction of Japan was a deep mole in KMT. He managed to be selected as the President. His 12-year rule followed by 8 years of his protégé 'literally' poisoned and divided the people in Taiwan, with a small but vocal group opposing CSR. This internal complication has created a silent majority being taken hostage by the pro-Japan and anti-China faction. But this internal complication, a social psychological disease can be cured with a simple solution. As the people in Taiwan and Mainland China are embracing the Internet and opening to historical facts and rational diagnosis like this kind of article, the internal complication will be removed and the external interferences will be stopped since they don't make sense. I venture to claim that the majority of people in the U.S., Japan, Taiwan and the Mainland will eventually see that a peaceful resolution of CSR will create a stable China which will continue fine-tuning her reform (one nation multiple political systems) and making economic progress. This is the basis for a friendly US-China relation and world prosperity!

CHAPTER 43

Space Law Should Be Established Before
Space Colonization Takes Place

—ɯ—

ABSTRACT

SPACE EXPLORATION IS EXCITING AND plenty of enthusiasm was stirred up ever since the Apollo landed on the moon. However, the international space programs are not coordinated nor in close collaboration. Although plenty of investment dollars seem to be available to put people in space as tourists or to establish space colony, people have not given deep thoughts on there might be some bad consequences if space colonization is succeeded or what condition the Earth should be before embracing successful space colonization. The title question and other related issue such as preventing space colonization turning to be a space threat worse than nuclear threat deserve our serious attention before pouring billions of dollars into space race..

—ɯ—

The Economist is a reputable journal and its recent Technology Quarterly, Sudden Light, has a number of interesting articles related to space technology. This comment article is inspired by reading those articles, especially by the one on Human Space Flight: The Orphans of Apollo. One central point the article questions is the need or justification for making human presence in space, be it on the moon or Mars for whatever motivation. The article talks about scientific dreams inspired by science fiction and various rich folks ventured into space exploration motivated by different reasons, profit, scientific fame or even Earth benefit (public good), for example by sending power back to Earth or moving heavy industry from Earth to space so that Earth can be a pristine human colony. I must say that the article touched on a nerve: are the billions of investment spent on putting humans into space really necessary and beneficial to human? But the article failed to press further to discuss the question, under what condition space exploration resulting in human presence in space will be guaranteed to be beneficial to the entire Earth? We will make an attempt to extend the discussion to the above question.

A generation of children watched the Apollo landing with Neil Armstrong, Buzz Aldrin and Michael Collin standing on the moon and wondered what would be the next. Fueled by science fictions, star war movies and comic books, people continued to wonder for more than four decades and expect people to be in space. Science needs this kind of zest to make breakthroughs. Today, some people are taking their wondering into action, not satisfied with breakthroughs shown in space launch, robotics technology, or satellite communication, they want people in space, motivated by different reasons not necessarily for profit. Elon Musk, boss of company SpaceX, is one of the strongly motivated; he has talked about being able to drive the costs of space travel lower than the US government can. He also talked about the need for a self-sufficient colony of people on Mars to ensure that the human race could survive on Earth. His purpose is not to maximize shareholder value but to make history, a road map for Mars colonization fueled by methane powered spacecraft.

Peter Diamandis, co-chairman of an asteroid-mining startup, Planetary Resources, had set up in 1996 the Ansari X prize, a $10m reward for anyone who could build a vehicle able to lift three people 100km into space twice in two weeks. It was won in 2004 by SpaceShipOne, an experimental aircraft built by Scaled Composites, financed by Paul Allen, now aiming to build the world's biggest aircraft as a platform for launching satellites and people into space. (Google has also raised a $20 million prize to motivate space research)

Richard Branson, founder of Virgin Galactic and Jeff Bezos, Chief Executive Officer of Amazon.com are into the space-tourism business. Branson's SpaceShipTwo could let six paying customers fly into the zero gravity space and has attracted 700 people paying deposits for tickets. New Shepard, the small reusable rocket built by Mr Bezos's private company, Blue Origin, is capable of taking a roomy space capsule to the same height as SpaceShipTwo. Mr Bezos's ambitions have been influenced by Princeton Prof. Gerard K. O'Neill envisioning moving all heavy industry into orbit taking advantages of the unlimited and uninterrupted solar power with spare to beam back to Earth.

In the above scenarios, workers would live in vast space settlements; the raw materials for manufacturing would come from the Moon and the asteroids with industry waste swept away by the solar wind - an inversion world with orbital space becoming a swarm of industrial satellites employing millions of workers while the billions below restore Earth to a pristine environment receiving much of the living supply from the space. While possibility of realization of such a dream is still scientifically debatable, it would be clear to social scientists that such a scheme only works if the Earth has become a harmonious entity. The serious question troubling every intellectual is then, how does human race achieve such a condition on Earth?

Internationally, space programs are not coordinated, more in wasteful competition. China, Russia and Europe's space agency all aspire to putting people on the Moon. The United States talks of Mars as its next destination, but seems to be moving slowly for lack of funds. It is good for doing interesting science, be it Moon or Mars, but focusing on putting people in space and building colony has questionable merit, especially when the programs are in competition with no collaboration. Most troubling thoughts on human space flights and space colonization are that no one seems to pay attention to what might be any bad consequences if such an endeavor is succeeded or what condition the Earth should be before embracing successful space colonization.

Reviewing human history on colonization on Earth, it was not a pretty picture, especially recalling the recent Go West or colonialism practiced in Asia and Africa a couple centuries ago. The fighting among colonizers was quite bloody. Although space colonization may not have any aboriginal 'beings' to deal with in space, but the successful space colonizer may pose tremendous danger to Earth beings on Earth. One could simply imagine the devastation on Earth subjecting to an attack from space. Parts of Earth may be vulnerable to such stacks by other parts of Earth beings succeeded in space colonization.

Predicting future is hard. Daring experiments are the bases for scientific advances, however, civilization can only advance incrementally with a sound humanitarian footing, a footing must be good for the entire human race. Space colonization can only occur when there is no friction among people on Earth. So before we continue to invest billions of dollars into space exploration, we must study, research and define a sound and ripe condition on Earth for accepting the possible fruits of future space colonization. Should Space exploration be a cooperative endeavor free of secrecy so the fruits will be received by earthlings all together not by just a few? Should Space Laws be established, say by the U.N., to prevent space pollution? And to remove the possibility of turning space colonization into space threat worse than nuclear threat? Should we define the condition of a harmonious Earth so it can be ready to accept space colonization? Space exploration is an expensive investment; it is wise for Earth beings to adequately understand the above questions before plunging billions of dollars more for space race.

CHAPTER 44

Historical Development and Future Significance of G20 Following The Meeting in Hangzhou, China

—⚹—

G-NUMBER CLUB IS A NATURAL creation as the world is advancing in economy and size. There were obvious needs for the biggest world economy to have a forum to dialog on issues related to economic development. Hence at the 200th anniversary year of the establishment of the United States, 1976, the U.S., Japan, the U.K. France, Germany, Italy and Canada formed the G7 with each nation's Chief Minister of Finance, and/or Economics Affairs or Treasurer or Head of National Central Bank participating. Being a club member is a honor representing the country's economic accomplishment and its implied obligation for helping maintaining the world's economy. G7 was functioning for 21 years until 1997 when the economic crisis occurred in Asia, collapsing its finances which drastically affected the world economy.

By the suggestions of the finance ministers and central bankers of G7, the Ministers forum was increased to 20 nations in December 1999, adding Argentina, Australia, Brazil, Canada, China, India, Indonesia, (South) Korea, Mexico, Russia, Saudi Arabia, South Africa, Turkey and EU (included the significant 5 Gold Bricks, Brazil, Russia, India, China and South Africa). Nine years later, just before the 2008 global finance crisis occurred, the finance ministers, to their collective wisdom and credit, decided that their national leaders should be invited to the G20 meeting as well. Each country would take turn to host the meeting, last year the G20 was held in Belek, Serik, Antalya, Turkey.

This year 2016, China is hosting the G20 from September xxx4-5 in Hangzhou City, a city famous for its picturesque West Lake and rich Chinese literature and cultural heritage. Instead of selecting her biggest top four cities, Beijing, Shanghai, Guangzhou and Shenzhen, famous for hosting international events, China has deliberately selected Hangzhou as the host for G20. Judging from the preparation that Hangzhou has put in for G20 and B20, a summit of business leaders of G20 nations with focus on industrial innovation, one can naturally appreciate why Hangzhou as a top ranking civilian industrial city full of enterprising and entrepreneurial spirit is selected as the G20 host. The world biggest online enterprise, Alibaba, is headquartered in Hangzhou, which is a testimony to Hangzhou's industrial power and innovation capability. Sure enough Hangzhou has not disappointed the G20 and B20 attendees.

Before the meeting begun on Monday, 9/4, there were already news-highlights hitting the world press. The arrival of G20 leaders and their meeting with the Chinese leader Xi Jinping were prominently featured not only on Chinese television but certainly on their own national TV. It is definitely a busy and tiring week for the host H.E. Xi Jinping, who attended a marathon of receptions and meetings with the leaders of the G20 nations and their business and industrial leaders. The host was addressed as H.E. Xi Jinping on his nameplate, many Chinese have wondered whether H.E. means anything other than His Excellency, an unusual title used in China.

By being physically in China visiting Beijing and Shanghai in the first half of September, the author had the opportunity of witnessing the continuous coverage of the G20 event by the visual media as well as hearing the sideline discussions off the mainstream media. Firstly, the TV coverage of the G20 event is extremely educational for the Chinese general public, especially for the young people who received a heavy dosage of international affairs. Rightly so, the news and discussions were more related to the bi-lateral encounters between the leaders of China and another country but there was also a significant focus on security issue in the world. For example, the placement of THAAD anti ballistic missiles was bright on the media's radar screen. The exchanges of dialogs between Presidents Xi and Obama and Xi and Park would certainly make impacts on the future course of the event even though the parties stuck with their pre-meeting official positions. Perhaps, this is the significance of G20 and the value of having annual G20 meetings where courses of international events and relations could be modified by physical encounters of G20 leaders. The news media of course had a exciting field day at the G20, while they were anxious to grab the headlines resulting from G20's major resolution, plenty of gossiping report such as the missing red carpet for President Obama or bitter verbal exchange between security staff between the visiting party and the host.

Other than the political significance of the G20, exemplified above, other significance is in the impact on world economy and a side benefit of cultural interaction exhibited in its art performances. The impact on business and industrial development can be seen and projected into the future from the meeting agenda of the G20's companion B20 meeting. The continuity of B20 as an annual event will sure make positive influence on business and industrial cooperation across national boundaries.

Of course, the main focus of G20 is on economy with twin emphasis on trade and investment which are the two main locomotives for propelling economic growth. 2016 G20 meeting have concluded the following solutions:

The G20 shall provide clear direction and planning steps for world economy; Inject new energy into and create innovative method for economic growth; improve financial management and raise ability to resist financial crisis; reenergize international trade and investment and expand their impact to construct an open world economy; and promote inclusive and interactive economic development and let the fruits of G20 benefitting the entire world. Under the above broad principles, the specific benefits to the global citizens expected are jobs creation, more pocket money, better and cheaper goods, and economic growth for everyone and cooperative efforts for dealing with climate change.

One other significant impact brought on by 2016 G20, perhaps not deliberately intended in its initial intent, is culture. Although culture was not specifically included in the agenda of the G20 meeting, but through the G20 entertaining event, culture had always been prominently highlighted. The water theatric show presented on the famous West Lake in Hangzhou for entertaining the visiting dignitaries of G20 and B20 was a spectacular performance. The show was created and conducted by the world-known movie and theater director, Zhang Yi-mou, with hundreds of talented Chinese artists participated presenting a variety of art shows full of western and eastern culture elements. The daring, rich and impressive innovation of arts, music and technology shown through the theatric presentation on water set a great milestone in art performance and integration of Eastern and Western culture. Such an event not only highlighted the intended focus on the theme to push new economic growth through innovation and creativity but also sets example exhibiting mutual cultural impact from multiple nationalities. No doubt this impressive Hangzhow G20 show, inherited and inspired from previous G20 cultural shows and expanded by incorporating more creativity, innovation and cultural elements, will make a lasting impact to future G20 cultural performances as well as a significant contribution to creating a boundary less world culture.

Similar to other international fora such as APEC, G20 Hangzhow offers a great platform for dialog among world leaders to gain understanding of global issues and to reach consensus for solving problems and promoting international cooperation. For the 2016 G20, one can cite a number of meaningful initiatives: First, the development issue has been prominently placed under the global policy framework. Second, concrete action plan has been put in place to realize the UN 2030 sustainable economic development. And third, a new growth has been articulated as an important agenda to define a new growth blue print and specific action plans for achieving new world economic growth through innovation. These new emphases were remarked by the host leader Xi Jinping in the closing session of G20. Indeed, this new focus on innovation is expected to be the key for new economic growth.

CHAPTER 45

Why People Say Donald Trump Is the Peace Candidate

—⚒—

ABSTRACT

NATIONAL SECURITY AND FOREIGN AFFAIRS have become important issues in the 2016 presidential election. The two candidates, Donald Trump and Hillary Clinton have been compared as who may be more hawkish or more dangerous as the next President of the U.S. While Hillary is touting to be more experienced and tougher than Trump to be the Commander-in-Chief, there are voices to express concern that she could be too militant. In contrast, some are saying Donald Trump is the peace candidate. This article collects thoughts expressed on this issue and discusses why people say that Donald Trump not Hillary Clinton is a peace candidate.

—⚒—

Trump appears as a presidential candidate with tough language and he vows to make America great again. One may wonder why we hear that, Trump is the peace candidate. One example is Rosa Brooks who published an article (Foreign Policy, 7-26-16) entitled, Donald Trump Is the Peace Candidate. I read her article and agree that she did make sense in branding Hillary hawkish but she had not much to contrast Donald with Hillary. Rosa claims Hillary is not persuasive as the peace candidate by citing facts related to Iraq, Libya and Syria against her and referred to another in-depth article by Mark Handler in NY Times on 4-21-2016, entitled, How Hillary Clinton Became a Hawk, where Mark said, "Clinton's more activist philosophy had already collided in unpredictable ways with her boss's instincts toward restraint. She had backed

Gen. Stanley McChrystal's recommendation to send 40,000 more troops to Afghanistan, before endorsing a fallback proposal of 30,000 (Obama went along though stipulated that the soldiers would begin to pull out again in July 2011, which she viewed as problematic). She supported the Pentagon's plan to leave behind a residual force of 10,000 to 20,000 American troops in Iraq (Obama balked at this ….). And she pressed for the United States to funnel arms to the rebels in Syria's civil war (an idea Obama initially rebuffed before later, halfheartedly, came around…).″

Handler's article further described another episode, "In Obama's first high-level meeting on Russia in February 2009, …. Clinton, the last to speak, brusquely rejected the idea of making a symbolic concession to Russia, saying, "I'm not giving up anything for nothing." Clinton's hardheadedness made an impression on Robert Gates, the defense secretary, who later said to Handler, "I thought. This is a tough lady." Brook also remarked on Russia, "Worst of all, Clinton seems utterly determined to bait the Russian bear. She denounced Russia's 2014 annexation of Crimea as illegal and she even once compared Russian President Vladimir Putin to Adolf Hitler." Based on Hillary's militant track record as the Secretary of State and her attitude wanting to demonstrate she is a tough lady and tougher than man, no wonder Brooks declared, "I'm voting for Donald Trump, peace candidate! It's simple. Donald Trump is the only candidate we can count on to end 70 years of dangerous tensions with Russia — the only candidate who is actively extending a hand of friendship to our longtime adversary."

The above arguments say more about Hillary's hawkish nature but do we have enough evidence to say Donald Trump is a peace candidate? What about his repeated slams on China on his campaign trail? His message appears to be resonating with many folks in the country. Why isn't this being viewed as hawkish? Since Trump has no foreign policy track record to be compared with Clinton, few analysts can make definite judgment on Donald as they could on Hillary. However, "Trump has boldly laid bare flaws on foreign policies of past presidents undermining U.S. interests and American prosperity", paraphrased from an article by Peter Morici, The Genius of Donald Trump's

Foreign Policy (Breitbart.com 8-29-16). People seem to appreciate his smarts in criticizing the past mistakes and allow latitude for him to learn on the job. Comparing his remarks on China and Russia, his toughness is more directed at trades than at military confrontations. Donald has no preference in liking Russia over China, even though Hillary has attacked Donald's 'kind' words about Putin and accusing Putin helping Trump.

Brooks imagined "a world permanently freed from the once omnipresent fear of nuclear conflict between two great superpowers. Imagine a world in which Russia and the United States stand together as friends and allies — a world in which Donald and Vladimir stand together, hand in hand. With a Trump presidency, we will finally see two great nations, once bitter enemies, co-sponsoring Miss Universe competitions together.... a Hillary Clinton presidency would be a catastrophe, dangerously increasing the risk of deadly military confrontation with Russia." Even though Brooks' article is written with plenty of sarcastic phrases not certain of her beliefs or imagining; nevertheless, sifting through the facts, one may conclude that Hillary is going to be a far more hawkish president than Donald.

Since we have no concrete evidence to pin Donald to be a potential hawkish President, we must find strong evidence to say Hillary would be a hawkish President. First, let's follow through Handler's long article in which he gave a biographic sketch of Hillary's exposure to the military and how she became a hawk. Hillary was born as a daughter of a Republican Naval Officer growing up through post WW II years. She was a motivated political student and went through a transition in the sixties from Republican to Democrat by attending both party conventions. In her own account, after she was married to Bill Clinton in Arkansas, she tried to enlist in the Marines to serve her country but got rejected when she was a lawyer at 27.

When she became the first lady living in the White House, surrounded by service men, she deepened her feelings for the military, exhibited by her visit to Bosnia. After being elected as the Senator from New York, she became close to General Buster Hagenbeck and protected Fort Drum military base from closure. In 2002, Hagenbeck led operation Anaconda, an assault on Taliban and Al Qaeda and became Hillary's personal briefer in military affairs. When Hillary advanced in seniority in the Senate she was offered a seat on either Senate Foreign Relations Committee or the Senate Armed Services Committee, she chose the latter (deviated from the tradition, Daniel Moynihan and Jacob Javits chose the more prestigious Foreign Relations Committee) to deal with Republican hawks like John McCann. Handler remarked that it was a perfect training ground for a woman aspired to be commander-in-chief. Jack Keane, another general, one of the architects of the Iraq surge became the greatest single influencer in Hillary's thinking about military issues, way into her term as the Secretary of State. Hillary had appeared more hawkish as contrasted with Obama.

Micah Zenko in his article, Hillary the Hawk: A History, (FP 7-28-16), has given even stronger statements about Hillary's hawkish track record by review-ing seven prominent situations where she considered the use of American mili-tary force, Haiti (1994), Iraq (2002), Pakistan (2007-2008), Afhanistan (2009), Libya (2011), Osama bin Laden (2011), and Syria (2012). Other than Haiti her opinion was indirectly quoted, she was supporting using military forces in all six cases. Zenko remarked, "Unlike Donald Trump, who has wildly shifting positions and alleged "secret" plans to defeat the Islamic State, Clinton has an extensive track record upon which one can evaluate her likely positions. By any reasonable measure, Clinton qualifies as a hawk, if a nuanced one. "

Another recent article by Paul Craig Roberts (Institute for Political Economy, paulcraigroberts.org, 8-29-2016), Can Americans Overthrow The Evil That Rules Them, stated, "The combination of Hillary with (Paul) Wolfowitz should scare everyone in the entire world. The prospect of nuclear weapons being in such crazed hands as those of Hillary and Wolfowitz is the most alarming though imaginable." Whoever elected on Nov. 8th will have to assume the commander-in-chief responsibility with the power to order, covet actions, drone strikes, raids, long interventions and nuclear attack; from the above about Hillary and Donald, we should understand why people say Donald Trump is a peace candidate.

CHAPTER 46

China's New Work Permit System for Foreign Employees

—⚏—

ABSTRACT

A WORK PERMIT SYSTEM IS tied with immigration policy, industrial and social needs as well as the education system of a country. While China has recognized the need to develop a new work permit system with clear categorization and value points for foreign workers, the government must be cognizant of the changing and reforming nature of industries, societies and education systems from K-12 to tertiary schools. This article presents a glimpse of China's new work permit system and provides some relevant comments.

—⚏—

A recent news appeared in international news media about the subject title has caught people's attention. Naturally, foreigners working in China or having interest in working in China are very much alerted by this news. In my recent travel through China and Southeast Asia, I not only had opportunity reading and hearing this news piece, but I also had occasions talking to some people including taxi drivers, students, business people and foreigners who are currently working in China. Yes, there is definitely some anxiety for some people who very much like to work in China for various reasons such as love of China's culture, the country's social fiber, people's spirit, the language, etc. In this paper, I would like to present the facts (as far as I have learned about the new work permit system) and some relevant comments (based on deductions) of interest to anyone who may be interested in this topic.

China will rank foreign workers in A, B and C, starting Nov. 1st, this year, in nine cities and provinces, including Beijing and Shanghai, then nationwide on April 1st (Be aware, CCP does not honor April fools). It is said according to official sources that the new work permit system is to better serve the overseas talents to work in China, presumably designed to be beneficial to China and the foreign workers. The new system aims to support the nation's drive to promote her economy through technology innovation; hence it will be encouraging the top, regulating the middle and limiting the bottom category of workers to be classified by A,B and C. The official intent is clear and we will discuss more specifics below, however, the implementation details will not be very clear perhaps till next year.

The current work permit system consists of two types of permit for foreign employees. One employment license is issued by the Ministry of Human Resources and Social Security and the other issued by the State Administration of Foreign Experts Affairs (SAFEA). The present system does not provide a clear guideline for a foreign specialist; say from IBM, to apply which work permit from which government channel. The new system will consolidate all applications under SAFEA. Consolidating the bureaucracy is a good thing; however, the integration of the evaluation, approval, data digitization and administration steps probably will take time to develop in order to produce a consistent process nationwide based on the point system described below.

According to China's most recent official census in 2010, about 200,000 foreigners worked legally in China and perhaps with additional 400,000 were dependents. However, an unofficial estimate quoted by a consultant in HR service business today placed the figure of foreign workers at two million with more than 300,000 working illegally, mostly on tourist visa. As the US illegal immigration issue being high on her presidential election debate list, it is no surprise that the Chinese government is looking ahead to avoid an explosive illegal immigration problem and wants to tighten the control of foreign employees both from economic development point of view and from national security concern. China's minority populations are mostly in the north and the west bordering less developed nations, for example, Inner Mongolia bordering the independent Outer Mongolia presenting a special situation very different from foreign workers say coming from the Western countries or Japan, Korea, Vietnam, India, Singapore or Africa. One may point out that the foreign work permit and immigration policy towards Mongolian deserves special attention from the government, perhaps requiring exceptional rules deviated from the general point system, simply because an 'affirmative action' type of work/immigration policy will be helpful for Mongolian integration in China.

With China moving towards an internal consumption driven, industry upgrading and innovation stimulated economy, the country needs more talented foreign workers, in state owned enterprises, private companies and foreign corporations operating in China. The new system naturally will streamline the administrative process of foreign work permit application, but it does cause concern among some current foreign workers. For example, an American high school teacher teaching English in a Chinese elementary school is wondering how will teachers be categorized and what kind of scoring system will be used in categorizing teachers into A,B or C work permit?

On this teacher's concern, I can offer some relevant comments. It is not the color of the skin or hair or surname or birthplace that is critical in teaching English to Chinese children, it is the other elements, such as cultural background, parenting experience, educational level, teaching methods, of course, plus the fluency and good pronunciation of English that determine a good English teacher (especially to kids). As an example, I would rate an oversea Chinese, Mr. Wang, retired at age of 65 lived and worked forty years in the United States with confidence and desire to teach English in China higher than Mr. Smith, a 25 year old native born American or Britton or Ausie. Sadly, the current value system in China would pay a 25 year old Mr. Smith double the salary than a 65 year old Mr. Wang even Mr. Wang speaks just fluently, having a PhD with more knowledge in history, science, and Chinese culture than Mr. Smith. The sad value system is obviously a result of public perception. The government's point system must consider the above situation to correct the public perception in order to benefit Chinese children on learning foreign languages. In my opinion, Mr. Smith is better qualified to teach millions of Chinese English teachers who needs to improve or correct their English pronunciation.

In a publication by the Ministry of Human Resources and Social Security in China's Organization Personnel Newspaper, some clarifications of the classification system are given as follows:

A point system will be used to classify work permit (jobs) according to salary, education level, special skills, Chinese language skills, age, etc into three categories: 1. Class A, top professional, innovative and creative talent with 85 points or more; 2. Class B, professionals needed in China's economic development plans, short-term gap fulfillment, including management and technical skills with 60 points or more; and 3. Class C, unskilled and service workers with less than 60 points. There will be limits in class B in international trade, sports, culture and education areas and Class C will be strictly limited. The above point system is what I know so far; I am sure more details will be available nearing its implementation.

Logically, a point system is perhaps necessary for administering the millions of foreign workers in China, but the implementation must contain thorough considerations including examples cited above (foreign language teachers and workers with ethnic background same as Chinese minorities). Hopefully, the SAFEA organization bestowed with the work permit responsibility, will keep an open mind to fine tune the system to work for China's needs in tabbing into foreign talents like the U.S. has been benefitted from the talented foreign workers for many decades and not burdened by illegal immigrants. The key is the Chinese government must design a flexible work/immigration policy not only according to China's industrial and social needs but also must respond to and to some degree dictate China's reforming education system, where foreign workers are both needed (more in K-12 schools) and produced (more in tertiary schools).

CHAPTER 47

From President Obama to Dr. Sun Yat Sen on Political Philosophy

—ɷ—

Abstract

Dr. Sun Yat-Sen (11/12/1866-3/12/1925) and President Obama are alumni of the same high school in Hawaii. Obama has become the 44th President of the U.S. whereas Dr. Sun had devoted his entire life to the Chinese revolution. Being a unifier and loving person, he yielded his Presidency to another ambitious politician in order to prevent the infant Republic nation to be fractured. He had to lead a second revolution when the warlords tried to revert the Republic back to an imperial nation. He did not live to see a united China but his political philosophy and doctrine live on. The successes of modern Chinese governments in improving their citizens' economic welfare are largely due to practicing of his political teaching. With further adaptation of his political philosophy, China is expected to rise peacefully and is able to guide the world to 'Global Harmony'.

—ɷ—

Mr. Barack Obama as the first black American president carries a big halo over his head. He even won the Nobel Peace Prize on October 9, 2009, 'for his extraordinary efforts to strengthen international diplomacy and cooperation between people'. Now at the end of his second term, President Obama receives less respect and attention as a leader though still a good orator. His election victories had a lot to do with his educated and devoted campaigner wife and his opponents' messy divorces. In 2004 Senate race, his primary opponent, Blair

Hull (D) and Republican opponent, Jack Ryan, both failed their campaign by scandalous divorce history. With George Bush's approval rating dropping owing to Middle East wars and a financial crisis percolating, Obama projected as a 'change' candidate with powerful campaign speeches emerged as the Democratic nominee and beat the weak Republican McCain-Pellan ticket. Little accomplishment had he achieved in his brief one term Senatorial career as well as few proud accomplishments had he made through his presidential campaign promise of "change". No coherent vision had been cast regarding global peace and prosperity. His signature program, "Obamacare", met with numerous technical problems and may be overturned if Trump won this Presidential election.

Obama's Middle East solution can hardly meet the expectation of the Nobel Peace Prize and his 'Pivot to Asia' foreign policy may go down in history as a 'kimono dress', pretty but impractical (only Japanese like it), rather than as an intended waterproof steel curtain (navy strategy) to contain China. All the maneuvers of creating a Trans-Pacific Partnership (TPP), military exercises/alliances, and diplomatic initiatives regarding South China Sea seem to achieve no global objectives other than flexing the U.S. military muscle for restating her superpower status. Understandably, Obama has received a lukewarm reception at the 2016 G20 meeting and a declining approval rating at home from the American public. Never the less, Obama, being the 44th and a two-term American President, is still a distinguished alumnus (1979) of the first rate Punahou High School in Hawaii, renowned for its graduates becoming great achievers in many fields, arts, sciences, medicines,....... engineering, military, philosophy and humanities including numerous elected representatives and government officials with Obama topping the list.

This brings me to Dr. Sun Yat-Sen (11/12/1866-3/12/1925) who had attended Punahou in 1883 for a year. So Dr. Sun is technically a 'quasi-alumnus' nearly 100 years senior of Obama. Dr. Sun might not have been ranked high on Punahou's list of achievers, might even be ignored by contemporary Punahou graduates perhaps more sadly by all American people, but Dr. Sun was a great political philosopher regardless. I said 'sadly', because, Dr. Sun, as a statesman and a revolution leader, deserves more respect than most political leaders, not only for what he had done, said and published in his time but more importantly for his profound political philosophy which will continue to impact the world, through the rise of China, on account of the Chinese people and hopefully the entire global citizens following his political philosophy and teachings.

Dr. Sun Yat-Sen studied medicine and was a great doctor. He gave up his profession and started and devoted his life to the Chinese revolutionary. He inspired many people to follow him and eventually overthrew the Qing Dynasty in 1911 and founded the Republic of China (ROC). He was appointed as its first Provisional President. To prevent a prolonged civil war and possible foreign intervention from undermining the infant republic, Sun yielded his President position to Yuan Shi-Kai, a warlord in the North. Yuan attempted to turn the Republic back to an Imperial state. Sun had to lead a second revolution by founding the party, KMT. Sun was a unifying figure but he did not live to see the unification of China. He died in 1925. He was a unique selfless stateman with high ideals, widely respected and honored by being referred as the "Father of the Nation" or "forerunner of democratic revolution".

As a person, Dr. Sun was a charismatic gentleman, having many admirers and respectful patients. When he launched the revolution against Qing, he received funds and assistance from his teachers, colleagues, and friends including Americans, Chinese, Malaysians and Japanese. His high ideals, intelligence and charisma attracted many folks to his cause and some devoted their lives to his revolution. A lady, Ms. Chen Cui-feng (1873-1960), became Dr. Sun's revolution companion for two decades (1892-1912) knowing that he had an parental-arranged marriage (1885) with Ms. Lu Mu-zhen (1867-1952) who had bound feet unable to follow him in his revolution endeavors. When Dr. Sun failed in his initial attempt (1898) and escaped to Japan, a young Japanese girl, Kaoru Otsuki (1888-1970) had madly fallen in love with him. This brief romance (1903-1906) allegedly took place despite of the initial objection of Kaoru's parents but ended when Dr. Sun returned to China for his revolution work. Otsuki later married twice hence she did not receive any recognition by Chinese historians. When Dr. Sun succeeded in his first revolution,

Ms. Soong Ching-ling (One of the famous Soong sisters,1893-1981, elder sister of Soong Mei-ling, wife of Chiang Kai-Shek) 27 years younger than Dr. Sun insisted in marrying him (1915) despite of her parents objection. As Christians, Dr. Sun had to divorce his first wife in order to marry Ching-ling in a church. Ms Chen, his devoted companion, never sought formal marriage, left and remained as friends with Ms Lu. The three women in Dr. Sun's life all devoted their lives to him in different ways.

Although Sun is regarded as one of the greatest leaders of modern world, his political life was not so smooth compared to George Washington who succeeded in fighting for US Independence and became the first President of the United States. Dr. Sun's life was in constant struggle and frequent exile, to Hong Kong, Japan, Malaysia and the United States. The Chinese revolution he led was extremely treacherous, partly due to ambitious warlords fragmenting the country and partly due to foreign interference, especially Japan and Russia with intentions to carve up China. Japan's victory in the Japan-Russia war fought in the battlefields in China emboldened her ambition to conquer the entire China, leading cause to WW II in Asia. The current status of China is the direct result of the incomplete revolution, interfered and interrupted by foreign powers through WW II and Cold War till today.

Dr. Sun was exceptional in his political philosophy. He integrated both Western and Chinese political theories and amalgamated Confucianism and Christianity, which can be summarily represented by Bo-Ai (fraternity, worldly fraternal love), Tian-Xia-Wei-Gong (the world belongs to everyone) and Shi-Jie-Da-Tong (global harmony). These concepts may be ahead of Dr. Sun's time but they are certainly the desired political philosophies today. Based on these concepts, he developed a political doctrine known as The Three Principles of People: Nationalism, Democracy, and Social Welfare, prescribing the priorities and foci for people to build and maintain a peaceful and prosperous Republic nation 'of the people, by the people and for the people'. According to this doctrine, the ROC developed a constitution prescribing a government of five branches, Executive, Legislative, Judicial, Qualification and Surveillance, which absorbed the three-branch government system practiced in the U.S.

but added with an independent qualification branch responsible for qualifying and grading personnel of all government and professional positions to assure people with right skills matching the right positions and an independent surveillance branch responsible for monitoring key public officials to be free of corruption and cronyism. Judging from rampant corruptions and disastrous economic crises happening in governments today, it would be wise for people to study Dr. Sun's political philosophies and teachings and urge Chinese governments to fully implement Dr. Sun's doctrine to reach 'Global Harmony'.

CHAPTER 48

The Real Effect of the 2016 Presidential Debate

—⚏—

ABSTRACT

THE FIRST PRESIDENTIAL DEBATE DID not seem to have created much effect on the undecided voters, but the mainstream media would have you thought otherwise. There are two more debates to come but if the debates would still stay at substance less level then voters would be vulnerable to money controlled media and could not make a good decision. Moreover, a candidate especially a career politician could not be pinned down on any policy with these meatless debates. In this article, we suggest to voters to use a "Ten Dollar Challenges A Million Dollar Ad" strategy to pin down candidates on their positions and future actions.

—⚏—

The first 2016 presidential debate between Donald Trump and Hillary Clinton took place on September 26 at Hofstra University in Hempstead, N.Y. Since the two candidates are both from the New York State, it is logical that the first debate took place in New York State even though the Republican Party and Donald Trump know very well that New York State is a democratic state and all its universities are liberal leaning towards Democratic Party. Hofstra University is no exception. Be that it might, the first debate took place smoothly with Lester Holt of the Washington Post as the moderator. The format was a free exchange debate following each candidate given a two minute statement on a number of issues allotted to six 15 minute time slots.

I watched the entire debate. My impression was that neither candidate made any statement that we had not heard before. There was no new substance, actually hardly any substance at all, a very disappointing presidential debate. The moderator's questions had no depth and the candidates did not volunteer offering any in-deep discussion. Trump maintained his usual style and Clinton were very prepared in make-up, notes, and mannerism, carrying big smiles all the time whether she was quizzed or attacked, for example, with her outstanding issues such as the erasure of thirty thousand plus of her emails from her private email server which she was not supposed to use for doing her job as the Secretary of State. Donald did remark that Hillary did not have the temperament to be the President but Hillary tactically handled his accusation with her big smile.

Post debate, the mainstream almost unanimously wanted you (the audience) to believe that Hillary won the debate hands down. I was wondering, Hillary won by what, a calmer poise than her usual stance or her emotionless big smile? Winning a presidential debate must win by content, message and intellectual political substance, but we heard none. Did we hear the difference between reducing taxes (Donald) and raising taxes (Hillary) in how exactly it will be implemented through what tax system, how exactly the government budget will be affected, what exactly the impact it will have on what people and be exhibited where? We heard none of that other than Hillary saying: read my website. Shouldn't a president be able to articulate any issue and solution to the public in speeches?

As time moved on, more sensible analytical comments about the presidential debate should emerge, at least for the sake of or the benefit of the next debate to be held on October 9th at the University of St Louis, St Louis, MO. In another paper, I have commented about how citizens especially Chinese Americans should vote on issues and not by party line. In American politics, party doctrines have become so politically correct and far from the politicians actual deeds (reality of their actions not their words). The voters must watch, examine and predict the politicians' deeds not from their words; of course, that is very hard for voters especially when the mainstream media dwell mostly on the 'political correctness' rather than evaluating on past behaviors and performances of a politician. It seems that the mainstream media are more eager to preach than to investigate to give the public the materials to watch, examine and predict who may be a better candidate.

So what can voters do? Yes, there are some organic media which are trying to do an honest job by refusing to accept 'political' donations or to be bought by 'Ad money'. But we all know it is hard to find organic media totally free from money hand. So what shall voters do? Unfortunately, my answer is also to use money, but I am talking about small amount of money to counter the big money like millions of dollars spent on TV, newspapers, radio, etc. I may have mentioned this before, but I will get into more specific here for this Presidential election so we may make a wise decision in selecting our next President.

Let's face it, we know politics are influenced by money so we have no choice but to join the game, but we must use our money wisely, based on an old idiom, "Four Ounce Tips Over Two Thousand Pounds" or translated in today's language, "Ten Dollar Contribution Challenges A Million Dollar Ad". Is this possible? I think so, if more people understand how to do it. The method isn't difficult and can be illustrated by a few examples below.

If you were a Sanders supporter before, you are now facing the choice between Hillary and Trump, all you need to do is sending Hillary a ten dollar (or twenty five) contribution attaching a number of questions on the check demanding receiving answers before they cash the check. For example, you support Bernie's free tuition idea, ask how exactly Hillary can realize that now she is in favor of it. Another example, Hillary wants to increase taxes on the 1%, ask her which tax avenue will be used and how much are to be gained and which loop holes must be plucked in order to realize the effect she claimed? If Hillary cashes the check without addressing the questions then you should demand a refund through public media if necessary. If Hillary returns the check, at least you know she is honest and won't be able to keep her promises.

Likewise, if you (say, a Ted Cruz supporter) want to ascertain whether Trump is truly conservative, you can send him a small check with a few questions. Now that Ted Cruz announced his support for Trump with six reasons and Trump has welcomed Cruz's support, then you can challenge Trump on any of the six reasons, asking him which one he will support, pinning him down so to speak. Another example, now Paul Ryan is openly supporting Trump, you may send a small check to Donald with a question: how is he going to work with Ryan, ask him to name some potential cabinet appointees. The above questions are just suggested examples, surely you should ask your own questions. If you are really concerned with America's future, our democracy, we, the majority, must counter the big money which has control over the major media to rig the election. We, the majority or any voting bloc must use the "ten dollar against million" strategy to steer the politic correctness to the truth. I believe that a half million voters sending their questions with ten dollars will have a bigger impact on the candidate than a five million dollar individual donor or money group.

Send the ten dollars by certified mail and demand a reply for cashing your check has a tremendous power, you will find out more about the candidate than reading news from the mainstream media. If a candidate would refuse to take your money, it represents an answer as well. Send these answers out through public or organic media to amplify the message. In a true democracy, the candidates must be accountable to the majority of voters.

CHAPTER 49

Why Do the U.S. and China Do War Studies Against Each Other?

—m—

ABSTRACT

A RECENT RAND REPORT COMMISSIONED by the Office of Undersecretary of the Army has raised many eyebrows since it touts that the war with China may be inevitable. The report analyzed four scenarios and concluded that the U.S. will win without causing nuclear war if the U.S. initiates the war the sooner the better. At least two articles have criticized the report for making dubious assumptions and suggesting questionable conclusions which may embolden the hawks to prepare war with China within 3 to 8 years.

—m—

For national security and defense, it makes sense to be cautious making broad assumptions and taking long-term view as well as near-term events seriously. Therefore, the Defense Department must conduct war studies based on hypothetic assumptions and targeted enemies. In making assumptions and choosing enemy target, conflict of interest is logically the primary concern. Thus it is fairly easy to understand that, if two countries have serious conflicts, they would likely be hypothetical enemies possibly entering war if conflicts are not solved. In order to prevent or minimize conflict, each country should clearly define her core interests so that other countries would understand and could avoid escalating a conflict. Often, a serious condition is defined for a particular interest as a 'red line'. We would hope other countries would not step over the 'redline' defined by us, if it was defined and declared rationally.

Among countries big or small, all have their own interests defined by their national or societal ideology, economic endeavors, geopolitical or territorial concerns with neighbors or other countries. Redlines are drawn on certain interest to highlight the seriousness. When a country steps over the 'redline' defined by another country on an interest issue, chances are serious conflict or confrontation will result possibly leading to war. Hence logically war studies are usually made when a country perceives that her interest and redline may be challenged. For example, in 1962, the Soviet Union was going to install missiles in Cuba which obviously threatened the U.S. security, a clear redline being stepped over by the Soviet and Cuba. President Kennedy took a decisive position to confront them, entering war if necessary. In the end, the Soviet backed down. Presumably, a war study had been done by the U.S. before the crisis; the Soviet Union would never be able to win a war against the U.S. on the battle field of Cuba and in the Atlantic Ocean so far away from the Soviet Union.

Recently, Rand Corporation published a war study, entitled, War with China – Thinking Through The Unthinkable. This study was sponsored by the Office of the Undersecretary of the Army, conducted by the Strategy, Doctrine & Resources Program at Rand's Arroyo Center, and authored by David C. Gompart, Astrid Stuth Cervallos and Christina L. Garafola (ISBN 978-0-8330-950-0 2016). While I was pondering on the purpose of this study, why it becomes public and how could such a serious study be based on wrong assumptions, analyzed with wrong parameters and concluded with wrong implications (worse! leading the readers to think a war with China is to our advantage, sooner the better, strike first to win and no concern of escalation to a nuclear war), a number of authors beat me to it in criticizing the report. One article, entitled, Rand Corporation Lays Out Scenarios for US War with China, by Peter Symonds, was published on 8-5-2016 on the World Socialist Web Site (wsws.org as well as strategic-culture.org & usfriendship.com). Another article is entitled, Making A US-Sino War 'Thinkable', by Amatai Etzioni (9-12-2016, Diplomat). Peter Symonds, a staff writer of WSWS and a member of the Socialist Equality Party, the Australian section of the International Committee of the Fourth International (ICFI), writes with a socialist view against war; however, his arguments of war being not inevitable and too many uncontrollable variables (beyond 'intensity and duration' of the war being considered by Rand) making the Rand report implausible. Amatai Etzioni, a professor of international relations of George Washington University and a military analyst, also questioned the validity of Rand's report because of its dubious assumptions and questionable conclusions (no possibility of nuclear war and US will sure win with first strike sooner the better); the report may erroneously embolden the hawks to prepare war with China eagerly.

Not only am I in agreement with the above points the two authors made but also I want to emphasize that this report gives no regard on two important aspects, one is there was no credible analysis on why a US-Sino war is inevitable based on conflict of interest and what redline each one may be crossing to justify a war. Furthermore, I agree with Prof. Etzioni that the Rand research never bothered to think through what will the U.S. gain in making a first strike and winning a severe war with China? Professor Etzioni questioned 'regime change' as a valid objective, since we have failed in many of our regime change endeavors in the past. China is a big country rising rapidly. The conflicts with China are like competition in the Olympic Games; the redlines are lines defining the race track. So long no one is crossing the red track line to stop the other from racing fairly, there is no serious conflict. Recently, the U.S. declared that the South China Sea (SCS) as our critical interest trying to elevate SCS issue as redline to the interest of the U.S. Let us think about it, the U.S. has no territorial interest in the South China Sea, why should we draw a redline there. The new President of the Philippines, Mr. Duarte, seems to understand that; hence, he is distancing from the U.S., not wishing to draw redline to provoke China. After all, China has kept her SCS interest soft, taking a position that any conflict can be negotiated bilaterally at a negotiating table.

A bible in the Art of War and Diplomacy, Sun Tze War Strategy, is well known in the world and it is taught in many military academies and universities. Sun Tze said unequivocally war is the last resort between nations; leaders must exhaust all other means to resolve conflict before thinking of war. Even under circumstances of looming war, smart leaders must prepare measures to minimize war, however possible, rather than to maximize the war, never provoking war. The leaders of the U.S. and China must honestly analyze each nation's critical interests with people's welfare in mind, carefully define red-lines in a rational rather than an arbitrary manner and truthfully anticipate compromise rather than provoking confrontation. The back-off of the Soviet Union from the Cuban crisis was the blessing of all mankind, a valuable history lesson. Placing Termial High Altitude Area Defense system (THAAD) in South Korea and agitating the SCS issue bear some similarity to the Cuban crisis. A compromising posture will lead to peaceful solutions more likely than beating the war drums and preparing for war. If war would be inevitable between the U.S. and China, battle ground occurring on the U.S. homeland might also be inevitable, an all-out nuclear war might also be inevitable as well. As said by Prof. Etzioni,"as someone who has been to war, I join the many who observe that all assumptions and scenarios about how a war will unfold, hold only until the first missile is lobbed".

The hypothetic war dates mentioned in the Rand report are 2015, 2020 and 2025. 2015 was already passed, fortunately, no war other than military exercises took place in South or East Asia. 2020 and 2025 are only 3 and 8 years away, wouldn't it be insane to urge our government to prepare for war with China?!

CHAPTER 50

Americans Have the Right to Know Why the U.S. Treats Japan So Differently

—⚏—

Abstract

SOMETIMES THE U.S. AND HER politicians have been accused of having double standards, say one thing and do the other, worse hiding the truth. A short documentary video on Youtube by Dr. Rhawn Joseph raised a serious question whether the U.S. had dealt the surrender of Japan and its occupation with high moral standard and ethics. Specifically, Dr. Joseph questions what happened to the $100 billion worth of treasure which was looted by the Japanese Imperial Army during the war? Did the U.S. make an unethical deal with Japan to protect the Japanese Emperor from war crime prosecution in exchange for some secrets, such as the treasure that was sunk in the Tokyo Bay or hidden elsewhere? Why Japan persistently denies her war crimes and the U.S. stays mute as a bystander? This article raises many more questions and urges Americans to find out the truth for the sake of healing war wounds and holding Justice.

—⚏—

A seventeen minute video (https://www.youtube.com/watch?v=Le7SCVNA7Z8) is available on Youtube featuring an interview of Dr. Rhawn Joseph, Director and Producer of Rape of Nanjing. The video is entitled, Hirohito & Asia's Stolen Treasures (Why the World Forgot the Rape of Nanjing & Japanese Atrocities). As a Chinese American born during the WW II, I do not particularly like to watch this kind of videos containing horrible images. I would get very upset by the cruelty and atrocities the Japanese Imperial Army committed during the war. I would rather forget the sad past though I do wish Japan would (like Germany) come forward openly and sincerely admitting her war crimes, apologizing to the victims and asking for forgiveness. I believe that 'to forgive and then forget' would be the best medicine to cure the terrible historical wounds inflicted by the Japanese war criminals. But this video's subtitle, 'Why' (the World Forgot the Rape of Nanjing & Japanese Atrocities), caught my attention. I sure want to understand the 'why' and hope to find an answer to why Japan has persistently refused to accept the responsibility of the war atrocities and to apology to the world (Asians and American WW II veterans) seeking forgiveness.; Doesn't this matter to Japan and matter to Japanese conscience? I chose to watch the video.

The horrible crime images shown in the video were very disturbing; I had to make an effort to block them off my mind. However, the central message that the U.S. was responsible for being lenient to Japan from covering up her war crimes, protecting her commander-in-chief Emperor Hirohito, and changing Japan's international image with post war PR work, not for the reason we were led to believe (feel sorry for Japan because we'd dropped the atomic bomb on her) but for a different reason so evil, deceitful, and shameful that we Americans should have the right to know exactly what is the truth. There is no excuse for hiding the truth especially for healing the war wounds and upholding the justice and honor for the American veterans died for WW II plus their families, descendents and millions of American children - to have a clear conscience regarding WW II and the US-Japan relations..

Dr. Joseph is a neuropsychologist and writer with interest in brains, origin of life and cosmology. Although many scientific publications are attributed to his name, very little biographic data is available in the public media. Based on www.thereachapproah.co.uk, Dr. Joseph obtained his PhD from Chicago Medical School and completed his training at Yale University in the Department of Neurology and Neuropsychology. Dr. Joseph has aroused some controversy from his view on the origin of life and his claim of alien life existed on Mars blaming NASAfor burying it. Perhaps because of his controversial character, the above video available in the organic medium never entered the mainstream. However, Dr. Joseph's principal claim is that General

McArthur was fully aware of the war crimes committed by Imperial Japan under the command of Emperor Hirohito but made an immoral and unethical deal with Japan to protect Hirohito from prosecution in exchange for certain secrets from Japan. One of the secrets is the loot of treasures (of the order of $100 Billion) taken from many of the Asian countries; some were brought back to Japan, some were deliberately sunk in the Tokyo bay for lack of time of hiding it and some were hidden in the country they were looted from or shipped to. Dr. Joseph's claim could be corroborated with other claims, for example, tons of construction wood and coal were hidden in the mountains in Taiwan before the Japanese Imperial army surrendered. Other secrets charged by the Chinese were the files of biological weapon experiments performed on Chinese civilians and soldiers including American prisoners of war.

Secret deals in current foreign affairs are often protected from public knowledge in the name of national security, a reasonable excuse. However, when time passes, those secrets should be revealed to the public especially when justice is at stake. Americans have the right to know what happened to the billions of gold, diamonds and valuables the Japanese Imperial Army looted from everywhere under the command of the Emperor? Were they divided up secretly? Was part of the treasures given to the unprosecuted war criminals in the name of restoring Japan's economy (Dr. Joseph claims that is the reason Japan could recover from the war faster than all other Asian countries)? Did the U.S. receive part of that treasure and how was it spent? These questions matter not in the domain of national security but in the domain of justice and ethics.

What happened to the secret files of the Japanese biological weapon development and bacteria experiments on human? Why is the Japanese Imperial Army unit 731responsible for the deadly bio warfare work completely immune from prosecution from the war tribunal court? Why was the Japanese Emperor, Hirohito, the real commander-in-chief of the Japanese aggression, completely free from prosecution? What were the secret agreements made between the U.S. and Japan for helping Japan to recover from WW II? Despite of mountains of evidence showing the cruelty and atrocities committed by the Japanese on Nanjing Massacre (and many massacres that followed under the order of the commander to – "kill all, loot all and burn all"), sex slavery (Japanese call it the comfort women program necessary for military morale), and human biological experiments, Japan constantly denies them and the U.S. keeps very quiet as a bystander? Why the U.S. as the standard bearer of freedom and justice for the world has always been mute when comes to Japanese war crimes? Why weren't there any significant war reparation demands for Japan to compensate the damages caused in many Asian countries? These are not just curiosity questions; the American people have the right to know the truth.

The U.S. was the occupier of Japan and the Philippines post WW II, but the U.S. (at least General MacArthur) did seem to treat Japan, the culprit of WW II in Asia, better than the Philippines and other Asian regions. It is reasonable to have alliances with Japan, Korea and the Philippines against the Soviet communist bloc, but it was not at all logical to favor Japan over the other Asian countries especially when there was no clear definite enemy target in Asia threatening the U.S. at that time. Japan was a strong economy and competed, in many ways along with other Asian countries, with the U.S., so with Japan's aggressive militant track record towards her neighbors why was the U.S. picking Japan as the favored ally in Asia? When the U.S. offered the administrative rights of the Liuqiu (Okinawa) Islands and the Diaoyu Islands to Japan, it was puzzling to many Asian countries.

We, Americans, freedom lover and justice holder, must know the truth what actually happened seven decades ago; only the truth can keep the U.S. on the side of justice crushing the image of a country with double standard. We have the obligation to bring the organic media to the mainstream to serve the justice.

CHAPTER 51

Macao and the Philippines – Implications
on Political Governance

—⚹—

ABSTRACT

MACAO AND THE PHILIPPINES ARE located in Asia with different cultural background but sharing one common fact - colonized by the Western powers. Macao has now a population of nearly 600,000 and a GDP over $46 Billion and a GDP per capita of $55,860 (and kept growing since One Country Two Systems (OCTS) took effect) whereas the Philippines has a population of about 100 Million, a GDP of $300 Billion and a GDP per capita of $3,050 after being independent for 70 years. Certainly, the OCTS worked very well for Macao (Hong Kong too!) but the Philippines has not fared so well. This paper reviews their history and governance models to find implications.

—⚹—

The two regions are located far apart with different cultural backgrounds but sharing one common fact -- colonized by the Western powers. They have evolved into their present politico-economic status under very different political governance systems. Reviewing their history, examining their governance models and comparing their economy allow us to treat them as two case studies: Can we deduce some implications? Let's first proceed with a brief review of their history and governance models then discuss any implications.

Macao, like Hong Kong, is also a Special Administrative Region (SAR) of China in the proximity of Guangzhou city; the two regions are located at the west and east side of the ocean exit of Zhujiang (Pearl River). The Portuguese at the early sixteenth century were the first to sail to the Pearl River Delta and showed an interest in doing trade with China. It was not until 1557 that the Portuguese established a permanent settlement in Macao at an annual rent of 500 taels (~20 Kg of silver). The Portuguese continued to pay a tribute to stay in Macau up to 1860's. Portugal tried to declare Macao as a part of the Portuguese State of India jurisdiction after Hong Kong was sadly ceded to the British after China lost the Sino-British first Opium War (1839-42). On July 3rd, 1844, the U.S. signed a treaty with China in Macao to officially open a Sino-US relation, but the Portuguese declared Macao Independence (from China). The Portuguese colonial aggression eventually forced China to sign a Beijing Treaty (Protocol of Lisbon.12-1-1887) to accept "perpetual occupation and government" of Macao by Portugal with Portugal's promise of "never to alienate Macao and dependencies without agreement with China". In 1911, the Chinese revolution established the Republic of China (ROC) but she still endured foreign aggression including the 1st (1931-32) and 2nd (1937-45) Sino-Japanese wars. Even at the end of WW II after Japan surrendered to China, Macao and Hong Kong were still occupied by Portugal and the United Kingdom respectively.

Post WW II, the Chinese civil war resulted (1949) in ROC's retreat to Taiwan and People's Republic of China (PRC) controlling of the Mainland China. Then the PRC declared the Protocol of Lisbon invalid but was not ready to settle the unequal treaty issue. On 2-8-1979, China and Portugal established diplomatic relations with China acknowledging Macao as "Chinese territory under Portuguese Administration". Then through years of negotiation, agreement was reached in 1987 to return Macao to full Chinese sovereignty by 12-20-1999. Since then, the PRC has applied her "One Country, Two Systems" (OCTS) formula as the governance model. Macao emerged as a gambling city in the 1960's with gambling industry as her main economy. The Basic Law of the Macao SAR was adopted by the National People of Congress on 3-31-1993 as the constitution of Macao effective 1999 ending the European Colonization of Asia.

In 2002, the Macao government ended the gambling monopoly system and up to 6 casino operating concessions were granted. Under the OCTS formula, Macao not only survived the 2007-8 financial crises but also began to emerge (with casino and city real estate developments) as the main gambling hub in Asia rivaling Las Vegas as the biggest gambling city in the world. Recently, the 5th Ministerial Conference for Economic and Trade Cooperation between China and Portuguese-speaking Countries was held in Macao (10/12-14/2016) where Chinese Premier Li Keqiang delivered a keynote speech and the Portuguese Prime Minister Antonio Costa also attended after visiting China. The Sino-Portuguese forum was established in 2003 by seven Portuguese speaking countries, and now having a permanent Conference Secretary located in Macao. This showed that Macao under OCTS played a central role in trade and investment with Portuguese speaking countries and served as a key trade exhibit center for products from the Portuguese world. Macao's ever growing GDP is a testimony to Macao being a successful example of the OCTS governance model.

The Philippines unfortunately had been a Spanish colony over three centuries from 1521 to 1898. During that period, outside raids by Dutch, Japanese, Portuguese and British forces and internal revolts were all unsuccessful to remove the Spaniards. The Spanish used the medieval European feudal system in governing the Philippines by relocating native inhabitants into settlements. The conquerors, friars and native nobles were granted estates for serving the Spanish King and given privilege to collect tribute (taxes) from the inhabitants. The feudal system evolved into a provincial governance system with cities (plaza) emerged. On the national level, the Philippines were governed by the King's representative, the Governor-General of the Philippines as the head of Supreme Court, Commander-in-chief of the army and navy and the Economic Planner of the country. The country economy depends on trade that benefitted mostly the Spaniards and Spain with little advantages to the natives. The Spanish did induce some commercial exchanges between Asia and America leading to introduction of new agriculture crops and animals to the Philippines.

The Philippines revolution started by Emilio Aquinaldo in 1897 was most fierce and successful against the Spanish among other rebels. Aquinaldo was elected president of the insurgent government in May 1897 but by December, the revolution had developed to a stalemate between the colonial and the rebel governments. By mediation, the condition of truce dictated the self-exile of Aquinaldo to Hong Kong. On 4-25-1898, the Spanish-American war broke out and the Spanish navy was defeated by the U.S. navy. On May 19, Aquinaldo returned to the Philippines and took command of the Filipino forces which had liberated much of the country. On June 12, Aquinaldo issued the Philippine Declaration of Independence establishing the First Philippine Republic. Then in August, the Americans won the 'rigged' Battle of Manila (with the agreement of Spanish) and took control of Manila. (Obviously the U.S. had no intention to help the Philippines to gain independence!) In the treaty of Paris ending the US-Spanish War, the Spanish agreed to sell the Philippines to the U.S. for $20M, later ratified by the U.S. Senate.

On February 4, 1899, the Philippine-American War broke out. On March 23, 1901, Aguinaldo was tricked and captured by the U.S. troops, a force of 65000. Aguinaldo pleaded allegiance to the U.S. but the rebels fought on. In the end, after the infamous Massacre of Samar, the U.S. took over the administration of the Philippines in 1902. The U.S. rule lasted until 1935. The U.S. approved "the Common Wealth of the Philippines" and granted the Philippines real full independence on 7/4/1946 after the end of WW II. In 1962, Philippines changed her National Day from July 4th to June 12th commemorating Aquinaldo's Declaration of Independence on June 12, 1898. Today, the Philippines has a government system resembling that of the U.S. but her economy is weak, comparing to Japan (which also has a US like government but received a significant US aid post WW II).

What are the implications? Macao has a population of nearly 600,000, a GDP over $46 Billion and a GDP per capita of $55,860 (and kept growing since OCTS took effect) whereas the Philippines has a population of about 100 Million, a GDP of $300 Billion and a GDP per capita of $3,050. Certainly, the OCTS worked very well for Macao (Hong Kong too!). Both Macao and the Philippines have much better economy now than their colonial days, a testimony that colonization is bad, but why China's OCTS produces better economic outcome for Macao and Hong Kong in contrast to the Philippines (even Puerto Rico, still under US trust surviving under a federal tax aid) is worthy of economists studies. No wonder the Philippines' new president is bringing a huge group of over 400 businessmen along with his first State Visit to China to explore economic cooperation. Taiwan, another China's potential SAR, should seriously ponder on the merit of OCTS: Does OCTS only work for people having Chinese blood, culture and DNAs? These are the implications!

CHAPTER 52

The Final Presidential Debate and
Election Outcome Analysis

—ɯ—

THE U.S. FINAL 2016 PRESIDENTIAL debate took place on October 19 at the University of Nevada (UNLV) in Las Vegas, Nevada. As usual, the debate was 90 minutes. The debate was conducted by Chris Wallace of Fox News as the moderator. The format is ten minutes of open discussion following a two minute Q & A for each question asked by Mr. Wallace. The simplest conclusion can be made about this debate is that Mr. Wallace did a better job in moderating the debate session. He had asked fair and penetrating questions, shown no bias against any party and controlled the debate process. Comments from viewers of both parties and independents claimed that Mr. Wallace had conducted the best presidential debate among all three debates.

Before the final debate, the media survey and opinion poll overwhelmingly giving Hillary Clinton a lead over Donald Trump as much as ten points or more. According to the American Presidency Project, compiled by John Wooley (UCSB) and Gerhard Peters (Citrus College) with a history dated back to 1999, there were 45 major newspapers with 10,306,701 circulations endorsing Hillary and zero for Donald Trump as of October 18. The list included the largest newspapers, USA Today, Wall Street Journal, NY Times, LA Times and NY Post. This is unprecedented and the effect or impression that the American media had made in the 2016 election was that they wanted so badly to influence the outcome of this election - Defeat Trump - to the point to be willing to sacrifice the sacred 'neutrality' of the media. As a voter, you must wonder why? Is it just because Trump with his free speaking mouth has angered the media or Trump's macho and anti-establishment behavior broke the ethics of the American society or as Trump has said that the media was biased for not so honorable reasons? Media's preference on reporting more on negative news to catch more eyeballs is well known, but why prefer Trump's negative news to Clinton's does raise a big question.

During the debate, the following main topics were asked and debated mostly with expected opposing positions (my comments are put in brackets) : Supreme Court Justice Appointment, Gun Control and 2nd Amendment, Abortion and Roe vs. Wade, Building Wall and Immigration, WikiLeaks on Hillary's 'Open Border' (Hillary blamed on Russia's espionage that had led to the leak. Wallace subsequently followed with a no-punch question: Do you condemn foreign interference on US elections?), Economy and Candidate's Plan to Induce Growth (candidates debated around reducing versus increasing taxes, smart policies/negotiations versus more funds for stimulation), Trump's and Clinton's Conduct towards Women brought up in the last debate and now more women came out to accuse Trump (A tough question for Trump, Trump claimed that the new charges were false and brought on by dirty campaign tactics like the violence disrupting campaign rallies instigated by Hillary's campaign and Hillary never touched Bill Clinton's women issue nor on campaign violence other than enumerated Trump's character faults), Conflict of Interest and Clinton Foundation (A tough question for Hillary, Hillary defended Foundation's charity work and deflected to Trump Foundation; chose not to respond to Trump's suggestion that Clinton Foundation should return the huge donations made by foreign countries with unacceptable positions on woman; Question on This Presidential Race Being Rigged and Whether Both Candidates Would Accept the Election Result (Trump said he had to look at the result and kept Wallace's Question in suspense. This has become the headlines of the media immediately after the end of the debate), Middle East and Placing US Troop Issue, and the final question on National Debt, Entitlement and Social Security (cutting taxes to grow economy versus taxing the wealthy to fund the Social Security benefits and the Medicare services).

After viewing the entire debate and C-SPAN's call-in comments, I was surprised how diverse the issues were considered to be important by the voters. Hence, it is very difficult for anyone to predict how this debate has changed the voters' minds. However, the media did not hesitate at all to come out with surveys and poll numbers right after the debate to indicate that Hillary had won and gained supports in significant percentage points. In this debate, Hillary appeared to be refreshed, dressed in a smart white outfit with broad smiles delivering the rehearsed script lines (sometimes reading), whereas Donald appeared more tired than his previous debates with lips zipped most of the time restrained from taking his usual aggressive stand. Overall, Trump tried to focus on substance and being consistent and Hillary was trying to emphasize experience and plead for votes. After the debate, one particular 'independent' caller stroke a resonant cord with the following remarks: For the first time, he had to do his own research on the candidates since he cannot get truth and facts from the media. The media was so biased that it was scary to him. So for this election much credit must be given to C-SPAN for covering the debates without commentators. Not the same credit can be given to the major TV networks and newspapers syndicates.

Although the final outcome of this election cannot be predicted for certainty, the following scenarios are plausible enough for readers to keep in mind and to reflect on them after the election:

No national landslide victory for the 2016 Presidential Election, in fact, there may be quite a few opposing landslides won on States and Cities reflecting a divided country.

A contest of the election result may actually take place more serious than the 2000 Bush-Gore Presidential Election. The fact that the media raised the 'acceptance' question in the debate may signal that the media may know more than they let the public know.

More embarrassing leaks may come before even after the election with the purpose of warning and correcting the American Democracy (a good intention) or exposing the corruption in the American election process (an evil intention).

If you had read to this far in this article before the election, I plead you to pay more attention to the Organic media and speak out wherever and whenever possible to demand a fair democracy then cast your vote. If you read this article after the election, then you would have witnessed enough and you should have more time to right the wrongs!

CHAPTER 53

Where and What Can the U.S. And China Collaborate?

—⚋—

ABSTRACT

THERE ARE SO MUCH VALID arguments and so many examples for the U.S. and China to collaborate. Beyond the 'global warming and climate change' where the two countries have agreed to work together to reduce pollutions, there is a host of opportunities for the two great powers to collaborate. A few examples are discussed in this paper. Our world has been poisoned by the 'hegemony theory' for too long; it is time for the world powers to understand 'world harmony' (Shi Jie Da Tong) and explore collaboration rather than confrontation.

—⚋—

As the Presidential Election Day arrives, President Obama's two terms will draw to an end in a couple of months. What will his legacy be when he leaves the White House? This is a question many political analysts and historians will ponder, since Obama has had a miraculous rise to become the most powerful individual on Earth for the past eight years. In my view, President Obama's greatest achievement, which will be his legacy, is his effort dealing with 'Global Warming and Climate Change'. The fact that he had met with the Chinese leader, Xi Jinping, and successfully collaborated with China to mutually commit to a significant reduction in environmental pollution in the coming decades is the most positive accomplishment for the Obama Presidency. This effort induces the world to follow as evidenced by the ratification of the Paris Climate Change agreement by both the United States and China announced at the G20 summit in September 2016 which no doubt will lead the world to pay attention to environment thus benefiting the Earth and all its inhabitants.

The benefit of US-China collaboration is tremendous as we all can see in the handling of the 'Climate Change' issue. But where and what else can US-China collaborate for mutual benefits and world welfare? Amid much China bashing, American citizens seem to be brain washed that there is no way to collaborate with China other than target her as an enemy. The hostile rhetorics towards China uttered by the two Presidential candidates, Trump and Clinton, in their campaign speeches are especially disappointing and misleading. On the above title question, I see an American phenomenon of burying our heads in the sand. People use outdated arguments and ignore the facts in assessing China; not only being inaccurate but also leaning towards blaming China for our domestic setbacks such as losing competitiveness in our manufacturing industry and even in research and innovation. A recent set of documentary films shown in Discovery Channel, entitled, Smart China (Exec Producer, Kyle Murdoch, Producer, Verity Mackintosh, Director, Robin Singleton and Presenter, Josh Klein, in Youtube, https://www.youtube.com/watch?v=-h8y3b5NTt0&feature=em-share_video_in_list_user&list=PLbPCj8kYQM0DkgaL3WzQBczJ5PBok2Sq-) clearly depicted a correct impression we Americans should have, that is, the real challenge to the U.S. is how we may revitalize our industrial power by collaborating with China and treating China as a giant market place with talented people, manufacturers and consumers, rather than targeting China as an enemy.

Where and what can the United States and China collaborate then? If we lift our heads up from burying in the sand, we can see that there are plenty of areas and specific projects we can work together for mutual benefits and for world prosperity. Let me list a few categories below and focus one or two domains for more detailed discussion:

(I)   Terrorist Threat: No doubt the Islamic terrorism has become a global imminent threatening which drives hundreds of thousands of refugees running away from their home countries in the Middle

East to Europe, America and elsewhere. China has a significant population of Muslims and years of experience in accommodating Muslims as Chinese citizens under China's constitution. Naturally, China is very much concerned with the current 'terrorists problem'. From world peace and a long term point of view, it makes great sense for the U.S., China, and the EU leading countries to work together to deal with this issue.

(II)   Maritime Pirating: It is amazing with today's advanced maritime technologies, we still see pirates capturing commercial ships in the open sea. The U.S. has the most powerful navy in the world; why isn't the U.S. making demands and providing protection on freedom and safety of navigation in the open sea? This is an action China and many Asian countries would appreciate more than seeing the US Navy conducting military exercises in the Asia pacific. The recent outcry of the Philippines' new President preferring focusing on domestic economic development to foreign military alliances should make us rethink our Asia policy. More than 60% of China's trades depend on safe sea lane transportation. The U.S. Navy can easily lead a global maritime alliance to eliminate pirates and maintain ocean safety.

(III) Developing Countries: China is emerging to become a developed country. She has decades of experience in trying to lift her out of the developing country status. There are so many countries needing help to develop their economy. This is an area that the U.S. and China can perfectly collaborate to promote world prosperity and obtain mutual benefits as well. Opening dialogue and collaborate will produce many win-win projects on Asia, Africa and South America.

(IV) Anti-Drug War: In a 2013 study, it is reported that an estimated of 24.6 million Americans above age 12 were current illicit drug users which is an increase of 9.4% over previous year. The actual number of drug addicts in China is not known; estimates suggest that it is between 2.3 and 20 million people. This may seem like a very small number when compared to China's population, but because of how fast drug abuse has risen, China may surpass other countries that currently have the most drug abusers. Both China and the U.S. are drug transit (and money laundry) regions and huge drug abuse market places. If the U.S. and China could collaborate in prevention, education, eradication, interdiction, rehabilitation, treatment and law enforcement, the positive effects will be tremendous.

(V)   Science Research and Space Exploration: The above mentioned Discovery Channel video offers convincing arguments that the U.S. and China should collaborate. On space exploration, the U.S. adopted the policy of excluding China when the International Space Station was launched in 1998 as a seven nation joint project. China was forced to go it alone in space research. Less than two decades, China just demonstrated her capability of launching a space station of her own and the launching of manned spacecraft. In the past month, China has launched her Tiangong 2 space lab and this month she demonstrated a successful docking of a manned spacecraft Shenzhou 11 (2 astronauts, a man and a woman) with the space station Tiangong 2. The EU space research organizations have expressed interest in collaborating with China, unfortunately there may be some system incompatibility issue. After witnessing China's achievement, even a layman can conclude that collaboration between the U.S. and China in space exploration will be beneficial to mankind.

The above is just a few examples of a host of opportunities for the two great powers to collaborate. The world has been poisoned by the 'hegemony theory' for too long; it is time for the world powers to understand 'world harmony'(Shi Jie Da Tong) and explore collaboration rather than confrontation!

CHAPTER 54

The Immigrants and Minorities in the United States and China - A National Issue Needs A Correct Policy

—ɷ—

ABSTRACT

IMMIGRATION AND MINORITY IS A hot topic in this presidential election. Indeed it is a national issue touching upon our domestic and foreign policy. This paper makes a review of the U.S. immigration laws and their discriminating nature and compares with a far more accommodating philosophy regarding immigration and minority. The author agrees with many Asian Americans in questioning the motive behind any legislation to disaggregate race data of Asians, a mere 3.6% of the US population, into seven categories. Reviewing the historical discrimination and current 'data disaggregation movement' aimed at Asians do raise a flag whether or not the U.S. is making some fundamental mistakes in dealing with a rising Asia.

—ɷ—

The United States and China, the two great world powers, have lots of differences, especially from historical perspective, but they also have many similarities, particularly from national issues point of view. This paper in its limited space will focus on the immigrant and minority issue, an important national topic both nations face but have very different approach to deal with the issue. Since it touches upon many other domestic and foreign policy issues, it is best to start from a broad background review before we enter a serious discussion.

The United States is a young nation formed largely by immigrants making the native Americans now the smallest group of minority among other minority immigrant groups. The majority of immigrants in the United States are mainly coming from Europe naturally bear a common culture customarily called Western even though upon closer examination, they are not as homogeneous as the term Western or White suggests. The United States 2010 Census (race/ethnicity data) classify and show her citizens and residents by (1) White (75.1%), (2) Black or African American (12.3%), (3) American Indians and Alaskan Natives (0.9%), (4) Asian (3.6%), (5) Native Hawaiian and Pacific Islander (0.1%) and (6) some other race (5.5%). The total adds up to 97.6 % with 2.4% defined to belong to two or more races.

As stated by the Census Bureau, information on race is required for many federal programs and is critical in making policy decisions, particularly for civil rights. States use these data to meet legislative redistributing principles. Race data are used to promote equal employment opportunities and to assess racial disparities in health and environmental risks.

The Census Bureau's classification of race categories has been expanded to 15 with 7 to sub-classify the 3.6 % Asians (Asian Indians, Chinese, Filipino, Japanese, Korean, Vietnamese and other Asian) and 4 to sub-classify the 0.1% of Native Hawaiians and Pacific Islanders (Native Hawaiian, Guamanian or Chamorro, Somoan and other Pacific Islander) and left alone the 75.1 % white (European, Middle Eastern, North African, ...), the 12.3% Black and the 2.4% multiple race categories. Does the Census Bureau really believe the 75.1% white is so homogeneous as a single race just because their skin is a little whiter and the 2.4% mixed race people is an unimportant group so they can be left alone. Why Asians must be further sub-classified? What is the real purpose?

I ask the above questions because recently in California, a Data Disaggregation Bill, AB-1726, was introduced by the Democrats to require the government (and California university system which was removed by protest) to collect data on workers, employees and students based on Census 2010's race classification, i.e. further dividing the 3.6% Asian category into seven sub-divisions. This raised a big protest from the Asian community which already felt that the higher education system in the nation is discriminating against Asians in its college admission process. It is a legitimate concern that the Disaggregation Data Act (mysteriously nick named as Ahead Act) will be used to discriminate against Asians rather than benefit them. We will come back to this point later.

We all know that as the US immigrants, Asians had been systematically discriminated, especially in the state of California. California used unfair taxes to discriminate against Chinese immigrants, starting from the Foreign Miner Tax in 1850. In 1852, $3 monthly surtax and $50 per head port entry tax were applied to Chinese. The 1862 Anti-Coolie Act stated, "the act is to protect free white labor and to discourage the immigration of the Chinese into the State of California". The discrimination eventually led to the Chinese Massacre in Los Angeles in 1871. In 1882, the Congress passed the infamous Chinese Exclusion Act, which was renewed for ten years by the Geary Act in 1902 extending it to cover also Hawaiians and the Philippines. The Exclusion Act later was extended indefinitely. In 1907, there was a Gentlemen's Agreement with Japan limiting Asian immigration to the U.S.; later in 1920, there was the Japanese Exclusion Act. The Chinese Exclusion Repeal Act also known as Magnuson Act was adopted on December 17, 1943 as Chinese and American became allies in WW II. After reviewing these historical development regarding US immigrants, it is clear that the U.S. had maintained a white superiority attitude towards other races, Asian, Black and others.

China is a nation with a huge population and a long history naturally involved with absorbing immigrants over her 5000 years of history. Today, China has at least 56 races or ethnic groups with Han being the majority. The famous Great Wall China built and the marriage diplomacy practiced towards neighboring and/or minority races simply explain China's philosophy about immigrants. This philosophy is a honorable one, that is, towards races who were militant or hostile to China, China would not welcome them (However, they would rather build a massive wall to keep the outsiders out instead of having prolonged border wars) but towards races or neighbors who were friendly, they would be welcomed (China either granted them Suzerainty status or accepted them as tributary state allowing free immigration. China often accepted or proposed royal marriages). Within China, the 56 ethnic groups maintain their historical culture, but largely they are integrated into the Chinese society by inter-marriages. Perhaps, because the Chinese people do not emphasize the color of the skin as a measure of superiority rather they consider fair skin only as a beauty factor in assessing females but never on males. In fact, calling a male with a very fair skin, Xiao Bei Lian, (little white face) is not a compliment at all. It is a derogative term reserved to describe a man as good looking but incompetent, dependent, weak and feminine.

As an Asian American, I am puzzled like many others by the new push to disaggregate racial/ethnic background information (data) on the 3.6% Asians with no intention to dissect into the racial/ethnic data of the 75.1% white which consists of different groups of Europeans, North Africans and Middle Eastern (all Arab nations). There are so much inter-mix and integration among Asians and census defined whites as indicated by the 2.4% (likely a minimum indicator) mixed race Americans. There is no justification in further disaggregate Asian data even for healthcare purposes. With the past history of US discrimination against Asians and the interment of 100,000 Japanese Americans during WW II, it is no wonder that the Asian community will question the motive behind any Data Disaggregation of Asians into Asian Indians, Chinese, Filipinos, Japanese, Koreans, Vietnamese and other Asians.

The McCarran-Walter Act, an immigration and naturalization law enacted in 1952 retained a quota system for nationalities and regions. This Act established a preference system which determined which ethnic groups were desirable immigrants and placed great importance on labor qualifications. The spirit of this law is vividly revealed by McCarran's speech in the Senate: "I believe that this nation is the last hope of Western civilization and if this oasis of the world shall be overrun, perverted, contaminated or destroyed, then the last flickering light of humanity will be extinguished." Such a biased concept runs deep in American politics which may be the root of our domestic issues and foreign policies in dealing with a rising Asia. We Asian Americans have a responsibility to correct the government's mistakes.

CHAPTER 55

A Citizen's Open Letter to the Next President of the U.S.

—◆—

ABSTRACT

No MATTER WHO GETS ELECTED as the next US President, we hope that the President will keep an open mind to listen to the American people while sitting in the Oval Office. This election was distracted by too many negative smears which overshadowed many important issues. This letter discusses citizens' views on some important issues in a form of an open letter to the next President of the U.S.

—◆—

This letter is written while the country is sitting on the edge about the Presidential election on November 8th. The two candidates are running such a close contest with different pollsters giving Donald Trump and Hillary Clinton each a lead of a few points over the other. The author of this paper may have his own hunch but can't be certain enough to make the prediction who will be the next US President. One thing is pretty certain that the winner will be either Hillary Clinton or Donald Trump. Hence this letter is addressed to both.

Dear Ms Clinton,

Since you have 30 years of political experience and you are proud of your career record serving our government, you would be running this country your way and the old way. In campaigning for the top job of this nation, you presented yourself as the best candidate for the Commander-in-Chief job. You said repeatedly in your campaign speeches, you knew what you were doing and you know how to continue the work of the past 8, 16 and 24 years to make the U.S. stronger and better. But from this citizen's point of view, our country has not been on a positive trajectory, we need some real changes, serious changes. So, if you became the next US President, I would not be hopeful that you would be a "Change' President but I sincerely wish that you will pause and ponder what were the voices that disagreed with your campaign speeches, by at least reflecting on this letter on its entirety. The remainder of this letter is addressed to Mr. Trump on many issues you sure will face as the first woman President of the U.S.

Dear Mr. Trump,

You claim that you are not a politician; in many ways you are not but you do have some political senses that got you at least 50% of the popular support. However, as the President of the U.S., you must become a polished politician. Taking the Oval Office is very different from taking a Trump Tower Office, negotiation skills and acute financing capabilities are necessary but not sufficient to run the White House. We hope that with your smarts you will climb a fast learning curve and be humble to surround you with many capable people from all walks of life cross party line, since your cabinet must work in a non-partisan manner to make the U.S. great again. A new book, titled JFK and Reagan Revolution -A Secret History of American Prosperity, written by Lawrence Kudlow and Brian Domitrovic, is a good bedside book to read. It discusses how tax cuts, elimination of tax loopholes and bi-partisan support lead to economic growth and American prosperity – a goal you (and citizens) would like to achieve.

Mr. Trump, you have got a number of things right that attracted a solid support; that is impressive. However, this election was distracted by too many negative smears which overshadowed many important issues. Your debates and campaign speeches were not nearly as solid as the votes that you received. Therefore, we present you with our views on a number of issues which were scarcely covered by the media on your campaign trails.

(1) American Economy

You knew our economic ills, deteriorating manufacturing capability, dwindling challenging jobs, and a problematic economy, but neither the cause nor solution is a simple one. One cannot blame it all on free trade or NAFTA or cheap Chinese imports. Sure, trade negotiation must be done smartly for US benefits, but what kind of benefit and who gets it, do we know? When the U.S. economy was the world strongest, capital flew into our productive economy. The US currency remains as the most desired and sought after currency worldwide. When we misuse funds for nonproductive causes bloating our budget running up a huge debt year after year, things changed to create our economic ills. The government spent more on weapon development, military alliances and foreign wars and never made adequate investments in productivity enhancing infrastructure and human resources development. The government allowed our economy to become a hedge or bubble economy led by financial industry and used monetary policy, allowing the Fed to print and pump the market with greenbacks at a record speed never seen before, to fix recessions and financial crises, still hoping to draw capitals to the U.S. to continuously cover our debts and deficits. This model no longer works as foreign countries have become wiser and begun to trade with other currency than just the dollar. We cannot accuse China, Japan or Korea manipulating their currencies, since the soundness of a currency is tied to the nation's GDP. Mr. Trump, we must change our economic model, hopefully your tax cut will also cut the tax loopholes and regulations to bring corporate cash stashed abroad back home to stimulate growth and make the U.S. great again.

(2) Foreign Policies

You are right about our failed Middle East policies. We wasted too much money in wars that got us nothing. Your idea of asking Japan and NATO to pay more for their defense sounds reasonable. However, the issue is deeper than negotiation and accounting. We must review our fundamental strategy of building military alliances all over the world. Do we really need them? Is our security really at stake? What happens if we don't have these alliances and thousands of military bases in the foreign land? The new President of the Philippines, Mr. Rodrigo Duterte gave us a wakeup call on the alliance issue, a longtime ally finally realized the alliance didn't do any good to them (and us!?). The Cold War was over 26 years ago, now we are facing a rising Asia, not just China, it is Japan, it is India, it is South Korea, even Malaysia and Vietnam. Does 'Pivot to Asia' with military presence and adding more military alliances help our national security, GDP and world prestige? Mr. Trump, to be a real change agent President, we urge you to probe this type of fundamental issues.

(3) Supreme Court Justice, immigration, Healthcare and China Issue

You have recognized them as important issues. People will thank you for appointing a conservative judge for preserving our constitution. Repealing Obamacare with a new healthcare insurance law to stimulate open insurance competition across state line to mandate accountability, productivity and efficiency and to keep the healthcare cost from ramping above the general inflation rate is right on. As for immigration, building a strong 'virtual and physical' wall by enhancing existing immigration and naturalization laws are the right directions. This country does need good immigrants.

Both you and Ms Clinton made hostile rhetoric about China although from somewhat different angle. A correct China policy is vital for the U.S. to let us revitalize our economy and avoid futile military actions. The present 'target China' strategy has no valid justification other than hinged on an old legacy 'anti-communism' doctrine. China not only long departed from the Soviet style communism but earnestly embraced capitalism making such economic progress causing us nervous. China's progress is no justification for us to plot an anti-China foreign policy. Many countries (for instance, the U.K.) want to collaborate with China for mutual benefits and world peace, so should we! We urge you to forget rhetoric and focus on reality.

Finally, in closing, no matter who gets elected as the next US President, we hope that our President will keep an open mind to listen to the American people while sitting in the Oval Office.

CHAPTER 56

Singapore - Colony to Independence to the
Future between the U.S. and China

—⚏—

ABSTRACT

AS A HIGHLY DEVELOPED SMALL nation situated at the geopolitically important Malacca Strait between two Muslim countries, Singapore needs to conduct a delicate foreign policy not only minding her neighbors but also caring about the great powers in the world to maintain her stability and security. In the past decades since her independence in 1965, Singapore had adopted a pro-US foreign policy when China was weak having no economic competitiveness in the world. Now China is a very different nation, Singapore needs to reassess the reality and cultivate a role to bring the U.S. and China into a collaborative rather than hostile relation for the benefit of the stability and economic prosperity of the entire South East Asia, of course, including Singapore herself.

—⚏—

Singapore is a small city gaining her nation status only in 1965. Singapore was a British colony. Like many territories in Asia, Singapore was captured by the Imperial Japanese army during WW II. The British military surrendered to the Japanese on 2/15/1942, a Chinese New Year day. The Japanese rule was brief but brutal killing hundreds of thousands of civilians. After Japan surrendered to the allied forces in 1945, all former British colonies including Malaya, Singapore, Borneo and Sarawak were returned to the British Empire in 1946. Post WW II, nationalism emerged and promoted self-governance movement in South East Asia which led to Malaya's independence in 1957 and Singapore's self-governance in 1959. Singapore declared independence in August 1963. Out of economic considerations, Malaya, North Borneo, Sarawak and Singapore joined to form the Federation of Malaysia in September, 1963. However, the Malay centric policies caused friction between the Chinese populated Singapore and the Muslim dominated Malaysia Federation. In 1965, Malaysia parliament voted 126:0 to expel Singapore. Singapore then declared to be an independent nation that year. China and India helped Singapore to become a member of the United Nations.

Lee Kuan Yew (aka LKY) was the founding Prime Minister of Singapore and the leader of the People's Action Party which is the dominating party in Singapore. LKY held the Prime Minister position from 1959 to 1990 for three decades, then maintained a senior minister position during Goh Chok Tong's tenure as Prime Minister from 1990 - 2004 and as a Minister Mentor from 2004 - 2011 when his son Lee Hsien Loong (LHL) became the Prime Minister. LKY died on March 23, 2015 at age of 91; his funeral received over a million mourners and hundreds of international dignitaries. So no doubt Singapore owed her success as a developed nation to LKY for his six decades of government service.

Since Singapore's independence, LKY focused on economic development; he brought Singapore from a poor nation having an unemployment rate over twenty percent, per capita GDP $428 (1960) to a prosperous country of per capita GDP of $3880 in 1979 (nine fold increase over his prime minister tenure) and $53120 in 2011 (14 fold rise at his retirement). Presently, Singapore is ranked 3rd in the world with per capita GDP over $58000. Of course, Singapore also owed her prosperity to her geopolitical position at the Malacca Strait, a conduit of 50% of world trade and over 12.5% of world's oil transport per day (15.2 M barrels per day).

Singapore is situated between Indonesia and Malaysia, two Muslim countries. From LKY through LHL, Singapore maintained a delicate foreign relation with her neighbors on the one hand and sought after the U.S. military presence in South East Asia on the other hand. Hence, it is no surprise that

Singapore welcomes the US 'Pivot to Asia' policy and supports earnestly the Trans-Pacific Partner (TPP) program. However, there is a new changing factor that LKY recognized but did not live long enough to alter Singapore's foreign policy. This changing factor is China. Over the past three to four decades she has risen from a war-torn poor country to a fast developing nation not only surprised many of her neighboring countries but also alarmed the U.S. feeling insecure about her leadership position in Asia.

China's rise is predominantly in her economy, now being the second largest in the world. China has a long history being at the center of the world (The Middle Kingdom). But the two centuries of modern time gave China a humiliating status as a weak nation, militarily unable to defend herself from the Western invaders thus suffered from numerous unequal treaties. Worst of all, she was invaded by her smaller neighbor, Japan, with ambition to conquer the entire China using unspeakable atrocious killings to achieve it. Of course, this part of history should be in the hearts of the Singaporeans since Singapore was also Japan's victim. During China's plight; many Chinese fled from China and emigrated to many parts of South East Asia including Singapore, Indo-China, Malaysia and Indonesia. This history gives bondage among many oversea Chinese immigrants all over the world, including some Singaporeans, who are glad to see the rise of China.

China works hard and is rising fast despite of severe challenges to a poor and populous nation. Bearing the dual entity of a glorious ancient Chinese history and treacherous modern eras of humiliation, China is reviving with a clear mandate - focusing on the welfare of her people to fulfill a Chinese dream - prosperity for her citizens. This Chinese Dream is the reason why China repeatedly insisting that she will rise peacefully. However, the dreadful war memories also taught China an unforgettable lesson - she can never be weak again. This firm belief creates an auxiliary mandate to the Chinese Dream. The Chinese people and most Chinese immigrants worldwide do understand this.

China's twin mandates are coupled. China is trying to chart an economic development path to be inclusive and beneficial to the world as well as to herself. This noble goal is contained in her grand vision of building One Belt and One Road connecting Asia to Europe and beyond. China's military development is by and large defensive in nature; she achieved her nuclear and space capabilities despite of being excluded by the Western military alliances and international space development community. Understanding this background and China's history, one can easily appreciate that China's rise is not a threat to her neighbors or to the world except when someone is purposely trying to thwart her economic development and threatening her national security, she must defend and take counter action.

Singapore had adopted a pro-US foreign policy when China was weak having no economic competitiveness in the world. Now China is a very different nation, Singapore should have seen that coming. From a small country point of view (especially Singapore with a population predominantly Chinese), it is more meaningful to talk heritage binding than talk nation alliance. LKY's foreign policies towards neighbors and the U.S, were smart but now it is time to reassess the reality and review the above mentioned history. Singapore must understand the true meaning of hegemony and national independence from a point of view of large country (such as China and the U.S.) versus a small nation (such as Singapore).

Singapore certainly has options in adopting her foreign policy but the choice must be made with careful analysis focusing on reality not following a legacy. What made it successful in the past may not be in the future. Singapore was ruled by the British Empire. The foreign policy change of the U.K., such as Brexit and Engaging China, and the other ASEAN nations such as the Philippines, Malaysia and Indonesia exhibiting signs of resetting their foreign policy towards China are case studies for Singapore to learn from. Singapore with her majority of population having Chinese heritage should have a even brighter future with China's peaceful rise than other Asian countries. This conclusion is obvious unless Singapore is taking part in any action against China's rise. At this juncture, when the U.S. just elected a new President, Donald Trump, who carries no 'legacy' baggage in foreign policy; it is the most opportune time for Singapore to reset her foreign policy regarding China and the U.S. Singapore could play a significant role in bringing the two great powers to a collaborating and friendly relation and reap the benefits or Singapore could take sides causing more friction between the two great powers and suffer the worst consequence. Apparently, Singapore's bright future hinges on her making a clear and wise choice.

CHAPTER 57

Trump Movement, Phenomenon and Victory - Post Election Analysis on <u>Why</u>, How and What I. Why Trump Represented a Movement and a Phenomenon?

—⚬—

ABSTRACT

TRUMP WON THE PRESIDENTIAL ELECTION to be inaugurated as the 45th President of the U.S. a surprise to not only many Americans but also many folks worldwide. This author has been following this election closely from the primary to conventions to debates and finally to the election. As hundreds of post-election analyses are surfacing in the media, this paper makes a comprehensive review of the Trump movement, phenomenon and victory in three parts: (I) Why Trump represented a movement and a phenomenon? (II) Why and How Trump won the Election? And (III) How and What Does the Trump Victory Mean to the U.S. and the World? There was a lot to learn from this election. The following is part I.

—⚬—

Trump has become the President-elect to be the 45th President of the U.S. and to take office on 1/20/2017. This author has published a number of articles about the 2016 presidential race, the candidates, their campaigns, party conventions and 'A Citizen's Open Letter to the Next President of the U.S.' in anticipation of the outcome of the election. Making prediction on Presidential election is fun but not as useful as post-election analysis on the election process, the winning campaign, the voting and non-voting public and especially the possibility of improving our future Presidential elections. As hundreds of post-election analyses are surfacing in the media, I beg my readers' pardon for using a boastful title to catch your attention. I will try my best to live up to your expectation.

I. Why Trump represented a movement and a phenomenon?

Trump is smart, paid his tuitions in politics his way, donated to both parties, supported many campaigns and then ran for elections himself and learned plenty of the American political system. Trump carefully studied the people and determined to represent them; hence his campaign for Presidency was a movement and the silent majority became his loyal followers and created a phenomenon.

Real Trump: Despite of his flaws and what the media's selective reporting, Trump was a handsome youth excelled well, a bold, shrewd and successful businessman, a best-seller writer and publisher, and a popular TV show-man. Trump has a beautiful family with well groomed children. He is a doer (accomplished tough NY city projects). His political ambition developed after he amassed a fortune, unlike career politicians using solely political ambition to make a fortune. The real Trump is a loving, kind and generous individual and a frank, outspoken and fearless person.

Trump recognized a few right things, anger and fear, stress and despair and disappointment in government in the people and listened to them on their frustrations; he improved his campaign as time progressed whereas Clinton ignored grass-root signals, kept up with the same message in synch with biased mainstream media and never improved her campaign tactics. She paid more attention to the rich and powerful than to the grassroots.

Trump's messages were continuous and consistent with personal follow-up in twits (a huge number of followers), even though not in eloquence.

Voting for Trump is voting against war. This notion emerged during and after the debates where Clinton appeared to defend the war and will have more military actions whereas Trump uttered tough stand on foreign issues without committing specific action. For example, The U.S. will continue to be in Asia for a long time and we will defeat ISIS.

Yes, Trump created a movement, but it is not a revolution but a restoration to true American conservative capitalism, American first, which resonated with the common Americans, the slogan, Make America Great Again sounds more honest than Clinton's Together We Will Be Strong.

Clinton put fuels to Trump's movement and other Republican candidates failed to see the sign of silent anger especially the white middle class - feeling poor and neglected. The more the media and Clinton be littled Trump, the more they fueled the angry flame. Trump became the lone target and he reacted with his anger and earned a martyr image.

Even the usually subdued Chinese Americans got excited by the movement. Usually the young generation Chinese Americans identify with Democrats; their action will overwhelm their parents' votes. But this time more Chinese Americans broke silence and spoke. They identified with the Trump phenomenon. In the 2016 election, more Chinese Americans left the Democratic Party line they usually identified with.

California Democrats sponsored SCAS education bill (2013) limiting college entrance to be proportional to population in the state definitely benefitting White, Latino and Black over Asian Americans. The Race Data Disaggregation Bill (2016 CA Democrat introduced) further angered Chinese, Japanese and Korean Americans who were suspicious about the bill's motive.

Obama accepted 5 million illegal immigrants (interpreted, although incorrectly, as to get votes for Democrats) whereas Trump took a firm anti-illegal immigration stand and at the same time an anti-color bias position.

Trump received too many unfavorable media reporting in contrast to media being mute on anything negative about Clinton (plenty in her 30 years of political career). An amusing phenomenon in this election: New York Times made biased reporting and apologized after the election.

America does not have a uniform value system despite of the American elite waving the flag of political correctness. There are classes and different views clearly shown by the Presidential campaign started two years ago. Trump's defying political correctness hit a chord. For example, Berkeley campus phenomenon and Harvard student's observation: no one can say anything opposing Clinton or supporting Trump, it would not be politically correct – this fueled the anger of the silent majority.

Politically correct attitude and arrogance exposed hypocrisy to people. For example, Peter Thiel, co-founder of PayPal, a gay, made a speech supporting Trump and got excommunicated by Clinton supporters denying him a gay.

Old Democrats despised Clinton's past deeds and hawkish world view. Democrats became party of war opposite to the Kennedys' beliefs. For example, Adam Walinsky, former Assistant of the Kennedys, came out to denounce Clinton and support Trump: Trump dared to say the truth and not being afraid of generals or the activists.

Democratic Party is no longer a party of working class; it did nothing about wages, stood by free trade harming the blue collars, and focused on fund raising from the rich and powerful and painting a false economic picture. For example, former Secretary of Labor, Robert Reich's article: the public see the link of power and wealth and declining wages undermining democracy.

Online media 'trumped'(term in bridge game) traditional media. Despite of a fairly well orchestrated mass media behind Clinton, the Trump team outperformed in online media and twitter communication to voters and small donors, keeping them informed all the way to the finishing line. Also see below how Cambridge Analytica helped Trump to win.

Trust in Government and current administration dropped. (2007 UN study, over 40 years, developed democratic governments, trust in government continuously dropped, even Sweden and Norway is dropping since the 90's) Shown by US Gallop polls, since 70's trust drops in 12 out of 17 institutions, banks, congress, president, schools, media and church, this distrust and fear for the worse are the basic undercurrent that tilted the election towards the political outsider Trump.

Trump phenomenon is the reaction of middle class Americans to attacks on their values by the intellectual and academic communities. Trump had the hunch how big the anger was there and he led and ride with the movement.

CHAPTER 58

Trump Movement, Phenomenon and Victory - Post Election Analysis on <u>Why</u>, <u>How</u> and What
II. Why and How Trump won the Election?

—✵—

ABSTRACT

TRUMP WON THE PRESIDENTIAL ELECTION to be inaugurated as the 45th President of the U.S. a surprise to not only many Americans but also many folks worldwide. This author has been following this election closely from the primary to conventions to debates and finally to the election. As hundreds of post-election analyses are surfacing in the media, this paper makes a comprehensive review of the Trump movement, phenomenon and victory in three parts: (I) Why Trump represented a movement and a phenomenon? (II) Why and How Trump won the Election? And (III) How and What Does the Trump Victory Mean to the U.S. and the World? There was a lot to learn from this election. The following is part II.

—✵—

II. Why and How Trump won the Election?

Even though Trump was not using all the politically correct vocabulary, he resonated with the angry silent majority. He spoke what they did not dare to speak under the political correctness shroud. Then in the course of debates and rallies, Trump spoke and listened and was able to amplify the resonating emotions and built a loyal group of followers which grew day by day while Trump team kept them informed and maintained contacts along the way.

Media ignored the true public and focused on a fake public favoring the activists' agenda. (Even polls were conducted on 'fake' public) Trump took a gamble to fight Clinton and the media at the same time and linked them together with the word 'crooked'. The word stuck!

Clinton and media over played the woman card, not only annoyed the male but even some of the women who did not wish to be viewed as victims who needed protection or affirmative action. Clinton's own image as a tough fighter having no glass ceiling whatsoever just did not lend any credit to the woman movement – most women want glass ceilings in their workplace removed but the White House did not really have a glass ceiling. Her nomination was the proof.

Clinton also over played the LGBT issue and unavoidably tied it to the abortion issue, thus 'having no baby and killing baby' created a difficult position further divided the women voters and most critically lost the conservative religious groups. The continuous attack on Trump regarding his past behavior towards women backfired when Clinton and Trump were put on the same ethic scale.

Rumors can help but also can backfire. Organic and mainstream media generated plenty of rumors but rumors need time to brew or to get clarified. One example of an inconsequential rumor is a quote attributed to former U.S. Attorney General, Janet Reno: "Donald Trump will never be the U.S. President in my lifetime". She died on 11/7/2016. So the rumor had no time to produce any effect on Trump's victory. Plenty of rumors and truth were derived from Wiki Leak on Clinton's deleted emails; they definitely had enough time to do damage to Clinton.

Primary to Trump is like Miss USA pageant and talent show, his experience is no match by Jeb, Ted, Mario, etc. The exchanges of personal attacks did not hurt Trump. For example, Picture of Mrs. Cruz vs Mrs. Trump was a clever way to respond to the 'semi-nude' professional model pose of Mrs. Trump used in campaign ad by his opponent.

Trump has selected Mike Pence (born June 7, 1959 Christian, Conservative Congressman from Indiana) as his running mate who has the right temperament and ideology to support Trump. Pence had done a great job in the campaign winning supporters. Tim Kaine, the Democrat VP nominee flip-flopped on the abortion issue which did not help Clinton's campaign.

The biased mainstream media was somewhat if not largely responsible for creating the Trump Phenomenon and victory. Trump took advantage of online media and did an end run on the traditional media. This will have very significant impact on how and what kind of media will be used in our future elections.

Trump's daughter Ivanka made a powerful and moving speech at the Republican Convention which was viewed by millions of American voters. So did the rest of the Trump family, they earned an up-right impression from the American public.

Email-gate and WikiLeaks haunted Clinton throughout her race. On March 16, 2016 WikiLeaks launched a searchable archive for 30,322 emails and email attachments sent to and from Hillary Clinton's private email server while she was Secretary of State. Out of a total of 50,547 pages of documents span from 30 June 2010 to 12 August 2014. 7,570 of the documents were sent by Hillary Clinton. The emails were made available in the form of thousands of PDFs by the U.S. State Department as a result of a Freedom of Information Act request. The final PDFs were made available on February 29, 2016. The founder of WikiLeak, Australian, Julian Assange (who came to global prominence in 2010 when WikiLeaks published a series of leaks, allegedly provided by Chelsea Manning, an army soldier court-marshaled for disclosing military documents. These leaks included the *Collateral Murder* video (April 2010). Assange had been targeted by the FBI but he escaped to Ecuador under political asylum and continued exposing Clinton's deleted email incriminating her throughout the campaign to the last day prior to election.

FBI Director James Comey who investigated Clinton's email issue, gave her a pass then reopened the investigation eleven days before the election and then gave her a second pass on Sunday barely two days before the election day. The Trump team seized the opportunity in every campaign rally. Clinton blamed the FBI Director for losing her campaign momentum in the last stretch but the fact that she never apologized nor admitted any guilt on the email-gate might have influenced lots of voters to vote for Trump.

Trump is a great Twitter and the Trump campaign out performed Clinton's in email, Facebook and Twitter. Facebook co-founder Dustin Moskovitz donated $20M to Democratic groups to stop Trump but Mark Zuckerberg, Facebook Founder and CEO, defended Peter Thiel, his board member, for supporting Trump. Zuckerberg and Facebook should have seen the data change on the social media regarding Trump phenomenon and possible a sign of victory. Now Peter Thiel is on the Trump transition team which will definitely not hurt Facebook at all.

During Bill Clinton's era the union membership is about 22% and now only 12% of the labor force, thus losing bargaining power against corporations. Democrats buried their heads in the sand and did nothing for workers. They were the majority of angry Trump supporters.

Trump's good personal stories (charity and generosity, for example, he helped a distressed widow/Mom to avoid bank's foreclosure on her home) outweighed his bad manners or big mouth. Another example, 2006 Ms USA Tara Conner credits Trump for helping her to kick the drug addiction which quashed the story that he called 1996 Ms Universe Alicia Machado Ms Piggy for whatever reason.

George Soros was identified as a promoter of color revolutions and a shark in the currency and stock market and he had a close tie with the Clinton's.

Soros' money and color revolution tainted Clinton's image. Post election, some people even questioned why the Clintons wore purple at her concession speech, purple revolution?

Chinese Americans, especially mature age elites, for the first time mobilized in support of Trump on immigration and traditional values and they shouted: we vote for policies not personalities. For example, the group Chinese Americans for Trump was started by California resident David Tian Wang (not yet a citizen but a campaigner for Trump). He had members in 30 states, and many had raised funds to send those airplane banners through their skies. The fly-banner effort started with a 'Chinese-Americans for Trump' member in Arizona, who is also a pilot.

The popular vote is very close differing only by about 1% and the total vote is much less than 2012 election, but Trump won the electoral vote by 306:232. Trump team had far more accurate assessment and put the effort in the right states in the final week.

Excellent work by Cambridge Analytica, which studied the voters and modeled disenfranchised new Republicans versus the old Republicans (Paul Ryan, Mitch Mcconnell and the party operatives...). Trump stood for the new Republicans, caring more about law and order, immigration, wages, jobs and deep contempt for the reigning political establishment (in both parties) rather than status quo for the party establishment.

CHAPTER 59

Trump Movement, Phenomenon and Victory - Post Election Analysis on Why, <u>How</u> and <u>What</u> III. How and What Does the Trump Victory Mean to the U.S. and the World?

—ɯɯ—

ABSTRACT

TRUMP WON THE PRESIDENTIAL ELECTION to be inaugurated as the 45th President of the U.S. a surprise to not only many Americans but also many folks worldwide. This author has been following this election closely from the primary to conventions to debates and finally to the election. As hundreds of post-election analyses are surfacing in the media, this paper makes a comprehensive review of the Trump movement, phenomenon and victory in three parts: (I) Why Trump represented a movement and a phenomenon? (II) Why and How Trump won the Election? And (III) How and What Does the Trump Victory Mean to the U.S. and the World? There was a lot to learn from this election. The following is part III.

—ɯɯ—

III. How and What Does the Trump Victory Mean to the U.S. and the World?

Trump victory may seem to be a disappointment even failure to the Republic and Democratic parties, but in deeper and more rationalized analysis, Trump victory let the voting public vented their frustration and lessened their distrust of the party politics and party mechanism from nomination to primary to final election. Too many party elites were too righteous and shamelessly played sainthood in making judgments on personal flaws rather than listened to issues that were resonating with the voters. Hopefully the Republicans will appreciate Trump victory and correct their attitudes and forge behind him to make America great again. Hopefully, the Democrats will calm down and accept Trump victory with humility rather than anger or hatred through protests and mass demonstration. It is time for reflection not protest.

Many issues Trump raised in his campaign would require policy changes and fiscal budget revamping. Pentagon's budget was one of the items voters were concerned. Trump wanted America's allies to pay more to the U.S. for station and presence helping their defense. The Pentagon may be faced with a reduction of budget or shifting more funds to R&D and military infrastructure investments if the allies do not substantially increase their contributions. Trump must learn quickly about the different agendas foreign states promote. Example, Why is Japanese Prime Minister Abe Shinzo so eagerly flying to New York to meet with Trump. What is his agenda? To get Trump's support for Abe's revision effort of Japan's pacifist constitution (even willing to pay more to the U.S. for defense) or permission to develop nuclear weapon or testing Mr. Trump's plan about TPP? Hopefully Trump as a smart and great negotiator would decipher Abe's eagerness (Abe is in no way in Trump's league) and consider America's interest first not just for the near future but for the long haul. History is the best lesson for international affairs. Trump's statement: "The U.S. will continue to be in Asia for a long time" can be interpreted in very different ways by China, Japan, Korea and ASEAN. We will just have to watch what it really means.

Internationally, Trump's victory surprised many traditional media and public elites but this surprise will probably generate some positive effects. For one, this election, more so than the Brexit outcome, underlined the sacred claim in democracy that people are given opportunity to express their wish under a given democratic system. The American electoral system protects state(regional) interest and binds the federation. The majority of electoral votes represent a fair choice and they uphold justice rather than the growing belief that popular votes can be manipulated by money hands and elites. Trump, spending much less money than the Clinton machine by a wide margin about 1:2 ratio, and yet won the election and gave democracy the needed adrenaline.

One should also recognize that the Internet and social media offer the public a fairer tool to communicate and express oneself than the traditional media which is now proven to be more vulnerable to be bought and controlled. This election will have lasting impact not only on American future elections but also elections worldwide; thus it may be remembered as his legacy even though he has not completed his US 45th Presidency.

China has always been an issue in the U.S. Presidential election. Both Clinton and Trump had bashed and blamed China for US domestic and world problems. The majority of the American voting public may not be very well informed and versed on the complex love-hate US-China relations, but the following four issues, South China Sea, trade war, currency war, U.S. Pivot to Asia Pacific policy (including North Korea and Japan's militaristic ambitions and TPP) had reached sufficient public awareness level thanks to US and Chinese media. As proven by this election, the US mainstream media should not be relied on as the only controlling voice on issues. The internet organic media offered alternatives for justice. China has understood it and Trump has been a savvy Internet user and beneficiary of it. Trump will have to sift through the mainstream and organic media for public opinion in dealing with the four US-China issues currently on the table.

Trump's victory came as a surprise and Trump's transition team and future cabinet appointments are in the spot light. Appointing Mike Pence to be the Chairman of the transition team is a smart move and appointing Reince Priebus is a practical one (despite media's disapproval that he had no government experience) simply because Trump needs a rolodex to run his administration interacting with the Congress. Reince is that useful rolodex on all Republican legislators and some democrats too before it is updated and replaced by a Trump's own White House Rolodex. The media is not shy in making comments on hiring. One advice in hiring may be helpful is that don't load up with Ivy League resumes but pay attention to rural state university graduates who are likely less liberal, more conservative and understanding better the rural America problems. Regarding the Supreme Court Justice, Trump should pick a conservative, energetic, knowledgeable and youthful Justice to carry out the original intent of the constitution.

Will this country be further divided? It is hard to say how the U.S. will change to from a 50:50 divided situation in terms of conservative versus liberal or left versus right. Post Trump victory, we may see the country tilting more conservative but left versus right may have to be redefined from the legacy definition. Is making America great or strong a 'right' or 'left' statement? The post-election protests although significant in numbers but they are on different issues. I guess most likely the demonstrations will pass with no one paying much attention to them.

Will Trump make tax cuts? Yes, he will have to fulfill some of his campaign promises. Trump had a specific tax reduction plan, simplify seven tax rates to three, business, estate, dividend and capital gain tax reductions. Trump must work with Congress to get tax reduction bills passed. Reince Priebus has his work cut out for him.

The following has changed from speculation to prediction, that is, Trump will deal with illegal immigrants issue (building wall and deport illegal immigrant criminals), refuse to accept Muslim refugees (cut funding), repeal Obama Care (at least part of it), start infrastructure building (the stock market already rallied around that and healthcare), reduce taxes (the issue is which tax category to start with), and create jobs (industry elites will come around to Trump's table soon).

Media already speculated that the U.S. relation with Russia will improve. (not because of that Trump had a tie with Russia and Russia helped Trump to win as claimed by the media (that's all baloney). The reason is more likely that Putin will make an effort to improve relationship with the U.S. and the U.S. will welcome it for the purpose of working against IS, solving Syria problem, reducing military spending etc. The improvement of US-Russia relation may not come at the expense of US-China relation as time and condition have changed from the Cold War era.

Regarding China, lessen military pressure and confrontation, but continue economic pressure on China is likely Trump's policy. There were numerous scenarios expressed by analysts, adding tariffs to reduce debt, even renege on debt, and ditch Taiwan (Paul Kane) to get something in return from China; but Trump needs time to digest these complex issues. My prediction is that nothing drastic will take place in his first year or two. Not like Clinton, Trump probably did not and is not thinking about a second term right now. Interestingly, in Xi's phone call to Trump, Xi has mentioned four times the word, cooperation, which must have made an impression on Trump. If cooperation is less painful than confrontation, what would Trump choose? Trump's first 100 days challenge will most likely be focusing on the domestic issues.

Based on Trump's world view and political philosophy, I venture to say that the new President of the U.S. may make a quick impact on the United Nations by letting the UN gaining power and be more effective in managing global affairs especially in the area of regional peace and stability, education, science and infrastructure building.

Will violence protest become a norm after presidential election and other elections? Over 200 incidences of hate or harassment occurred in a few days right after the election. However, no concrete proposals on revising or fixing the election process have surfaced. I would like to voice a suggestion here. A rigid electoral counting method (Winner take all of congressional districts per state plus 2 per number of senate seat) is intended to protect small states with less population but hurts the minority population in large states (here minority means population in rural area but still can be larger than populations in small states) in large state, always losing to the majority population (city population) in every election. A simple amendment could be made to count the electoral votes of large states with population greater than the medium state population (~6.2 million) according to the voting split rather than by winner-take-all. For example, if New York had a split vote of 9 million to 7 million on two candidates then its electoral votes should be a split of 9:7 ratio rounding to whole numbers. This could be achieved easier by a federal mandate.

Did Trump strengthen or weakened the GOP? Trump woke up and strengthened GOP with his victory giving GOP control of both chambers. New Republicans want to crush the crony capitalism, need evenhanded support, and desire a transparent and accountable system where they can share rewards. Trump, not a career politician and party bureaucrat, is in a good position to really strengthen GOP in a fundamental way, but on the other hand, he may not want to do that if the old machine is too rusted requiring too much energy to repair. Trump did more in the campaign than Reagan did in his, hopefully the GOP party will rally around him to seek party reform for party's future. With new Republicans encouragement, Trump will be more motivated to fix the party for the long haul. This is another domain where Reince Preibus may make a mark.

Based on Trump's campaign rhetoric some may say that the US Allies in Asia may have to defend themselves on security, especially the wealthy countries like Japan and South Korea, Japan and the Philippines already increased their military spending. However, a serious arms race in Asia is not necessarily to the best interest of the U.S. even though we may want to sell our surplus weapons. Trump's asking US Asian Allies to pay more for defense should not be interpreted as the U.S. would be pulling out of Asia. Similarly so for Europe.

Trump's negative view on trade issue with China and his positive remark he loves Chinese people presented an intriguing question: How or should he increase economic pressure on China? (Trump encouraged her beautiful grand-daughter Arabella to learn Chinese; a video of her went viral in China) Trump's position on TPP actually will help China and consideration of joining AIIB as a good idea may just lead to a cooperative relationship with China as Xi appealed to Trump.

Coincidentally, Trump just won his 'Trump' trademark lawsuit defending his trademark application in China right after he won the Presidential election. Chinese court reversed its ruling previously ruled against Trump favoring a Chinese claim. Perhaps we will see much more Trump buildings and objects in China very soon.

Will the Clintons face charges and go to jail? Jason Chaffetz, House Oversight and Government Reform committee may hold the key rather than the new FBI Director or Trump himself. Trump is likely to step back to make a decent gesture to forget about the email-gate.

Will globalization take a back seat behind 'America first'? It may not be a mutually exclusive situation in the area of economic development. America first cannot be a closed door policy in this day and age. It is more about using our funds wisely and more productively. The world is studying Trump phenomenon and victory and waiting to see his economic and foreign policy. Kissinger has offered a good advice to Trump: To analyze and reflect to demonstrate that he is on top of the known challenges and the nature of their evolution. Again history offers lessons.

Trump has assembled a reasonable team with due diligence. There were some surprises such as Giuliani who had supported Trump full-heartedly but he did not become a team member. We expect the new team, no matter what their previous experiences were, will climb a learning curve to find a way to work as an effective team in the Trump Administration. The resumes of individuals will be less critical than the chemistry among people. With Trump's experience as a successful CEO and a head of family having all children devoted to him, Trump is likely to be able to build a competent team, by hire and fire, quickly if necessary. (Hiring is nearly complete and firing has already begun.)

There is a simple analysis in the organic media stating that Trump victory will make five losers (Japan, Germany, France, South Korea and Mexico) and five winners (Russia, North Korea, Israel, Turkey and China) in their relations with the U.S. Although the analysis is simple minded but it does have some logic. We certainly should keep a close watch on the future development of the relationship between the U.S. and these countries.

In conclusion, Trump did recognize the anger in the silent majority, a movement needed a Champion. He seized the opportunity and turned the movement into a phenomenon. He did a lot of things right, but most critically he had his own pollsters and used the social media and Internet smartly. He beat not only his strong opponent, Hillary Clinton, successfully but also the biased mainstream media brilliantly and won the victory. He certainly has a lot of challenges lying ahead but his surprise victory puts him in a good position to make a fresh start, permitting a learning phase, bolder approach and a few resets to achieve success as many of his supporters expecting. Trump may very well fulfill his promise to "Make America Great Again" and hopefully not at the expense of the world.

CHAPTER 60

From Kissinger-Trump Meeting to
APEC to US-China Cooperation

—〰—

ABSTRACT

TRUMP'S VICTORY WAS A SURPRISE worldwide. Even Henry Kissinger was surprised; he thought Hillary Clinton would win. Trump is now busy assembling his cabinet but he has found time to meet with Dr. Kissinger to pick his brain. There are a lot of challenges ahead of Trump. APEC, a successful economic development cooperation forum for Asia Pacific nations is held in Peru this month; the APEC leaders are waiting to see how Trump will shape his trade policy among many other issues dealing with US regional neighbors. While Japan is concerned about her defense treaty with the U.S., the Chinese leader offers cooperation to Trump in forging the US-China relationship. Cooperation needs specific actions. An US-China Infrastructure Development Conference seems to be an appropriate initiative to kick off.

—〰—

Dr. Kissinger is not only well known for his effort assisting Nixon to make their historical visit to China opening her door to the world but also known as a statesman well versed in international affairs and diplomacy. He has written many books about the world, China and international conflicts. In his giant autobiographic volume about his service in the White House, he has shown that he is a very perceptive, meticulous and honest person from the way he described the events and personalities he dealt with in his tenure assisting President Nixon in the White House. Kissinger was honest about his misjudgment on the election outcome during an interview by Jeffrey Goldberg of The Atlantic on 11/10/2016. In that interview, he was asked whether he will be meeting with Trump, he said, "I will not reach out to him, but that has been my approach to every president since I left office. If he asks me to come see him, I will." Then upon Jeffrey's last question, he offered Trump his advice to reflect and analyze to demonstrate that he (Trump) is on top of the known challenges and the nature of their evolution. Of course, this is the proper response a statesman should make, offering the President-Elect a polite invitation to meet with a suggested agenda.

The fact Trump is meeting with Kissinger on 11/17/2016, within a week of the above interview, suggests that Trump is a humble leader anxious to absorb whatever wisdom a veteran diplomat and statesman can offer him. On 11/17, Trump had a very busy schedule meeting eight guests starting with Henry Kissinger, then South Carolina Governor, Nikki Haley, Representative Jeb Hanvarling, Florida Governor Rick Scott, General Jack Kane, Oracle CEO Safra Catz, Admiral Michael Rogers, Former Cincinnati Mayor Ken Blackwell. Trump had to squeeze Abe Shinzo, the Japanese Prime Minister (who was anxious to be the first foreign head of State to meet Trump) into an evening meeting. There was no statement issued about the Abe-Trump meeting other than Abe's remark to the press, "the U.S. and Japan will be able to maintain a relationship of trust." Japan's concern about the US-Japan Defense Treaty is understandable in view of Trump's America First political philosophy. Whether or not the U.S. will interfere in the China-Japan Diaoyu Island dispute may become the real test case for the Trump Administration.

The Kissinger-Trump meeting was to talk about 'Events and Issues Around the World' and focused on Russia, China, Iran and EU as reported by the Hill quoting a statement, "President-elect Trump and Dr. Kissinger have known each other for years and had a great meeting. They discussed China, Russia, Iran, the EU and other events and issues around the world," the statement reads; "I have tremendous respect for Dr. Kissinger and appreciate him sharing his thoughts with me," Trump said, according to the statement. Dr. Kissinger was also interviewed by Fareed Zakaria on CNN after his meeting with Trump although disappointing to Zakaria, Dr. Kissinger did not elaborate on any content of his conversation with Trump. Kissinger has interacted with five Chinese leaders for forty years, it is almost impossible that Kissinger could give Trump a core dump about China in one meeting. We would expect that so long Kissinger can keep his health (he is 93 years old) in shape, he will continue to make contribution to the Administration on foreign policies.

Kissinger was surprised that Hillary Clinton lost the election and he remarked that the foreign countries were shocked about Trump's victory. Trump's hostility towards free trade was very explicit on his campaign trail. Hence, there is no surprise, in the 2016 Asia Pacific Economic Cooperation (APEC) Forum held in Lima Peru this month (Summit to begin on 11/19-20/2016), the minds of the world leaders are all on Trump while Obama is attending APEC for the last time. He will not be promoting the Trans Pacific Partnership (TPP) since he has already decided not to send TPP to US Congress for ratification. Both Trump and Clinton had opposed TPP during their presidential debates and campaign speeches thus its death had been prescribed. Obama probably would not be comfortable to field the questions about the new US administration's trade policy since Trump is yet to translate his campaign rhetoric to concrete policies.

Trade issues are very complex involving not only foreign trading partners but also our fifty states with different interests. Trump has attacked NAFTA and threatened a trade war with Mexico, Canada, China and the likes by raising tariff against their imports and designating China as a currency manipulator, but he may not be able to implement any effective solutions. For example, 48 out 50 states have either Canada or Mexico as their leading trading partner under NAFTA, therefore, it means tearing up NAFTA may be a politically impossible task. Regarding waging a trade war with China, neither side will win. Limiting imports or raising tariffs will not bring back manufacturing jobs since they were lost decades ago. In some industries such as garment or some other light manufacturing, low-skill, low wage jobs are actually moving away from China to other country like Vietnam for lower cost labor. On the other hand, China can retaliate on imports from the U.S. hurting our industry such as Boeing jets, high-tech products or American made high-end automobiles.

Trump as a king of real estate is most likely to succeed in accelerating a domestic infrastructure upgrade program. He was right to point that our airports, highways, bridges, transportation hubs, and shipyards are behind times compared to many countries including particularly China. He was also right to say that we need to entice U.S. corporations to bring their cash stashed abroad avoiding taxes back to homeland to stimulate economic growth. It seems that the solution to trade issue lies in the domestic policies such as business regulations and tax policies. We have to make the U.S. a competitive, business friendly environment to compete globally.

The Chinese leader Xi Jinping has congratulated Trump for his victory and called him on the phone for a conversation. In talking to Trump, Xi has mentioned four times the word cooperation for forging a more friendly and productive US-China relationship. It seems that in order to achieve cooperation China (and the U.S.) should take some specific actions. One example comes to mind which can be initiated immediately is to organize a US-China Infrastructure Development Conference. The agenda of this conference should contain business, finance and technology matters in 'infrastructure building' in both countries and in the One Belt One Road (OBOR) program where both nations can cooperate and bring forward their contributions. Certainly, there are cooperation opportunities in many other domains. As citizens, we look forward to seeing such initiatives to be taken up by both countries.

CHAPTER 61

Can We Compare Trump's Future Foreign Policy and Obama's Past Performance?

—⚏—

ABSTRACT

THE ARTICLE, TRUMP'S 'AMERICA FIRST' Is the Twilight of American Exceptionalism, by Max Boot, in Foreign Policy, November 22, 2016 compared Trump's foreign policy with Obama's and expressed concern over result even though both supported quasi-isolationism and non-interventionism. This paper begs for a different opinion based on an analysis of Obama's and Trump's personality and background. The world was surprised of Trump's victory. Trump now holds the key of the moment of surprise as well as the element of surprise. If he can resist the establishment and its old way of doing things, Trump's foreign policy may be more in sync with President Obama's (non-interventionism and quasi-isolationism) but in a good way in terms of achieving real beneficial results.

—⚏—

Rationally speaking, the answer to the subject title must be no, comparing unknown in the future to deeds done in the past has to fall in the speculation category. However, if one takes a serious analysis of President-elect's campaign speeches, one can certainly formulate some predictions. Max Boot, a Russian American writer, consultant, editorialist, lecturer, and military historian, has done just that and published an article; Trump's 'America First' Is the Twilight of American Exceptionalism, in Foreign Policy, November 22, 2016. In his article, Boot, based on Trump's campaign pronouncements, said that "Trump's foreign policy may be more in sync with President Obama's than either man would care to admit. And not in a good way: Trump shares with Obama a desire to pull back from the world but lacks Obama's calm, deliberative style and respect for international institutions." Boot, educated in UC Berkeley and Yale, currently a Jeane Kirkpatrick Senior Fellow at the Council for Foreign relations, has been an advocate of American values in foreign policy. (He once described his ideas as "American might to promote American ideals.) Boot thinks Trump's execution of foreign policy may not be a good way but I disagree. I shall explain my view later.

After reading Boot's article, I have mixed reactions to his arguments. Boot is fairly accurate in recounting Obama's deeds but his effort to predict Trump's foreign policy based on his campaign remarks is commendable but not credible simply because Boot did not derive his conclusions with due consideration of the personality and background of the two gentlemen which are very different. A president's personality and background shape his perception of the world and influence his decision making process in formulating and executing his foreign policy. Yes, both Obama and Trump want to pull out of Middle East and both do not see America has a mission of global intervention or world policing but their perception of the problems and their thought process of defining optimal solution differ. Hence, in the following we will offer a different analysis not so much as finding similarity between Obama's and Trump's foreign policy (Trump's foreign policy may not be so predictable as admitted by Boot) but more on the way of seeking solutions by Obama (hindsight) and Trump (probable approach).

Obama was the first black American President elected by an electoral vote of 365:173 (popular vote 69.5m : 60m, 52.9%:45.7%), an impressive victory over John McCain, a veteran war hero. Obama won the election with the 'change' slogan. Yet, in his two terms, Americans by and large were disappointed by his administration. As a great orator and idealist with liberal social ideology, it is understandable that he sees America as a flawed nation, not an exemplar of democracy rather as a nation needing to perfect herself. Hence his apologetic gesture to the world. Boot cited Obama as a Jeffersonian, a term attributed to Walter Russell Mead, to mean the U.S. should perfect her own democracy and not searching monsters in the world to destroy. However, Obama did not fulfill his 'change' mandate simply because he is a product of the establishment based on his education background and his short political career as a democrat. When he assumed the 44th US Presidency, he basically inherited the foreign policy and proceeded gingerly with his philosophy of 'pull back'. He may be a believer in international organizations and international laws, but his actions on foreign policy maintained the 'double talk' or 'double standard' practice that the U.S. had always adopted. He basically was not willing to challenge the establishment, the US Government-intelligence-military complex.

Although both Obama and Trump seem to support quasi-isolationism and non-interventionism, Trump's 'America first' and his American Exceptionalism (if he ever uttered the word) has to be interpreted from Trump's world perception and his unorthodox political background. Trump is a successful self-made wealthy business person with a different kind of ego and self confidence from Obama has. Being an outsider of the political establishment, a billionaire and a competitive winner with a strong personality, we need to understand his view of 'winning' and his definition of 'making America great again' in order to comprehend his foreign policy. In contrast with Obama, Trump has few strings attached to the establishment. His victory against the establishment surprised them but confirmed and endorsed his self-confidence which will lead him to act more independently and much more daring to upset the establishment in conducting foreign policies. Yes, he will pull out from Middle East but more likely to take an unexpected approach to produce quicker result and show a win for America. His definition of 'winning' is not for his personal gain for money (he is rich enough) nor for any imperialistic gain (not a hegemony believer) but more likely a gain for the U.S. Treasury or national budget interpreted simply as a gain for the American people. Perhaps Mead's term, Jacksonian, "not seeking foreign quarrel but will clobber if provoked", is an appropriate description of Trump, but more than that, Trump is likely to abandon the 'double standard' foreign policy practice and adopt a shrewd business negotiation practice to deal with foreign affairs in security and trade.

Boot and most analysts have said that Trump's foreign policy is not predictable because he has been too outspoken making many outlandish statements (build walls, renege debt, reduce emission accord, kill TPP, apply punitive tariffs, renegotiate NAFTA, reduce commitment to NATO...) Yet in diplomatic speeches, he has kept himself vague or non-committal enough and he is far more transparent and honest than many typical American politician with their double talk – do as I say but not do as I do (talk civil liberty and do killings at the same time). The fact that some Syrian rebels said: "Today, we know that [the Americans] are really and practically not backing us, whereas before, we considered them our friend while they were implementing our opponents' agenda." Trump's transparency and frank diagnosis of international problems may be a beneficial change to our conduct in foreign policy, we just hope that he and his new cabinet can live up to his claim to always make a good deal for American people, not for the establishment at the expense of the American people. The world was surprised of Trump's victory. Trump now holds the key of the moment of surprise as well as the element of surprise (as he repeatedly said in his campaign speeches that the US government must not give away the element of surprise). If he can resist the establishment and its old way of doing things, Trump's foreign policy may be more in sync with President Obama's (non-interventionism and quasi-isolationism) but in a good way in terms of achieving real beneficial results.

CHAPTER 62

Fidel Castro, His Legacy and Future US-Cuba Relationship

—ɯ—

ABSTRACT

THE CUBAN REVOLUTIONARY LEADER FIDEL Castro died at an age of 90 (8/13/1926 to 11/25/2016) for intestinal illness. He is well respected by many world leaders for his persistent struggle in defending an independent Cuba; his life-long revolutionary effort has clearly had impact on other Latin American nations. Castro left behind an anti-US legacy and an unknown future for US-Cuba relation. A review of Castro's life and his legacy may be useful for gauging the development of US-Cuba relation under the new 45ᵗʰ US President Donald Trump.

—ɯ—

The news of Fidel Castro's death came on 11/25/2016. The Cuban revolutionary leader Fidel Castro died at an age of 90 (8/13/1926 to 11/25/2016) for intestinal illness. Castro was loved by the Cuban people despite of criticisms from the West that he had failed in building the economy of Cuba. Castro relinquished his government positions in 2007 when he had health problems. His brother Raul Castro succeeded him. Castro was a firm believer of communism and a socialist government for Cuba. He is well respected by many world leaders for his persistent struggle in defending an independent Cuba; his life-long revolutionary effort has clearly had impact on other Latin American nations, especially Venezuela whose leader Nicolas Maduro is an admirer of Castro. The US-Cuba relationship had been hostile until President Obama announced on 12/17/2014 to normalize the relationship with Cuba leading to the establishment of a formal US-Cuba relation in July of 2015.

Castro lived to see the normalization of US-Cuba relation and the visit of President Obama to Cuba (May 2016) even though he did not meet with Obama. The French President Francois Hollande met with Fidel Castro at his private home in May 2015 and Pope Francis also held a private session with Fidel last September. Just before Obama's arrival, Fidel Castro received Venezuela President Nicolas Maduro who has become the most vocal anti-US Latin American leader. Regarding Obama's visit, Fidel Castro rejected Obama's words of reconciliation and wrote in his column in Granma: "We don't need the empire to give us anything." Apparently till his death, Fidel Castro wasn't ready to bury the past. So he left behind an anti-US legacy and an unknown future for US-Cuba relation since the new US President-elect Trump seems to have a different attitude (from that of President Obama) towards Cuba regarding Castro as Cuba's brutal dictator. Thus a review of Castro's life and his legacy may be useful for gauging the development of US-Cuba relation.

The most prominent legacy Castro left in Americans' memory is the 13-Day Cuban Missile Crisis. The Cuban Crisis is remembered as the Cold War crisis nearly brought a full-scale nuclear war to the world. In response to the failed Bay of Pigs Invasion of 1961, and the presence of American Jupiter ballistic missiles in Italy and Turkey, the Soviet leader Nikita Khrushchev in a secret meeting in July 1962 decided to agree to Cuba's request to place nuclear missiles in Cuba to deter future harassment of Cuba. In the end, President John F. Kennedy took a hard-line in the confrontation, the Soviet Union backed down by dismantling the nuclear missiles and returning them to the Soviet Union in exchange for a public declaration and agreement by the U.S. never to invade Cuba without Cuba's provocation and quietly to remove the nuclear missiles the U.S. placed in Italy and Turkey. Post this Cuban Missile Crisis, the U.S. led an effort to place economic sanction against Cuba.

Fidel Castro was the leader of Cuba's July 26th revolution (1953-1959) over-throwing the authoritarian government of Fulgencio Batista and established the government led by Fidel Castro. Castro's belief in communism and his struggle in defending Cuba's independence had made a deep impression on many world leaders. The Cuban revolution changed Cuba's relationship with the U.S. The 1961 Cuban Missile Crisis further worsened the US-Cuban relationship for 54 years. Over this long period of time, Castro had never wavered in his will in protecting Cuba to be independent against a severe economic sanction led by the Western powers. He built a communist nation at the doorstep of the U.S. which has been the flag holder of the anti-communism crusade ever since WW II.

Cuba has resisted a US led economic sanction through 11 American Presidents. Reagan was known for his aggressive militant stand against communism. During Reagan's terms, the Soviet Union collapsed under an economic crisis that had put huge stress on Cuba. Reagan put Cuba on the terrorist-supporter list and allegedly approved more assassination plans on Castro's life than any other US President. Ironically, Castro was credited for informing the U.S. an assassination attempt on Reagan's life hence saved his life. President George H. W. Bush had wanted to be the first US President to travel to a free Cuba; he had strengthened the sanction during his administration. President Clinton had refused to give US visa to investors who invested in Cuba. Clinton was known to ridicule Castro's long tenure as Cuba's president: "Castro was the president when I was in college, he was president when I was working, he was still president when I got married, he was president when I became the U.S. President, and he was still the president when my term for presidency was completed." President George W. Bush was also hostile to Cuba; he put restrictions on culture, science even sports exchanges with Cuba, limiting Cuban visits to grandparents, parents and siblings only and restricted Cuban Americans to send funds back to Cuban families if they were communists.

The present US President, Obama, fundamentally changed his foreign policy to Cuba. This year marked as the year the U.S. and Cuba had established a formal relationship. Obama expected to improve the US-Cuba relationship, however, to everyone's surprise, the US 2016 Presidential Election elected Donald Trump as the next US President. Trump is not a career politician and he was not a member of the Washington Establishment. Although, Obama's about face approach on US-Cuba relation was not debated in the Presidential debates, Trump's impression towards Cuba was clear from his brief tweet: "Fidel Castro was dead." and a statement after Castro's death: "Today, the world marks the passing of a brutal dictator who oppressed his own people for nearly six decades." "Fidel Castro's legacy is one of firing squads, theft, unimaginable suffering, poverty and the denial of fundamental human rights. While Cuba remains a totalitarian island, it is my hope that today marks a move away from the horrors endured for too long, and toward a future in which the wonderful Cuban people finally live in the freedom they so richly deserve." The statement added: "Though the tragedies, deaths and pain caused by Fidel Castro cannot be erased, our administration will do all it can to ensure the Cuban people can finally begin their journey toward prosperity and liberty. I join the many Cuban-Americans who supported me so greatly in the Presidential campaign, including the Brigade 2506 Veterans Association that endorsed me, with the hope of one day soon seeing a free Cuba."

While Fidel Castro is mourned by the Cuban people as a hero and his brother Raul Castro is trying to model after China in future development, the above statement is certainly not a conciliatory one in nature for burying the past and improving the US-Cuba relationship. In addition, the Cuban Americans represented by Senator Marco Rubio (Florida), Ted Cruz (Texas) and Robert Menendez (NJ) were making statements that Castro's death changes nothing and his Brother Raul (85 years old) has been in charge for nearly a decade. It will be interesting to see the development of the US-Cuba relationship after the new administration takes place on January 20th, 2017. Will Raul Castro groom a successor to emulate China in economic development and to be friend with the U.S. politically?

CHAPTER 63

Meaning of Burning Flag and Mocking Swear-in

—⚏—

ABSTRACT

MOCKING SWEAR-IN LIKE BURNING THE flag is broadly offensive to the citizens generating only hatred not giving any positive meaning. Hence, the ruling by a court disqualifying the elected legislators in the 'mocked swear-in' case in Hong Kong is perfectly justified. In this paper we discuss the significance of flag burning and mocking a swear-in for a public office.

—⚏—

Burning flag is an offensive act, looking from both the 'doer' and 'viewer' points of view. The one who burns the flag has the intention to be offensive to the people represented by the flag. One often sees this flag burning act on public television in news broadcasting. In one category, flag burning is committed by a person not-represented by that flag, for example, an American flag was burned in a war torn city in the Middle East by an al Qaeda terrorist/soldier or an angry mob not Americans. (One also recall during WW II, how offensive to Americans when American flags were burned by the Japanese Imperial army) This act of flag burning is expressing hatred and intending to be offensive to the people represented by that flag. In another category, flag burning is committed by a person or mob identified by the flag, for example, an American flag is burned by a mob of American citizens and protestors whether or not the protested issue is political or otherwise.

In the first case, the flag burning expresses hatred and will only receive hatred back or deep disgusts. Since the act is committed on a foreign land usually by a foreigner, this act is out of jurisdiction of the U.S. law thus can only be dealt with diplomatically or declared as an act of war. In the second case, burning an American flag is subject to the jurisdiction of American law. First, if the flag belongs to an institution or a private entity not belonging to the burner, the act can be charged as a crime - willfully destroying public or private property against the property owner. However, when the property right is set aside, burning an American flag becomes a controversial issue. To some Americans who put personal freedom above the meaning of a national flag (A flag is signifying a nation and government which bears the responsibility to protect its citizens' freedom and rights governed by the American constitution and laws), they argue that the flag burning is protected by the first amendment of bills of rights to protect freedom of speech. However, personally, I believe this interpretation is stretching beyond reasonableness. Freedom of speech can include words, speech, photos, images and acting (drama, play, music, movie, etc) but not actions such as burning (a flag or any other object offensive broadly with no restriction) or waving (a knife or gun or other object threatening with no safety concern). Therefore, I support President-elect Trump's idea to treat American flag burning as a crime threatening the American government the flag represents.

Recently, there is a comical but serious news about elected officials mocking their swear-in process by uttering offensive or unpatriotic words. This happened in Hong Kong where British colonial rule applied for 100 years without democracy (Hong Kong was returned to China in 1997) until recent two decades. I place the significance of 'mocking swear-in' more than 'an offensive act with no restriction' to the government and its people it represents. An elected office is a sacred position bestowed by the voting public. Any individual or political figure seeking that position is by definition accepting that position's responsibility - to serve the people under the constitution and laws governing that position and the people. Mocking the swear-in is to refuse to swear in or to deny the validity of the position to be sworn in. I am glad to see that the Chinese higher court has ruled that the swear-in was invalid hence denying the elected individuals to take the positions they deny or disrespect.

Examining further into the 'mocked swear-in' incidence, one realizes that the 'Hong Kong for Independence' is the culprit behind the absurd act.

Political dissent and cry for independence exists in every country or society whether the degree of democracy is high or low or unique. In the U.S., there were many such movements (Alaska 2006-, California 2000-, Florida 1952-, Georgia 2009-, Hawaii 2011-, New Hampshire 2012-, Texas 1990-, Vermont 2001-, Republic of Lakota: Montana, Wyoming, Nebraska, North and South Dakota 2008-), but the U.S. Constitution essentially made secession impossible barring revolution. The U.S. Constitution states: "All persons born or naturalized in the United States, and subject to the jurisdiction thereof, are citizens of the United States and of the State wherein they reside. No State shall make or enforce any law which shall abridge the privileges or immunities of citizens of the United States; nor shall any State deprive any person of life, liberty, or property, without due process of law; nor deny to any person within its jurisdiction the equal protection of the laws." This gives the U.S. the right and power to use force to squash any State secession rendering it impossible for any State to succeed.

In the U.S. one has freedom of speech to voice different political views by forming political parties, but one can not oppose constitution which places the welfare and benefits of the entire country (larger constituency) above any subgroup in the nation. So although there are many secession proposals in the U.S., there are not much different from a novel lack of reality. However, by stating the reasons for advocating secession it still serves a purpose by expressing to the public and the government that a group of citizens have certain dissatisfaction. Similarly, people in Hong Kong can express dissatisfaction about the government through political party and elected positions but must respect and accept the Chinese constitution governing the entire nation. Mocking swear-in like burning the flag is broadly offensive to the citizens generating only hatred not giving any positive specific meaning. Hence, the ruling by a court disqualifying the elected legislators in the 'mocked swear-in' case in Hong Kong is perfectly justified. The fact 'Hong Kong for Independence' exists (whether with external influence or financial support or not) shows it has been accepted by the basic laws in Hong Kong as a small society, but disrespecting national constitution and laws are clearly not acceptable. The fundamental principle involved in the above two cases relates to identification issue, being a citizen protected by the nation represented by its flag and constitution must identify with and respect the flag and constitution. One denies them is denying one's own citizenship, then one must accept the consequences.

CHAPTER 64

Must A 'Change' PRESIDENT Take 'Strange' Actions to Accomplish 'Changes'?

—⟋⟍—

ABSTRACT

THE TITLE QUESTION IS PERHAPS far more relevant to Trump taking the helm in 2017. As a business man, he is used to taking risk, sometimes gambling or bluffing a little and lots of negotiations mixed with calculated decisions. This background will not go away when he takes the office at the White House whether he lives there or not. He must focus on bigger issues confronting his office, stimulating the economy, creating jobs and building world relations leading to win-win situation not a zero-sum business game. His people must do their jobs with the understanding their super negotiator boss is watching and expecting them to not only make good deals for America but also be aware of the consequences – people's lives more than their money are at the stake.

—⟋⟍—

If this question is posted to political science students as an essay topic, I am sure one would receive dozens of beautiful essays with convincing arguments not only to arrive at a conclusion on Yeh and/or Nay as an answer but also to follow a thought process starting on any of the underlined, capitalized and/or quotation-marked words in the title. The authors are right to come up with different arguments and conclusions simply because Must must be confined with circumstances and what actions and their consequences may be as well as how significant 'changes' are expected. Furthermore, an author may first focus on the word PRESIDENT, what kind of personality he has, what kind of political situation he is in, whether he is mandated with a 'change' mission, and why and what 'changes' he has promised to make for his or her people. This article is taking such a thought process - <u>Must</u> really depends on many factors - to argue and draw conclusion for the title topic.

First, we are talking about the President-elect of the 45th US Presidency, Donald Trump. Trump won the election against many odds and won a surprise victory with an unorthodox campaign. Trump is a businessman and not a politician, certainly not an insider of the political establishment as proven by the fact he was opposed by his own Republican Party to run for the presidency. He had to plead to the silent majority to get elected. He had to find his mandates in the campaign and the election process. He did it but in a way very much deviated from the 'norm' which you may even say 'strange' in an elite-controlled politically correct environment. He not only fought the two major parties but also battled with the mainstream media. His victory was a strange phenomenon to the traditional political pundits, pollsters and activists; in reality, Trump recognized the hidden voice of the silent majority muffled by the political correctness. By defying political correctness with his own style of rough language, he resonated with the silent majority and rode with the growing movement to victory.

Trump had certain intuition but he learned a lot on the campaign rallies and trails. He made many outlandish statements and promises testing the voters. He amplified them when he received warm responses from the cheering crowd. He toned them down if he found them hitting the wrong chord. Tough stand against illegal immigrants (stand remains firm, but wall can be a fence even a virtual wall) and repealing Obamacare (repeal but reserve the right to define 'changes' later) are two examples. Tax cuts were proposed as his basic political (and business) philosophy but everyone knows that tax cuts require the entire Congress and Senate to cooperate. With both the Senate and the House in control by the Republican Party, President Trump may have an easier time to fulfill his tax-cut mandate without taking too much 'strange' actions to circumvent the Congress. He might just have enough credit earned from his presidential election and a surprising sweeping victory of his Party to make the Congress work for him on tax policies. Similarly it goes with his domestic job creation plans, a cooperating Congress can be expected.

Appointing Elaine Chao as the Secretary of Transportation is probably Trump's easiest decision in cabinet appointment. Elaine married to Senate Majority leader Mitch McConnell from Kentucky and served as two-term Labor Secretary in President George W. Bush's cabinet and as Deputy Secretary of Transportation in the President George H. W. Bush's cabinet. Stated in the public record, under her leadership, the U.S. Department of Labor undertook regulatory and legislative reforms in protecting the health, safety, wages, and retirement security of U.S. workers by recovering record levels of back wages and monetary recoveries for pension plans, and obtaining record financial settlements for discrimination by federal contractors. She also restructured departmental programs and modernized regulations. We expect Elaine will be doing a fine job in getting America great again in transportation if Trump can get her a decent budget.

On foreign affairs, the title question is far more relevant to Trump taking the helm in 2017. As a business man, he is used to taking risk, sometimes gambling a little (although he did not amass his fortune from gambling in his casinos but from building real estate), and lots of negotiations mixed with calculated decisions and bluffs. This background will not go away when he takes the White House whether he sleeps there or not. However, in foreign affairs, the stakes are far higher and cannot be just measured by money in dollar, sterling, euro or renminbi. Human lives are at stake and nations are at stake; the U.S. President must take deliberate decisions to avoid devastating consequences. It is not a win or lose situation in the bidding for a business contract, strictly measurable in dollars which are recoverable as Trump has proven in his business life. In foreign affairs, mistakes are not always recoverable; in fact, more likely irreparable, they may not only cost the Presidency or election (as we recall Benghazi) but also destroy lives, moreover in a severe conflict destroying countries or the world. Thus, in foreign affairs, the President <u>must</u> take considerate and safe decisions for the sake of mankind not just for his own country.

Recently, while Trump is preparing to take on his responsibilities, he has been diligent in meeting with people and conversing with foreign leaders. In a number of events such as receiving Abe Shinzo and taking a call from Taiwan's leader Tsai Yin Wen, Trump did it his ways that the State Department regarded them 'strange' violating the normal diplomatic protocol. Since he is not yet sworn in as the President and he needs every opportunity to hone his skills in diplomacy, I think he is testing the water smartly with matters he knew he could get away before taking office. Appointing the Secretary of State is really his most challenging task. Again, he took his time interviewing or considering at least a dozen candidates; sure he will be benefitted by this process by picking everyone's brains and their world views. He can also use this process to mend fences and reward his loyal supporters while formulating his central view on foreign affairs.

One thing concerns not only his critics with a watchful eye is when Trump takes on his job he must realize that the campaign must be ended in order to start managing the day-to-day business as the commander-in-chief. He will not have time to tweet freely anymore. He must forget about things such as bluffing Boeing to make a good deal on Air Force One (although it is a smart thing to say that we want Boeing to make money but not that much government money on a couple of Presidential planes) but focus on bigger issues confronting his office, stimulating the economy, creating jobs and building world relations leading to win-win situation since zero-sum business principle in contract bidding is not the best way of dealing with foreign affairs. Let the people do their jobs with the understanding their big boss is a super business negotiator watching and expecting them to make good deals for America but also be aware of the consequences – people's lives more than their money are at the stake.

CHAPTER 65

Not All Trump's Cabinet Members Are Gold Fixtures

—m—

ABSTRACT

TAKING A QUICK VIEW OF Trump's appointees, you may get a feeling that he is organizing a richmen's club. But on a closer look, we find that Trump's cabinet does not have all gold fixtures like his Trump Tower cabinets. Thus Trump is not going to run the country like a billionaire filling his top posts all with other billionaires. He has appointed a mixture of new and experienced people. It is interesting to review Trump's appointees and to assess how his cabinet under watchful eyes of the media will shape up a strategy to deal with our national security and defense strategy and domestic issues.

—m—

President-Elect Trump has almost completed his cabinet appointments with Rex W. Tillerman, another 'Yiwanren' (A Chinese term for people worth above one hundred million is an unique term having no equivalent vocabulary in English, that is between a millionaire and billionaire) named as his Secretary of State. Taking a quick view of Trump's appointees, you may get a feeling that he is organizing a richmen's club with names like Wilbur Ross (Secretary of Commerce), Betsy Devos (Secretary of Education) and Linda McMahon (Small Business Administration) all worth more than a billion dollars and many more millionaires. On a closer look, we find that Trump's cabinet does not have all gold fixtures like his Trump Tower cabinets. There are at least five members (out of 20 announced appointees), Mike Pence (VP), Jim Mattis (Secretary of Defense), John Kelly (Secretary of Homeland Security),

Mike Pompeo (CIA Director) and Reince Priebus (White House Chief of Staff) with publicly reported net worth less than one million. In addition, there were no published net worth data on Scott Pruitt (Environmental Protection Agency) and Michael Flynn (National Security Advisor, see post note below), so it is fair to chuck off the idea that Trump is going to run the country like a billionaire filling his top posts all with other billionaires.

Trump has always been cherishing his self-made billions and he is certainly proud to be called a billionaire; in his Presidential bid, he has recognized that the U.S. is broke and poor and prioritized his goal to fix the nation's finances. So, it is not surprising that he surrounds himself with experienced wealthy individuals capable of making money to fulfill his mandate to make America great again - really - rich again. Trump seems to believe that people with experience in building personal wealth will have better idea to make America rich again. But Trump also understands the value of being thrift to build wealth; this can be seen from his remarks calling the administration to reduce waste including his criticism of the billion dollar price tag Boeing has estimated for a new US Air Force One. Based on this light, we will review Trump's initial cabinet appointments and assess whether his team will collectively accomplish his mandate - to fix America's ills and make her rich again.

Trump's Vice President Pick of Mike Pence was a good move which helped significantly in getting him elected. Pence not a millionaire but had a proud record being the Governor of Indiana building a growing economy with a balanced budget, low taxes and conservative principles. So it is understandable that Pence has been trusted by Trump as his right-hand man to serve the chairmanship of his transition team replacing Chris Christie, Governor of New Jersey tarnished by the Bridgegate scandal. Christie had over staffed the transition team with lobbyists which Trump recognized and smartly removed them. Trump's transition team led by Pence is sizable having 13 vice chair expanded from original six and a 21-person executive committee including Donald, Jr., Ivanka (and husband Jared Kushner) and Eric Trump. Seven of the thirty four members in the transition team have been appointed with a cabinet position, they are Ben Carson (Secretary of Housing), Jeff Session

(Attorney General), K.T. McFarland (Deputy National Security Advisor), Steve Mnunchin (Secretary of the Treasury), Steve Bannon in addition to Michael Flynn (**post note:** Flynn had been removed from the position of national security advisor because he had misled Vice President Mike pence and others about his meeting with Russian Ambassador, Flynn was replaced by General H.R. McMaster, a military strategist) and Reince Priebus mentioned above. The much talked about names in the transition team, Chris Christie, Newt Gingerich and Rudy Giuliani did not receive any appointment.

Trump seems to rely on experienced business people to fix the financial problems of the U.S. Let's look at the following appointees: Steven Mnuchin was Trump campaign's finance chairman, a former Goldman Sachs banker and an investor with experience in turning around a failed mortgage company with aggressive foreclosure measure; he is a proponent of cutting corporate taxes, now named as the secretary of the Treasury. Wilbur Ross, a billionaire, made his name in restructuring steel and textile corporations; he is the architect of 'America First' trade vision, now named as the Secretary of Commerce. Linda McMahon, another billionaire, made fame and fortune in sports entertainment (World Wrestling Entertainment); she is a proponent for cutting red tape, now named head of the Small Business Administration. Rick Perry, twice Presidential candidate and former Texas Governor had experience with alternative energy in Texas; In his book, Fed Up!, he criticizes federal government taking too much sovereignty and wealth from the states, now named Secretary of Energy. It is interesting to see whether this team can create or bring industries back to the U.S. producing jobs for Americans and obtain a trade surplus.

On national security and defense, Trump has shown his distrust of the 'old ways of doing things', thus his appointments have a mix of new and experienced people. His choice of Secretary of State, Rex Tillerson, Chief Executive of Exxon, made extensive travel and contacts overseas, especially having a rapport with Putin; he is a proponent to improve relationship with Russia and playing Russia card against China, now heading the State Department with no government experience. Tillerson's first test is how he will deal with the North Korea nuclear threat issue. One must note though Trump has appointed Terry

Brandstad, Governor of Iowa, as the Ambassador to China before announcing Tillerson's appointment. This may suggest that Trump simply would like to use people who are familiar with the leaders of China and Russia to deal with them but not necessarily able to pre-meditate a strategy of playing one against the other. Trump appoints Jim Mattis, as Secretary of Defense, a career military man with war experience in the Gulf, Afghanistan and Iraq; he is known as a strategist and critical of the past Administration's Middle East strategy. Trump had tapped Michael Flynn, a retired army general and former director of intelligence briefly under Obama administration, as his National Security Advisor; heFlynn is famous for the chant, 'lock her up', and is firm against terrorists and Iran nuclear threat. However, as post noted above, Flynn was replaced by General McMaster. Trump's Chief Strategist, Steve Brannon, a banker with naval officer background, made a fortune producing the Seinfeld sit-com; Brannon is a nationalist with anti-immigration view. Mike Pompeo, a Congressman sitting on the intelligence committee, is picked as the Director of CIA; he is also a vocal critic of Obama Administration. John Kelly, a retired general, lost his son to a roadside bomb in Afghanistan is Trump's Secretary of Homeland Security. It will be interesting to see how this group of people with military background will shape up a strategy of national security and defense.

The other appointments so far included Scott Pruitt, Head of Environmental Protection Agency, Andre Puzder, Secretary of Labor, Jeff Sessions, Attorney General, Tom Price, Secretary of Health, Ben Carson, Secretary of Housing, Elaine Chao, Secretary of Transportation, Betsy Devos, Secretary of Education, Nikki Haley, Ambassador to UN and Reince Priebus, Chief of Staff. We expect the experienced Secretary Chao will do fine and the new ones must climb a fast learning curve to deal with our domestic issues. The media has been very critical about Trump's team formation. However, we should give them time to orient themselves and pick up speed to keep pace with fast changing world.

CHAPTER 66

Will Tweeter Trigger Or Prevent Nuclear War?

—⁓—

As IF 2016 WAS NOT exciting enough in the news world, the news media appeared to be pumped with adrenaline to finish off 2016 with more sensational news. The following news sequence certainly cast a dark cloud over the Earth chilling any holiday spirit people might feel about the coming of the New Year. First, President Putin of Russia in his annual meeting on national affairs reaffirmed his policy of refreshing and strengthening Russia's nuclear forces along a note that Russia's economy is recovering steadily with self sufficient agriculture production in 2016. Then, President-elect Trump, after a meeting with the generals about US defense hours after the above Putin news, twitted to the world that the U.S. must greatly strengthen her nuclear capability. The news media immediately latched on this tweet offering many interpretations from concerns about Trump's ignoring the 'protocol' language regarding nuclear weapons and nuclear threats to possibly a new U.S. nuclear policy.

When Putin was queried on Trump's tweet, he said, this was nothing new; Trump had said "to strengthen nuclear forces" in his campaign. The news media's interpretation of course was varied but one consensus implication was that Russia and the U.S. might be heading to nuclear arms race despite Putin's claim that he did not want one. Tweet is a powerful tool and it has been specifically proven in the 2016 US election. Trump was able to send direct messages to tens of millions of people repeatedly through his tweets to energize the 'Trump' movement. Since Trump's victory, his tweets were able to stimulate the US stock market. In fact, the Wall Street observers have coined a term, 'tweeter risk' referring the daily rise or fall of stock prices attributable to a tweet from Trump. Trump's victory owes to some degree to his tweet performance.

Twitter is a communication product or service offered on the Internet with 'push and pull' characteristics in one-way and cascading communication. A micro-blog like message can be sent to a large number of tweet followers (A communication being pushed out by the Twitter while tweets being pulled in by followers). The twitter's biggest appeal and attraction to a communicator is the fast speed by which one can send messages to a huge number of Twitter accounts directly with no filtering so long as the short messages are less than 140 characters a piece. The ease of use and friendly way for any Twitter to scan a great number of twitters and their messages allowing a Twitter to follow (tune-in) a big number of Twitter accounts and retweet. Trump claims that he has 25 million followers, thus making his tweets powerful in delivering messages. President Obama has also used Twitter for delivering his messages. Tweeting does serve a useful purpose if a precise articulated short message can be sent to one's followers, but it also has the possibility to cause a Twitter to be driven by vanity, to become addicted or to be triggered by impulse by sending inappropriate messages out. Of course, Twitter followers can freely select to de-follow any Twitter account; hence a Twitter can also easily lose his or her popularity by misbehaving on tweets.

Speaking about Twitter behavior, one cannot help notice a number of Twitter events created by President Trump's tweets. On December 6, Trump tweeted, "Boeing is building a brand new 747 Air Force One for future presidents, but costs are out of control, more than $4B. Cancel order." Within 10 seconds, the Boeing stock started dropping, eventually reaching 1.6% below its previous day closing. This drop might not be significant for Boeing. But a week later Trump tweeted on Lockheed Martin about costs of F-35 (not a new issue) causing its stock to drop 2.5%. Anyone who profited over these tweets is really behaving with questionable ethics since the trades are bordering on insider trading. Some were attributing the stock price drop of aerospace and healthcare industries since the election to Trump's tweets and/or his cabinet appointments. There were Wall Street brokers openly soliciting investors to profit on Trump's tweets.

In addition to Trump's tweet effect on financial market, one can also observe the impact Trump's tweets had on diplomatic and world affairs. Mr. Trump, by speaking with Ms. Tsai on the phone and referring her as "the President of Taiwan" in a Twitter post, created a diplomatic incidence which essentially violated the traditional American position on the "Taiwan Issue", known as the "One China" policy - respect and recognizing that Taiwan is a part of China. Using 140 characters to casually communicate about diplomatic affairs is obviously a dangerous action, which may be easily causing confusion in diplomatic protocol to seriously creating misunderstanding on foreign policies. Remedies of any damage cannot be made by another short tweet.

On December 22, Mr. Trump said on Twitter that the United States must "strengthen and expand" its nuclear forces "until such time as the world comes to its senses regarding nukes." This tweet may be a response to Putin's speech to his military's leadership in Moscow earlier vowed to strengthen Russia's nuclear missiles. But it's effect is very significant not only generating serious concerns in the world about an accelerated nuclear arms race but also wide speculation in our nation and diplomatic relations, domestically exhibited by the rising value of Uranium ETF in the Wall Street stock market and internationally demonstrated by numerous analysts' comments on possibility of nuclear warfare. These types of effects trigger-able by 140 character tweets issued by one individual not accountable by the U.S. Congress and her government system should be discouraged. From the above examples, one can easily see tweets as a one-way short communication that can lead to misunderstanding between governments and people a lot easier than repairing any damages. Under a tense circumstance, for example, in the Middle East Conflict (Iraq and ISIS) or in the South China Sea Dispute or in the North Korea nuclear missile crisis, an improperly versed brief tweet may very likely be misinterpreted to escalate the tense situation into war, even possible to trigger a nuclear war.

To answer the title question, we believe that an ill-versed tweeter will more likely trigger than prevent a nuclear war!

Conclusions

—ɯ—

As we are observing the two Giants changing, we sense the hostility between the two nations. China has been targeted as the enemy by the U.S. to the point that red lines are ignored and nuclear weapons are rattled like Sabers as if the consequences of nuclear war are acceptable or tolerable by the world. Yet, even common citizens should be concerned with this kind of development, not just for their own sake but also for the sake of the entire world. In closing, we would like to pose three questions to global citizens regarding why and how the two giants are changing and how we may respond or react. Question one is whether their changes are driven by insecurity if so who is insecure, the U.S. or China? Question 2 is whether their changes are driven by aggression, if so, who is aggressive? Question 3 is whether the two giants are marching to the land of no return - a nuclear war, if so what should we do to prevent it from happening?

This author has been devoting three years to US-China issues, following current events closely and analyzing analysts' opinions and comments all with the above questions in mind. In a nut shell, this author finds that the problem lies in misunderstanding. Chinese and Americans really need to understand each other and each country more. We Americans really do not have a free media as we proudly thinking that we do. In the process of searching answers to the above questions, we find that we have a rich news media but not a true free press. The Internet blogs and the global press seem to be far more objective in news reporting of world affairs but they lack the credibility and authenticity the mainstream media possess, especially on foreign affairs such as the US-China dealings and relations. The U.S. has more publications, TV stations and news papers than all other nations and continents combined, but the US mass media seem to be more controlled compared to, for example, the British media where you can find a fair view about the above questions which are sorely missing in the U.S.

In the following, the author would like to summarize a set of opinions expressed by foreign press and Internet blogs regarding the above questions. We Americans should keep an open mind to think about these opinions.

The U.S. is still practicing a 19 century foreign policy, a gun-boat diplomacy with a colonial mentality (said as much in John Pilger's well researched documentary film) The U.S. has the strongest military force and over 800 military bases all over the world. Yes some were leftover from WW II, but more were built after WW II and the U.S. is still building and expanding, for example, in Okinawa, despite of the opposition from local residents. Why does the U.S. maintain such a foreign policy? More foreign opinions are saying that the U.S. wants to maintain a world dominant position rather than saying that the U.S. is feeling insecure. The news media in the developing world (even some developed countries) would say that China was feeling insecure hence forced to build up her military. Naturally China's military build-up is not a desired consequence from her neighbors' perspective.

The military bases of the U.S. are mostly far away from America. They are built to surround certain targets the U.S. designated as threats, namely China and Russia as the major targets. In response to China's effort in Africa developing infrastructure and investing in local economy, the U.S. offers military solutions (weapons) rather than joining in a fair economic competition to help the third world. The U.S. reacted strongly to China's contract with the Horn of Africa country to have a naval base at Djibouti where the U.S. already has a 4500 strong counter-terrorism forces there. Djibouti serves a critical support role to China's commerce activities in Africa. China shifted her policy from inward-looking and non-interacting to making more contribution to the world. (Ironically, urged by the U.S. a few years ago) China has contributed to global peacekeeping operations with 8000 troops. The U.S. media paints China as an aggressor in the South China Sea, but never asked why China must build airstrips in the South China Sea. Is China an aggressor or is China feeling insecure? The foreign opinions seem to understand that better than the U.S. The U.S. has built so many military bases surrounding China from South Korea, Japan, Okinawa, Taiwan, Philippines to Singapore, literally like a steel chain around China's throat, chest, arms and legs. It is no wonder that the world opinions are more viewing the U.S. rather than China as an aggressor and showing sympathy to China's insecurity.

Surprisingly, the US mainstream media has been faithfully echoing the US Administration's outdated 19 century gun-boat foreign policy. Yes, there are different voices in the US press, but unfortunately, the mass media are more powerful and overwhelming in the press delivering the messages – China is a threat and China caused our domestic problems and is threatening our security. The mass media controlled surveys reinforce their messages making Americans so simple-mindedly accepting the American version of news report and interpretation. When foreigners traveling to the U.S., that is what they see and hear. They are genuinely concerned why is the U.S. leading the world to the land of no return by beating war drums, inducing arms race and practicing a nuclear weapon loaded gun-boat foreign policy.

The U.S. does have many military allies in the world but some of them are left-over from WW II and some of them are bought into the alliances with US aids. Now that the U.S. felt the financial burden of her over extended military engagement and began to demand her allies to pay for the military expenses. This turns out to be a wake-up call for some countries, for instance, Philippines and a few NATO countries; they are now wondering what is the real benefit for them to be a part of the US gun-boat foreign policy? No country would like to see its land to be the battle ground of a war, especially a nuclear war. The foreign opinions are clearly shifting. They realize that an adversary relationship between the two giants is not good for the world. They begin to see who is an aggressor and who is feeling insecure. They do hope that the U.S. and China can work together to deter any military threat, for example, North Korea, Iran and elsewhere. Do we Americans begin to see the same picture? Do we have answers for the above three questions? Why can't the two giants develop collaborative and friendly relations? Must WW III be the final destiny?!

APPENDICES (I)

—〰—

Image 1> 兩岸和平統一才能促進中美關係

Image 2> 大選后蜜月中看台灣未來

Image 3> 沒理念，國民黨等著泡沫化

Image 4> 記念周恩來先生有感

Appendices (I)

兩岸和平統一才能促進中美關係
張一飛

八月十二日參加了洛郡美國退伍軍人事務部和中美論壇合辦的二戰七十一週年紀念會。很榮幸應邀在其座談會上發表演說。此座談會的題目是中美合作促進更好的世界，我的講題的重點就是兩岸和平統一才能促進中美關係，有好的中美關係才會有中美合作，中美合作才會有更好的世界。在二十分鐘時間裡表明以上邏輯應當是夠了。沒想到當我開講，先點明我的結論，就立即有人發言反對，在我請求先不要打斷我的演講下，這個反對者，譚美生女士前蒙特瑞市長（Betty Chu），非常客氣的同意并表示歉意。我也答應她，會回答她的所有問題。很不幸，這座談會在南海和仲裁案上的討論超出了預定時間，我與譚女士沒能深談。

幸好紀念會會長張文基教授要我在中美論壇上寫篇短文總結我在會上的論點，我就在此報告我說的重點，並一併對譚女士的觀點做一個答覆。因為她的觀點在不少美籍華人，尤其在美出生者中頗有認同。她的觀點是大陸為專制政權，臺灣是民主社會不應統一。持這種論點的人說的是美國正義口號，但是沒有深刻了解兩岸和中美歷史源緣，而且忽略了探討為何中美關係會從二戰后，甚至一九七九美國承認一個中國并承認臺灣是中國的一部份之后，中美關係一直不能好。從此點來看，我上面所說的邏輯和結論就是言之有因了。我希望有以下的解說就更言之有物了。

兩岸之分，由於美蘇理念不同各支持中國的一黨積七十一年或可說二甲子之久。但兩岸都經歷了理念，政治制度的沖激和變化，經濟上兩岸也經歷了很大的轉型和成長。而美國依然守著舊思維(legacy)來對待兩岸，大陸不在變嗎？臺灣民主完全成功了嗎？可以像美國，日本一樣不必與大陸打交道了嗎？事實上，美日都不能與中國斷絕關係，中國已不是百年前，或五十年前的中國，她已經站起來了，有權利說話，辯護歷史，能夠也應該維護國家和人民的利益了。

在臺灣，大多數百姓與大陸有血緣，祖先，姓氏的密切關係，更不用說文化語言的根源了，但是他們被少數反中反華的人綁架，政治迷糊了，社會混亂了，經濟上明知與大陸合作有利，反要反服貿，反遊客，地緣歷史上明知與大陸有唇齒相依不可分離的關係，反要反對一國兩制，反對無時限的和平統一，**有道理**嗎？ 不錯，臺灣的民調，反中反華的人似乎越來越多，你想過為什麼嗎？大陸一直對台灣輸送利益，而民調反而不停下降，為什麼？**可信嗎?** 那來的影響，其實，不用仔細研究，海外華人都看的出這是外來的影響。臺灣內部的複雜情緒大都是受外來的影響。

美國對中國的敵意應當永遠不變嗎？美國為什麼要一直把中國當敵人？ 美國不是有很多人反對美國的中國政策嗎？ 美敵對中國才利用臺灣作島鏈**威脅**，要利用台灣，就不會贊成兩岸統一，這有道理嗎？反對<u>兩岸和平同一</u>就更沒有道理了。反過來說，如果兩岸和平統一了，美日就都沒有**辦法**和**理由**搞島鏈軍事威脅，自然中美關係會好，合作的機會就有了。 中美兩大經濟能合作而不對抗，那對全球經濟就有好處。 所以我在座談會上說<u>兩岸合平統一</u>是中美友善關係的基本要素，中美關係友善，才有真正合作可能，中美真正合作，世界才能和平，繁榮和更好！

大選后蜜月中看台灣未來
張一飛

民進黨蔡英文主席宣誓就職中華民國總統已經一個月了。政治上的蜜月當然不一定
限制為一個月，而是當選后一段時期勝選者用行動來證明他或她會對競選宣言兌現。
上任后對發生的事件的處理方法，當選者都會盡量順著民意，這段時期就是政治上
的蜜月期。蔡總統在蜜月中的表現如何，媒體是非常關注的，選民也會觀察和在公
私場合或經由媒體發話了。如果民聲抱怨，發出批評，指責和要求改變，那這蜜月
期也就完了。在蔡總統的蜜月中仔細考量她的新政府的表現，應當可以看出一些她
執政的走向也可以對台灣的未來作個評論。至少可以確定她是否還在渡蜜月？

在蔡總統的蜜月中發生值得選民關注的事件倒真是不少。先說她的新政府各部門在
立法院的答詢表態，從行政院長林全首用'中華民國台灣'新名詞到國防部長馮世寬
聲稱南海危機是大陸主動挑釁，外交部對沖之礁稱為島礁，教育部部長潘文忠廢除
課綱修改，行政院撤銷太陽花學運告訴等等，似乎蔡政府已經明確走向親日，甚至
是賣國媚日的方向。難道這是台灣的民意所向？不是吧，在選前蔡英文的言行盡量
模糊，對兩岸關係不作明白表態，對美訪問內容不敢透明公開，對日訪問也只是提
高國際身價，可是當選后，蔡政府似乎胸有成竹地往台獨，反中和親日方向邁進。
這一個多月來，真是蔡總統的蜜月嗎？

再仔細看看民間的聲音和表現，蔡政府是在渡蜜月嗎？先分析一下洪素珠事件，一
個老百姓的事件造成了全臺灣甚至海外的軒然大波，不但是一件對種族岐視，本省
人岐視外省人，的抗議聲音，更激起了反對日本皇民源緣的反中媚日言行。這種表
現就像對蔡政府打了一記耳光。因此事件，台灣民政府組織曝光了，一個沒有正義，
賣國的台獨組織，民進黨要認同和包容嗎？再看到中華愛國同心會的示威抗議，向
掛著日本旗的台灣民政府板橋基地圍堵，并領著拿五星旗的民眾高呼。這像是蔡政
府要的密月嗎？再看那高金素梅立委在立法院對蔡政府的質詢，為原住民發聲，質
問執政黨的轉型正義有何目的，問得林院長和馮部長啞口無言。還有民間對開放瘦
肉精的抗議也弄成走上街頭的情況，這不是又一巴掌嗎？

這一個月來蔡政府的表現不但是讓台灣居民感到失望和憂慮，對海外的華僑也產生了感觸，大家希望的是和平，不希望台灣變成一個麻煩製造者，美國華人這樣想，美國人更是這樣想， 那都是有民意根據的。然而蔡政府的作為太令人擔憂了，居然下令不讓剛退職的馬英久總統出國演講，這是那門子民主政治？台灣的民主在開倒車嗎？台灣的政治人物出國機會少，那是別人不請不歡迎，限制馬總統出國只能顯現民進黨沒有肚量，沒有自信。馬總統的一次演講能推翻執政黨嗎？這個事件加上通過縣市議長選舉要記名投票，只說明了民進黨對民主政治毫無信心。

作為一個關心世事的人，在今天通訊媒體發達的時代，可以盡覽各地新聞和評判事件。觀察了台灣大選之后一月餘，不免覺得新政府對台灣民意有很大的誤判，對國際華僑有更大的誤解。蔡政府的密月已經完了， 從今往後，蔡政府的日子說好聽的是有挑戰性的，說不好聽的是會把台灣領向焦頭爛額的日子過。當然，蔡政府也可能領取教訓，真正為全台灣的老百姓謀福利，而採取一個不製造麻煩的不反中的政策。老百姓拭目以待吧！

沒理念，國民黨等著泡沫化
張一飛

一個政黨的價值，首先必須要有鮮明的政治理念，其次，要有如何治理國家，訂定外交方向策略，提出內政問題處理方法，並對民生願景做出明確的表述，才能吸引同志入黨，為國為民服務，再經由全體黨員的努力和表現爭取人民信心，支持該黨從政。可是，從去年大選至今，我們看到了台灣政治的混亂，人民普遍對政局不滿。執政的民進黨不敢明確表明政黨理念，對選前承諾的事不但不兌現，甚至經常來個180度的髮夾彎。這個趨勢令民眾憂慮。

國民黨身為第一在野大黨，應當要把握這個時機，團結黨員，爭取人民支持。改選黨主席應該是一個改造自新、發奮圖強的里程碑。但是我們看到的是，國民黨把黨主席的改選當作去年大選一樣來進行。不能按照政黨的價值進行檢討：國民黨的理念該是什麼？如何針對執政黨的錯誤提出方案？如何團結黨內？如何向民眾顯示國民黨達成共識和團結的形象？相反地，國民黨陸續冒出幾個黨主席的候選人，大家不在黨內辯論、協調，以政見、個人的領導能力和過去政績及對外的吸引力說服黨員，反而是頻頻對外界媒體發話，重蹈去年失敗的覆轍。

國民黨的黨員應當本著政黨運行道理，要求黨主席競選人立即向黨員表述個人能力、號召力，取得黨內同志的信任。國民黨顯然在台灣有政治空間，不然中國大陸和美國也不會看重國民黨。但是如果國民黨不澄清黨的理念，凝聚共識，國民黨就會淪為泡沫小黨。

記念周恩來先生有感
張語人

二〇一七年一月八日是周恩來先生逝世四十一週年，周先生享年七十八歲
（3/5/1898 - 1/8/1976）如果活著他已是一百零八歲的老人了。人們每年記念他
正是因為周先生人雖死，可他還是活在人們心中。他的那一代人大多去世了，但是
比他晚一代，二代，甚至三，四代的人仍然記得他懷念他愛著他。就像今日新聞報
導說的，有的人活著像死人一樣，對世界人類無所供獻，而有的人雖然死了，他仍
然像活著一樣，鼓勵著大家為國家民族，為世界大同作出奉獻。周先生就是后者，
他一生為中國奉獻，他死了之後，仍然活在人們心中，勉勵著人們。這就是我們每
年都要記念他的誕誕日，不能忘掉一個中國偉人對中國的供獻和期望。

一百〇八年前，周先生生在中國的災難時刻，列強入侵中國，亞洲的日本也打敗了
滿清，強迫中國訂了馬關條約，把台灣寶島割讓了給日本。熱血的中國人都想發奮
圖強，留學各國，以期報國。周先生在 19 歲赴日留學時寫下了他的夢想給告別同
學： "願相會于中華騰飛世界時" 這是周先生在九十年前寫下的中國夢。

周先生的一生完全奉獻了給國家，他的革命事蹟，他對他的同志大公無私的忠心義
氣，他對待人的德行和真誠的愛心，他官居總理二十六年，擔負內政外交重任，一
切為國家著想，不為權力斗爭，他對上盡忠，對下愛戴，也只有周先生這樣的中國
偉人會有十里長街送行的場景，人們不顧公安的禁止，跪在天安門，跪在大街上，
在寒冬裡，悲泣著向周先生告別。周先生沒有子女后人，但是他有千千萬萬的人願
意奉他為先人，繼續他的遺願。這就是周先生死了仍然活在人們心中的原因。

周先生一生經歷了中國的災難，革命，建國，與世界各國的強人打交道，從史達林
到尼克森，他一心為國，他的事蹟和功勞，只有史家可以詳述，但是他是中國的一
個偉人已經牢牢的記在人們的心中。他為中國復興的夢作了祈禱，奉獻了一生，倉
造了契機，以至於中國走到了今天的地步。今日中國，雖然仍然有外交國際競爭博
弈的挑戰，但是中國站起來了，就像周先生一生的志願，中國已經向復興騰飛了，
中國人，全世界的華人都會記住你的期望：中華騰飛世界！

今天在周恩來先生的逝世記念日，我們記念周先生，我們會繼續周先生的宏願讓中
華騰飛世界！！！

APPENDICES (II)

Why Did I Publish the Book Series on US-China Relations?

—ᴍ—

The book, entitled, US-China Relations, Mainstream and Organic Views was published on 4-25-2015 now available on Amazon.com and other retailers. Ever since its publication, the author was asked by many of his friends, readers and prospective readers, why did he publish this serious book? Indeed, a thoughtful answer to the question is just as important as the context of the essays contained in the book. So the author would like to present his opinion and answer to the question for his readers and potential readers of this book and his future books.

This book is a collection of individual essays about the issues concerning the United States, China and between them; altogether, they portray a picture of current relationship between the two countries and their outlooks. The comments and opinions in these papers sometimes go beyond describing the picture of the relationship between the two nations; they delve into history, discuss media's analyses, right or wrong, and offer advice from a U.S. Citizen's point of view. This book contains 60 essays each having a distinct title of its own. As a whole, this book reflects the author's concern in his retirement life, (neither on personal health issues nor on the management of one's 401K which are not avoidable in retirement), on the future of our country and the future of our children.

Since the United States and China are now the two greatest economies in the world, what happens in these two countries do have impacts on other nations by intention or not. The relationship between the two countries is not only important to each other but also to the entire world. The U.S.-China relationship has profound impact to the future of our children and our children's children. When the author started to write a current event column a few years ago, he only focused on the affairs and issues relevant to the U.S. and China occurring at the time of his writing, but then he realized one cannot ignore the historical background to understand the present affairs. Moreover, one cannot analyze a current event without doing research on the history leading to the occurrence of such a current event. Gradually he understood that every article written by an analyst was built on his or her background and knowledge of the history. A Harvard graduate studied under a Harvard professor writes with that background. A blog written by a common citizen contains that citizen's background. Often, a common citizen with Chinese and American background and understanding of the Chinese and American history has a very profound, sometimes, unique perspective of the US-China relation, current and past.

The author named his column, Mainstream and Organic; because he could see the built-in bias the mainstream media has as a result of the media's historical background. One can easily see how the articles of New York Times are different from the articles of Wall Street Journal or Washington Post. On the other hand, the organic media in the Internet via blogs and emails carry the authors' backgrounds. The mainstream media tend to present a choreographed view with a concerted bias which could be resulted from a consensus of opinions of an active established group. Consensus in the mainstream media can be a good thing since it can influence the mass, except when its opinion is way off from that in the organic media. Organic media generally represent voices and opinions of individuals and small groups in the society, but collectively their views may represent the silent majority of the country. In discussions and analyses of current events, it is absolutely necessary to weigh in the organic views with the mainstream opinions.

The U.S.-China relation is a serious topic that the mainstream media have long dominated its presentation, discussion and debate. Even though there are opposing opinions in the mainstream media but they do not necessarily represent the organic views and the silent majority. For example, in the mainstream media, there is the school believing in 'China Threat' and there is another school believing in 'China's Dooms Day Is Here', but the opinions on 'China's Effective Reform' and 'Genuine Chinese Dream' in the organic media seem to be totally disrecarded. As a result, 'target China' becomes the main strategy touted by the mainstream and the collaborative G-2 idea gets trashed away.

US-China Relations draws information broadly from both mainstream and organic media and presents an independent, critical and objective view on the topics selected. It adds a fresh voice to the dialogue about US-China Relations. The author is a naturalized US citizen. He was born in mainland China. China, a vastly populated country, has always attracted him with its rich culture and long history, and as his ancestry land has constantly lured him to study her. The author was raised in Taiwan. Taiwan, a beautiful island where he lived sixteen years, often appeared in his dreams as homeland with familiar images. The author has spent the last 50 years in the U.S. (26 in Somers) witnessing her changes and being Americanized. Having lived through many of the events he discussed in the book, the author provides a deep and personal analysis of the historic moments and policies that have influenced US-China Relations over the last 70 years.

The author very much likes to share his views with his fellow Americans; hence he decided to publish his writings.

Taiwan was under Japanese occupation for fifty years (1895-1945) after Japan won the first Sino-Japanese war (1894 – 1895); Taiwan suffered from a systemic discrimination and a savage colonial rule but that part of history was very faint in the memory of the younger generation(s) in Taiwan.

History dealt Taiwan an unfair hand in her path of uniting with China; Potsdam Declaration was dishonored and the internal squabble between the Chinese Communist Party (CCP) and Kou Ming Tang (KMT) caused many decisions regarding war reparations to be made by world powers without the participation and approval of the governments of China. The U.S. supported the KMT based on the anti-communism policy even after KMT had lost the entire mainland and retreated to Taiwan. Taiwan became part of the U.S. military alliance in Asia and was protected under the U.S. – Taiwan Mutual Defense Treaty.

History dealt mainland China a worse hand forcing her to experience through Western invasions and Japanese aggression causing nearly one century long suffering and humiliation till the People's Republic was founded in 1949. However, the failure of the CCP to improve the mainland economy and the success of Taiwan's development with the U.S. aids, had accentuated their mistrust towards each other which retarded the effort of reunification between Taiwan and the Mainland.

President Nixon's ice-breaking trip to China in 1972 revived and redefined the US-China relation. President Carter's formal recognition of the People's Republic of China in 1979 and the US acknowledgment of only one China set the principal China policy: expecting a peaceful reunification of Taiwan with the Mainland. Recognition of China and a soft policy towards China had contributed to the final collapse of the Communist Soviet Union and the victory of the U.S in the Cold War! China also benefitted from the shaded help from the United States to open up and reform leading to China's miraculous economical development. However, Today, Taiwan's fate is still uncertain as much as the future of US-China relations, but it does not have to be, does it?!

Mainland China is the ancestral land and cultural roots of many overseas Chinese including the Chinese Americans living in the U.S. The Vietnam War left a deep scar on the U.S. as a war against communism, but ironically, it was Russia more than China backing the North Vietnam to a bitter war with the U.S. The Vietnam War in fact caused China to depart from the Soviet Union's style of communism and she eventually decided to 'reform and open up'. China's economical development, initially was gradual until recent decades that China had advanced significantly to be the envy of the world. Should China be the archenemy or just a rising competitor of the U.S.? Americans don't seem to have a clear idea and a precise principled China or Asia Pacific policy; it is certainly not clear from the mass media which tend to carry a bit of hostility towards China without honest justification.

China had shredded her paper tiger image by her fast impressive development; however, along with her economic success we also witnessed many of the ills and evils of a non-transparent governing body that exhibited amazing official corruption, judicial injustice, and widening gaps of wealth in societies. The recent leadership of CCP seems to be aware of these ills and have initiated party cleansing actions, to crack down corruptions, and to initiate reformative policies, to improve the social programs aimed at reducing the wealth gap. China is driving her economy to fulfill a 'China Dream' to bring more of her population to middle class. However, the U.S. doesn't seem to believe China, one wonders why?

The United States became the true country of immigrants after the Chinese exclusion act (1924) was repealed in 1943, even though there was only a small quota of 105 for ethnic Chinese regardless of nationality. Later, in 1946 the immigration quota was extended to Filipino and Asian Indian and in 1952 to all Asians. Finally, in 1965 the quota system based on National Origins was abandoned altogether. All immigrants appreciate the United States as the land of opportunities, where they live, work, get married and have a family and a career. However, like many Americans, the immigrants have independent views on political issues and do not necessarily agree with all US government policies, for example, on the invasion of Iraq, the support of the military government in Egypt, and permitting Japan to revive militarism. By encouraging Japan to re-arm and revise her peace constitution to permit first strike can potentially lead to uncontrollable situations possibly to wars. Was Japan or the U.S. the promoter of 'China Threat' to justify Japan's military expansion and to turn the US 'Pivot' policy into an arms race in Asia Pacific? Why are there vast different views in the mainstream and organic media on this issue?

As a US citizen, the author felt compelled to voice his opinions regarding the 'China Threat' and the many inconsistent China policies the US government is conducting, such as the Pivot, ASB and TPP. Especially alarming is that the mainstream media seems to have adopted a 'targeting China' position in beating the war drums daily hyping up a military conflict between the U.S. and China, ignoring the views expressed in the organic media. When the author wrote about issues concerning the U.S. and China, he always made reference to both views expressed in the Mainstream and Organic media so that the issues get a fair discussion.

Obviously, not all American citizens agree on every issue or be aware of all issues in the domain of US foreign policy, particularly, on the subject domain of the U.S.-China relation. However, the US-China relation is an extremely important issue to Americans and to America's future. Now China has risen economically as the second largest economy in the world. Does she pose a threat to The United States as repeatedly claimed in the mass media? Should the U.S. transform the Cold War strategy to target China? Is the U.S. China policy heading in the right direction? Is China being reactive to the U.S. 'Pivot to Asia' strategy or is she preparing an unavoidable war between the two nations? Should the U.S. embrace the rise of China instead of targeting China as the enemy? Is it possible for China and the U.S. to collaborate to create win-win opportunities for the benefits of both nations and world peace? These and many more are questions the author discussed and tried to answer in his essays by tracing the history of the past century and half to find causality roots for what happened and what might happen and by analyzing the current events without a legacy view of 'anti-communism equals ant-China' to project the trends of the U.S.-China relation development.

Americans cannot afford to be just led by the mass media. We need to keenly engage in the opinions of the organic media to make fairer and deeper analysis on the issues. The American citizens need to resonate in agreement or in opposition to bring out our citizens' views on the US-China relation issue. It is for this purpose, the author has decided to publish the book, The US-China Relations - in Mainstream and Organic Views.

APPENDICES (III)

Table of Contents of US-China Relations

—ɯ—

Acknowledgment

Preface

Introduction

Chapter 1   Why an Uninhabited Island May Draw the U.S. into a War

Chapter 2   True American Exceptionalism

Chapter 3   US-China Relationship and A Dangerous Xiaosan

Chapter 4   True Conflict in US-China Relationship

Chapter 5   A New Model for US-China Relationship

Chapter 6   ABC TV's Mistake Reflects Americans' Insensitivity To US-China Relationship

Chapter 7   Caroline Kennedy's Historical Mission

Chapter 8   Right Cyberspace Strategy and Policy For The U.S. With Respect To China

Chapter 9   Imperfect Diplomacy Evidenced by China's New AZID in East China Sea

Chapter 10 US Secretary John Kerry's Legacy to Be

Chapter 11 Should Obama's Administration Re-examine the U.S. Asia-Pacific Strategy?

Chapter 12 What Are the Intentions behind the Foreign Policies of the United States and China?

Chapter 13 New Year New Hope and New US-China Relationship

Chapter 14 From Mandela To Diaoyu Islands – A Lesson For World Leaders

Chapter 15 Why Is Abe Shinzo Following Junichiro Koizumi's Foot Steps on the Yasukuni Issue?

Chapter 16 The Difference of Germans and Japanese In Handling the Truth of WW II History

Chapter 17 Tom Clancy and US-China Relationship

Chapter 18 Debate on the Logic in Great Power Diplomacy - Diaoyu Islands Case in Point

Chapter 19 From 'Comfort Woman' Issue To US-China-Japan Relations

Chapter 20 Nation Development of The U.S. and China in Past 250 Years and Forward

Chapter 21 Interplay of US-China-Japan National Strategies – As Revealed By The Diaoyu Island Dispute

Chapter 22 Can Jade Rabbit (Yutu) Help Win The Space Exploration For Mankind?

Chapter 23 From Russia's Annexation of Crimea to International Diplomatic Play

Chapter 24 Should The United States Believe Or Not To Believe China's Message in Körber Foundation?

Chapter 25 Is Japan's Democracy Really Working for the Japanese People?

Chapter 26 State Visit of First Lady Michelle Obama to China – 'First' Comment

Chapter 27 Condemn Pity Or Exonerate Japanese Kamikaze Pilots?

Chapter 28 Don't Let Japan Highjack The US 'Pivot' Policy To A Japanese '3FN' Strategy

Chapter 29 Japan Can't Win the Diaoyu Islands Dispute by Increasing MOFA Budget

Chapter 30 The Illusion of Cyber Security and Privacy Protection for Citizens

Chapter 31 A Warm Bilateral Relationship Is Always Better Than A Hate Or Love Triangle – Vietnam and China Relationship

Chapter 32 Cold War I to Cold War II with A Changing Triangle

Chapter 33 Democracy Is Not An Ideology But A Method for Achieving the Goals of Ideology

Chapter 34 Will Hillary Clinton Win the 2016 United States Presidency -Views of Americans and Chinese and Bomb Shell Stories-

Chapter 35 Why Americans Need To Understand The Real China Issue? Watch the Historical Visit of Zhang Zhijun to Meet Wang Yoichi in Taiwan

Chapter 36 Japan Fast Copying President Obama in Circumventing Democracy

Chapter 37 A Stable World Under The Three-Legged Ding Structure

Chapter 38 Bipolar (Hegemony) and Multi-Polar (Post-Hegemony) World View and Foreign Policy

Chapter 39 Does Leader's Dream Match People's Dream? Comparing Abe, Putin and Xi's Dreams

Chapter 40 Bad Attitudes Impacting the US-China Relationship

Chapter 41 Worldwide Turmoil Viewed By Brzezinski and Wordman

Chapter 42 Why Does Japan Keep Denying Her War Atrocities? - The Nanking Massacre, Comfort Women and Unit 731 Biological Experiments -

Chapter 43 "In the Interest of the U.S." – We War!

Chapter 44 Robin Williams, Drug Problems and Opium Wars

Chapter 45 The US Leadership Transition at 2016-17 - Most Critical for US-China Relation

Chapter 46 Chinese Americans Should Vote on Issues, not Party Line

Chapter 47 Conclusion From The U.S.-China Commission (USCC) Military Assessment

Chapter 48 From Nixon-Kissinger to Obama-Rice on US China Policy

Chapter 49 Is War Between The United States and China Inevitable?

Chapter 50 Common Interest, Objective and Understanding (IOU) Policies Make the U.S. and China Win-Win

Chapter 51 Use Space Cooperation to Unite the Earth

Chapter 52 Who Is More Stupid to Engage in Arm Race and Repeat the Cold War? Is the U.S. or China?

Chapter 53 APEC Past, Present and Future - Sprouting of the Two Great Nations Relationship

Chapter 54 Significance of APEC-Beijing and Post-APEC Agreements between the U.S. and China

Chapter 55 Is China So Difficult to Understand by the West? Why? Why Not?

Chapter 56 Why Apologizing to Japan?

Chapter 57 American TV Should Provide Lifelong Learning In An Entertaining Manner

Chapter 58 Why Do Putin and Xi Cling To The Theme of Patriotism But Not Obama?

Chapter 59 Significance of Okinawa, Taipei and Hong Kong Elections

Chapter 60 The Near-Term Future of The U.S. and China

Table of Contents of Understanding the U.S. and China

—ɯ—

Acknowledgment

Preface

Introduction

Chapter 1   The Impact of Exporting Gasoline and Gas on the U.S. Economy and World Prosperity 22

Chapter 2   The Problem of Income Gap and Wealth Gap

Chapter 3   Hong Kong's 'Occupy Central', American Democracy and 'Baodiao' Movement

Chapter 4   Work Ethics, Style and Stress in the U.S. and China

Chapter 5   Global Competitiveness Ranking and No Free Ride in the World

Chapter 6   Arms Race of a 'Virtual Pentagon' under a New Cold War??

Chapter 7   Beheading Japanese and Serious Reflection

Chapter 8   Principles Affecting Wealth Gap Issue

Chapter 9   From Abenomics to Abelomacy - Japanese People Ought to Know

Chapter 10   Pressure Points and Sweet Spots (PPSS) Analysis of US-China Relations

Chapter 11   Justification of Military Bases on Foreign Lands – Camp Schwab to Cuban Missile Sites

Chapter 12   Transparent and Effective Governance, Debt Financing and China's 'Lianghui'

Chapter 13   70th Anniversary Sets Audition Stage for 2016 Elections and Future Outlook (I)

Chapter 14   70th Anniversary Sets Audition Stage for 2016 Elections and Future Outlook (II)

Chapter 15   Global Competition, Inventions, Innovations and Smart People

Chapter 16   Real Goals of Abe Shinzo's Washington Trip

Chapter 17   Chronological Account of AIIB and Its Significance

Chapter 18   Reflections on Lee Kuan Yew and Henry Afred Kissinger

Chapter 19   The Significance of Xi JingPin's Speech at Boao Forum for Asia

Chapter 20   To Apologize or Not To Apologize

Chapter 21   To Cooperate or Not to Cooperate (with China on Her 'Red' Interpol Notice)

Chapter 22   What is the Real Goal of the US Pivot Policy? Peace Pivot (I)

Chapter 23 What is the Real Goal of the US AP Policy? Evil Pivot (II)

Chapter 24 What is the Real Goal of the US AP Policy? Logical Path (III)

Chapter 25 Abuses of Navy Power and Wars - History Lesson

Chapter 26 Meaning of Being Chinese Today and Tomorrow

Chapter 27 Radical Ideas for Motivating Learning

Chapter 28 'Harmony' versus 'Hegemony' for Global Leadership

Chapter 29 US-Vietnam War, Sino-Vietnam-US Relations and South China Sea

Chapter 30 Agreeing with George Soros on China with a Different Tale

Chapter 31 Will The Hot Spots in South China Sea Ever Be Ready For Vacation?

Chapter 32 Tune RGB to Get a Bright Future for Taiwan

Chapter 33 Science and Technology in Education and Diplomacy for the 21st Century

Chapter 34 The World Scholars Should Confirm Who Really Discovered America!

Chapter 35 Comments on Forbes' Taiwan Needs a Strong Ally

Chapter 36 Americanization, Bigotry, China Threat, Doomsday, and Exceptionalism

Chapter 37 The Importance of Media in Election Campaigns

Chapter 38 Maintaining Empire in War versus Sharing Power in Peace

Chapter 39 US Citizens Troubled by Contradictory 'China Threat' and "Dooms Day'

Chapter 40 70th Anniversary of the Ending of WW II

Chapter 41 Is Economy or Security More Important in a Geopolitical Region?

Chapter 42 Understanding Divorce as a Social Disease

Chapter 43 'Comfort Women' - What Does It Mean To You?

Chapter 44 Examining the Taiwan Issue Post Obama-Xi Summit

Chapter 45 Think Tanks, State Visits and Foreign Policies

Chapter 46 China's Security: Who Is Targeting China?

Chapter 47 Who Cares About The Dreams of Taiwanese?

Chapter 48 China's World View

Chapter 49 Back To The Future to Forward to the Future

Chapter 50 A Chinese Dream - United Democratic People's Republic of China

Chapter 51 What Is the Real Significance of Trans-Pacific Partnership Agreement (TPPA)?

Chapter 52 Tough Talk of U.S. Presidential Candidates on China

Chapter 53 The Changing United States Over 240 Years

Chapter 54 Saving Capitalism by Preserving a Simple Concept

Chapter 55 Should Americans Be Concerned about US China Policy?

Chapter 56 John Mearsheimer's Theoretical Analysis of the Rise of China – Gospel or Fallacy

Chapter 57 Year-End Review on the World Affairs and the South China Sea Issue

Chapter 58 The World Will Be Better Off in 2016 and Possibly Beyond

Chapter 59 The 2016 US and Taiwan Presidential Elections

Chapter 60 View of China Rise by Kishore Mahbubani

Chapter 61 Decline of American Value and American Public School

Chapter 62 Obama's China Policy and Looking Beyond 2016

Chapter 63 Why Should the U.S. Accept a G-2 Relationship with China?

Chapter 64 Organic View on the US Democracy

Notes and References

—ш—

IN THE BOOK, US-CHINA RELATIONS, the author has included a fairly detailed notes and references section for each chapter to explain the special terms and people's names mentioned in the text. In the second and this book, only a few references are listed here for readers' convenience to look up any definition of a special term or a brief biography of a person. The following references will provide the readers either rapid search engines to find information you need or ready information in an organized manner:

US-China Forum, **http://www.us-chinaforum.org** or
     http://www.us-chinaforum.com
Wikipedia, http://www.wikipedia.org
Google Search Engine, http://www.google.com
Baidu, A Chinese Search Engine http://www.baidu.com
Foreign Affairs, http://www.foreignaffairs.com Magazine
Foreign Policy, http://www.foreignpolicy.com Magazine
Foreign Relations of the U.S. (FRUS),
    http://history.stste.gov/historicaldevelopments
New York Times, http://www.nytimes.com Newspaper
Wall Street Journal, http://www.wsj.com Newspaper
Washington Post, http://www.washingtonpost.com, Newspaper
Diplomat, http://www.diplomatmagazine.com Magazine
Economist, http://www.economist.com Magazine
e-International Relations, http://www.e-ir.info Website
Global Politics, http://global.politics.co.uk Magazine

Rand Review, http://www.rand.org Research on Policies

Tass, Russian News Agency, http://www.tass.ru/en
http://www.tass.ru/world

The Chinese Journal of International Politics,
http://cjip.oxfordjournals.org Peer Reviewed Academic Journal

Central News, http://www.cna.com.tw Chinese News

Xinhua News, http://www.chinaview.cn Chinese News
http://www.xinhuanet.com/english
http://www.news.cn/english

List of International Relations Journal,
https://en.wikipedia.org/wiki/List_of_international_relations_journals

www.ingramcontent.com/pod-product-compliance
Lightning Source LLC
Chambersburg PA
CBHW081356270326
41930CB00015B/3325